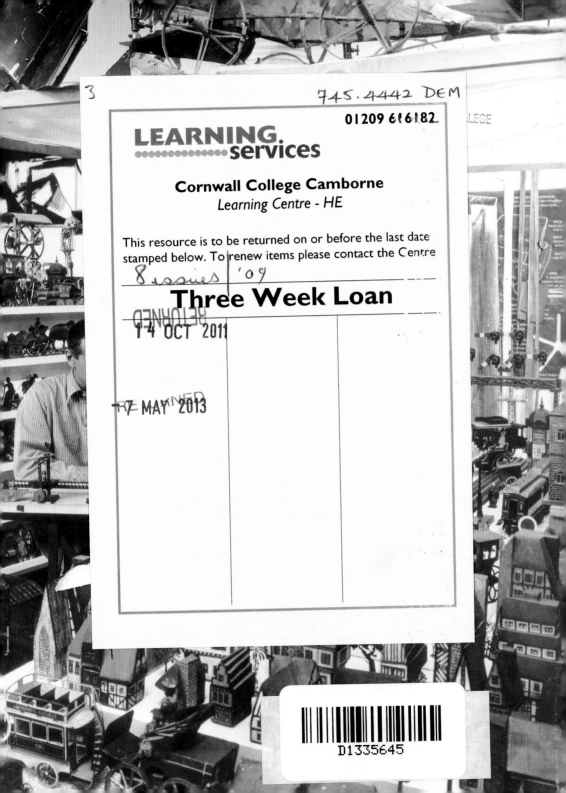

Eames Demetrios Selected Projects:

Books
*Wartime California* (fiction)
*Changing Her Palette: Paintings by Ray Eames*

Films/Videos
*77 Steps*
*Powers of Time*
*The Giving* (fiction)
*Common Knowledge: An Oral History of 1988*
*901: after 45 years of working*

Multimedia
Powers of Ten Interactive

# an eames primer

**eames demetrios**

Thames & Hudson

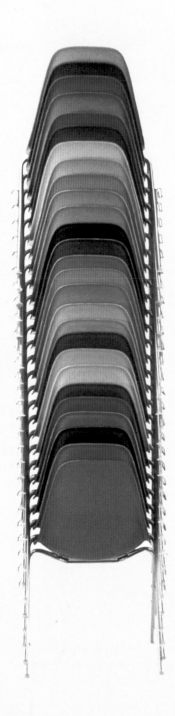

## Dedicated to Lucia Eames, and to the Seventh Generation

First published in the United Kingdom in 2001
by Thames & Hudson Ltd, 181A High Holborn, London WC1V 7QX

British Library Cataloguing-in-Publication Data
A catalogue record for this book is available from the British Library

ISBN 0-500-283-206

Printed and bound in Bath, England by Bath Press

All photos are by Eames Office © 2001 Lucia Eames dba Eames Office
(eamesoffice.com) with the exception of the following:
© 2001 Lucia Eames, dba Eames Office, courtesy of the Library of Congress: page
6, 13 (upper right), 15 (bottom right), 17 (nautilus), 20, 22, 23, 33, 70, 88, 100
(right), 101 (middle and upper right), 105, 108 (upper right), 113, 114, 118, 124,
135, 139 (upper left), 140, 141, 152, 153, 190, 200, 201, 214, 228
© Eames Demetrios: page 13 (lower right), 42 (molded plywood pilot seat detail),
49, 54, 61 (top image courtesy Adele Crispin), 61, 86, 114 (lower image) 117, all
901 flipbook images
© Vitra Design Museum: 4, 38 (Eames/Saarinen organic chair), 39 (molded plywood pilot seats), 40 (grouping of table, chairs, and folding plywood screen)
Shelley Mills: 9 (lower middle) 38 (Kleinhans chair), 157 (left middle), 182
All cover photos by Eames Office © 2001 Lucia Eames dba Eames office, except
Hang-it-All © 2001 Vitra design Museum. End papers: Dot pattern by Charles and
Ray Eames, released by Maharam © 2001 Lucia Eames dba Eames Office

Design: Ph.D

# Contents

|  |  |  |
|---|---|---|
|  | Introduction | 7 |
| Chapter 1 | The Worlds of Charles and Ray Eames | 11 |
| Chapter 2 | The Newton Deck of Cards | 21 |
| Chapter 3 | Lotas | 27 |
| Chapter 4 | Eames Chairs: A 30-Year Flash (Part I) | 35 |
| Chapter 5 | A Good Learner | 47 |
| Chapter 6 | Painting in the Broadest Sense | 63 |
| Chapter 7 | From Mexico to Cranbrook | 77 |
| Chapter 8 | Charles and Ray Eames | 93 |
| Chapter 9 | A 30-Year Flash (Part II) | 107 |
| Chapter 10 | Take Your Pleasure Seriously | 121 |
| Chapter 11 | Case Study #8 | 131 |
| Chapter 12 | Films as Essays | 143 |
| Chapter 13 | The Guest/Host Relationship | 155 |
| Chapter 14 | Constraints | 167 |
| Chapter 15 | Mathematica | 179 |
| Chapter 16 | 901 Culture | 191 |
| Chapter 17 | Modeling | 205 |
| Chapter 18 | "If the Office Were an Island" | 215 |
| Chapter 19 | An Image Can Be an Idea | 227 |
| Chapter 20 | Proposals, Sketches, and *Powers of Ten* | 241 |
| Chapter 21 | Ten Years Apart | 253 |
| Chapter 22 | Afterwords | 263 |
|  | Acknowledgments | 266 |
|  | Notes | 268 |
|  | Index | 270 |

Below: first image of a walk through the space at 901 Washington Boulevard, which continues throughout this book

# Introduction

When I was 14, I volunteered at the Steinhart Aquarium in San Francisco, and, through an elaborate set of circumstances, I was lucky enough to go on a trip to the South Pacific to swim on the back of a 30-foot whale shark. The night before I left, my grandfather, Charles Eames, showed up at our door completely unexpectedly. He came with a camera, one of those very basic 35mm models that came to market in the mid-1970s, for me to take on the trip. Charles told me that it was the least expensive one he could find and he wanted me to know that if it was lost or drenched it was no big deal. He said he and my grandmother, Ray, had gotten it for me because they knew that if I borrowed my parents' Nikon, I would be too afraid of dropping it in the ocean to do anything with it. In fact, he feared I might never take it out of the room. What was amazing to me even then was that this exact fear had been tugging at me—what if I destroyed my parents' valuable camera? Charles had brought precisely the right gift. I even took some pictures of that whale shark that were part of my own first publication.

This story is connected in my mind with another that my mother, Lucia Eames, told us about times a generation before when she and Charles, her father, painted together in the out-of-doors. To her, it was "perfectly natural to be sharing my father's paint and paintbrushes." But, later, she heard Charles respond to an onlooker's surprise at a five-year-old's having been allowed to touch, let alone use for the day, his expensive sable-hair paintbrushes. Surely such things were being "just wasted on a child." Charles observed that, on the contrary, letting her do so helped him; made him "darn sure to show Lucia, from the very beginning, how to properly respect and care for brushes and paints." So instead of creating bad habits, good practices such as taking care of one's tools could be taught from an early age.

Taken alone, each story could be about frugality in one case and extravagance in the other. One can easily imagine turning the stories on their heads: grandparents getting the fanciest camera around for a grandson setting off on an adventure, or a father buying the cheapest brushes for a five-year-old. But taken together in their actual orientation, these stories are about the difference between cost and worth. It is not just the actions, but

Three generations of the Eames family at the Eames Office, circa 1964: Lucia Eames, Eames Demetrios, Ray Eames, Charles Eames, Lucia Atwood, Carla Atwood, Byron Atwood

7

the thought behind them that is important and that is where the connection between these ideas lies. The story of the camera and the story of the paintbrushes are both ultimately about appropriateness.

Charles would often refer to this concept as "the need"—as in: the recognition of need being key to the design process. As I look back on these things now, after my work and research, I see many other echoes as well. I see how often the relationship between seemingly disparate Eames projects becomes apparent only when one steps back to see that kind of deeper connection. I think of their photography and 800,000 photographs in the Eames collection at the Library of Congress. I think of my grandparents' *Aquarium* project. I think of their friends. I think of my sister, Carla, about to board a plane for a long trip, and somehow Ray (by a kind of remote control) had gotten the perfect little present to the gate to surprise Carla. I think about "way-it-should-be-ness." I think about the way Charles always seemed to be working with the person at the top of whichever group he was dealing with. I think of Ray's painting and Charles's lesser-known painting and what common ground two such artists would have shared. I think of St. Louis and how Charles and Ray both grew up in cities of the heartland, which, despite ties to the great railroads of the nineteenth century, had ultimately lost their power by the middle of the twentieth. I think of how well Charles and Ray understood the meaning—and even the value—of labels without kowtowing to them.

The purpose of this primer is to give the reader an understanding of the key projects, themes, ideas, and arcs of the lives and work of Charles and Ray Eames. I will discuss the how and why of their work. I do not mean to force connections of stilted directness between their lives and work, but to sketch some key ideas about the Eameses' work and design approach. Above all, it is their design philosophy that I wish to communicate. My title for this book is adapted from the Eames film *A Communications Primer*, but it may be that the book's approach echoes the second version (of three) of *Powers of Ten: Rough Sketch for a Proposed Film on the Relative Size of Things in the Universe*. This book is a rough sketch of a primer on their work, taking the form of a thematic biography.

I bring to this book not just my youth but also my recent working life running the Eames Office, communicating, preserving, and extending Charles and Ray's work. I wear many hats at this work, but few are more wonderful than the many conversations with friends, relatives, and colleagues of Charles and Ray's, or reading old letters, watching their movies, going to libraries, pursuing loose ends, tracking wild hairs, scrutinizing chairs, studying the light at the Eames House, finding paintings, examining slides, listening to recordings, and much more. I want to thank all the people who talked with me about Charles and Ray over this time, because it has been an ongoing conversation. Charles died when I was 16, and Ray when I was 26. Time with them was wonderful, something we knew as grandchildren, but we undoubtedly would have been content to describe it as fun. Charles and I had a special connection, which probably evolved from my fascination with film. His loss was something I felt acutely. Our grandparents were not icons of design but simply our grandparents—we called them "Charlie and Ray." But it turns out they were teaching us design all along—I hope some of that comes across in this book. I sometimes think, on the one hand, that all of my interviews and explorations have been a subconscious compensation for not formally interviewing Ray myself, for taking her incredible life force for granted. On the other hand, the last few years of her life, as we got to know each other as two adults, one becoming a father, were priceless to me and filled with the wisdom of a woman who though proud of her life was always more interested in the future.

The author in the Eames Office graphics room, appearing in *Something About Photography* (1976), and filming *901: after 45 years of working* (1990)

This book does not focus on third-party endorsements. They are used from time to time, but the world has enough books and quotes and facts that acknowledge Charles and Ray's stature. Instead, I think it is time to look a bit more deeply at the seamless connection in all their work and how and—to some degree—why it was achieved.

Because, even beyond the specific connections explored in the narrative, I think of how often in their work they naturally bridged extremes, always staying focused on the need. Their La Chaise chair and their ESU were done within two or three years of each other. One is all curves, the other all right angles, and yet the connection is there, much deeper than the apparent geometry of their surfaces. The Eames House is a steel-frame structure made of off-the-shelf parts and filled with a rich broth of collections—some even call it clutter  The Lounge Chair itself took two years to design; the film *Lounge Chair* took five days. Charles and Ray were design revolutionaries whose slogan was "innovate as a last resort." They often sought the universal in the specific. Charles saw their work as an extension of his architecture, and Ray saw it as an extension of her painting. They eschewed self-expression for its own sake, but the work they created as husband-and-wife collaborators speaks with a single voice. And yet these pairings are intended not as paradoxes, but rather as dimensions of the same way of looking at the world.

I believe Charles and Ray constantly drew from this deeper well. This explains the seamless connection in all their work because, as important as any of the objects they created are, the philosophy behind them is even more important.

# CHAPTER 1

# The Worlds of Charles and Ray Eames

Most people enter the world of Charles and Ray Eames through the door of furniture. On these first pages you will almost definitely recognize at least one of their chairs, but even if you do not, you will be seeing some of the landmarks of their world and, indeed, of twentieth-century design. You may recognize the luxurious Eames Lounge Chair—probably the chair most people think of when they say "Eames Chair." Or you may recognize the fiberglass chairs, best-sellers in their own right, widely copied, and influential in their innovative use of the material. Or the LCW. Or, perhaps, the tandem seating—a comforting fixture of airports everywhere.

Some people come to Charles and Ray's work first through their classic short film *Powers of Ten*, a tool for thinking out of the box and almost literally mind-expanding. Grown men and women still vividly recall the first time they saw it at the age of 10, often in a science class. As the Eames films have become more widely available, young children have been weaned too on Charles and Ray's *Toccata for Toy Trains*, with its enchanting locomotives and exultant Elmer Bernstein score.

Other people will tell you about playing with the House of Cards as a child. Or seeing the Eames presentation at the IBM pavilion at the 1964 New York World's Fair: 22 screens of images and sliding on moveable bleachers up into the Eero Saarinen–designed theater (known at the fair as the "Egg"). Then there were the close to three million Soviet citizens[1] who in 1959 watched the seven-screen presentation *Glimpses of the USA*—their first experience of Charles and Ray Eames was for many their earliest and closest (ever) direct connection to the United States. Or the millions of parkas and winter clothes hung on Hang-It-Alls over the last few decades.

A small group, including, in a sense, Eliel Saarinen, entered the world of Eames through a simple brick church in Helena, Arkansas, still standing, that Charles designed in the mid-1930s. Others crossed the threshold at the 1938 showing of the American Abstract Artists Society in New York, when Ray's paintings hung in the Riverside Museum.

Several generations of children in Los Angeles (and Chicago, Boston, Atlanta, and

Charles and Ray, circa 1950. Self-portrait, night-time, reflected in the glass of the Eames House living room window

11

Seattle) learned their math at the Eames exhibition *Mathematica: A World of Numbers . . . and Beyond*. At the landmark Eames House in Pacific Palisades, California, natives of Los Angeles might humor visiting friends by driving them there for an appointment visit and suddenly find themselves connecting with its prescient and appropriate architecture. Generations of Indian designers touched the world of Eames through the National Institute of Design, which Charles and Ray founded in Ahmedabad. Countless numbers heard and saw this world sketched for them when they came to one of Charles's lectures. The English writer and architect Alison Smithson suggests that even the way we decorate today can be attributed to Charles and Ray.[2] If she is right, how many millions have unknowingly entered the Eames world through a friend's—or even their own—living room?

Huson Jackson entered it when he worked at Charles's office in St. Louis, and Charles wrote a song about their lunch order as he placed it over the phone.[3] Barney Reese entered in high school when she became friends with the young Ray Kaiser, and Reese's mother considered Ray's aesthetic influence a blessing for her daughter.[4] D. J. DePree and his son Hugh were instructed by their design director, George Nelson, to at least visit this world at the Museum of Modern Art in New York in 1946. The Eames furniture the DePrees saw there transformed their company, Herman Miller, Inc., forever.

Architect and designer Craig Hodgetts first entered their world when he visited their workshop in Venice, California, and, as he recalls, he didn't get it; it didn't look the slick way he expected a design office should look.[5] But twenty-five years later he codesigned the show *The Work of Charles and Ray Eames: A Legacy of Invention* with his wife and design partner, Ming Fung. Rolf Fehlbaum, head of Vitra, whose family has manufactured the Eames furniture in Europe since the 1950s, grew up with the furniture and at age 17 interpreted for his father on a visit to the Eames Office. Charles's advice on important things to do in California: go to Disneyland.[6]

Alex Funke was told the Eames Office needed someone to "pack the toys and shoot the fish."[7] He worked there for ten years, doing everything from filmmaking to timelines. Deborah Sussman entered the world of Charles and Ray when she was a student and heard them speak, recalling that "the students just went crazy. It was about things we'd never thought about before."[8] Her summer job at the Eames Office spanned almost a dozen years.

Here are a few more portals into the world of Charles and Ray Eames.

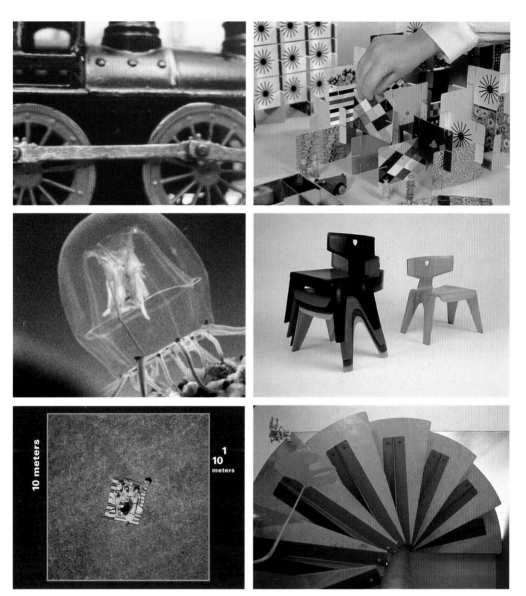

Various images and projects by Charles and Ray Eames, clockwise from top left: still from *Toccata for Toy Trains* (1957); House of Cards toy (1952); children's chairs (1945); Eames House spiral staircase (1949); *Powers of Ten* (1977); *Polyorchis Haplus* (1970)

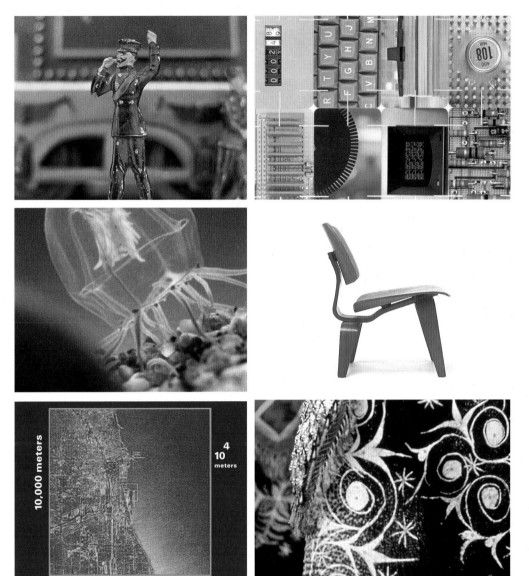

Left: a table setting by Ray photographed by Charles. This page, various images and projects by Charles and Ray Eames, clockwise from top left: *Toccata for Toy Trains*, continued (1957); eight cards from the Computer House of Cards (1970); Lounge Chair Wood (1945); detail of elephant, *India* slide show; *Powers of Ten* (1977), continued; *Polyorchis Haplus*, continued (1970)

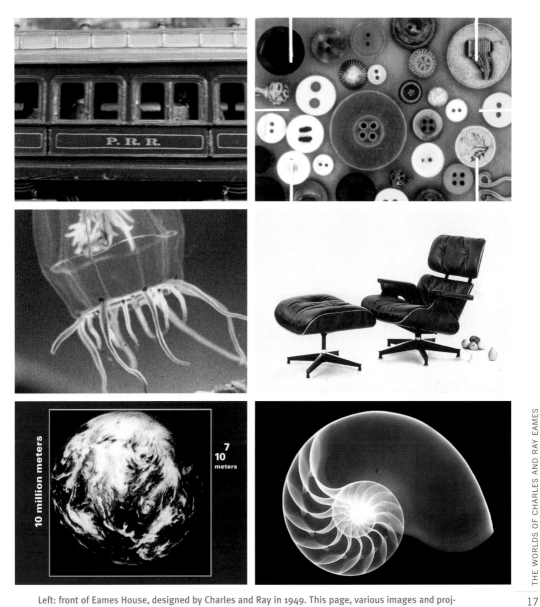

Left: front of Eames House, designed by Charles and Ray in 1949. This page, various images and projects by Charles and Ray Eames, clockwise from top left: *Toccata for Toy Trains*, continued (1957); buttons card from House of Cards (1952); Eames Lounge Chair and Ottoman (1956); nautilus photograph from *Mathematica* exhibition; *Powers of Ten* (1977), continued; *Polyorchis Haplus*, continued (1970)

17

Left: stacks of molded-plywood children's chairs, circa 1945. This page, various images and projects by Charles and Ray Eames, clockwise from top left: *Toccata for Toy Trains*, continued (1957); measurements card from House of Cards (1952); Eames Tandem Sling Seating (1962); Milky Way image from *Powers of Ten*; *Powers of Ten* (1977), continued; *Polyorchis Haplus*, continued (1970)

19

# CHAPTER 2

# The Newton Deck of Cards

In December 1973, the Nobel Prizes were awarded in Stockholm, Sweden. Among the winners was Leo Esaki, a scientist at IBM who won a share of the Nobel Prize in physics (he shared his part with Ivan Giaever for their work on quantum tunneling), the first time an IBM scientist had won a Nobel Prize. The following March, Tom Watson Jr., former head of IBM (who had only recently retired and was still quite powerful on IBM's board of directors), decided the company should hold a special dinner in honor of the physics laureates after their return to the United States.

Charles and Ray Eames were consultants with IBM. It was a special relationship that, from IBM's standpoint, was not only about the numerous films, presentations, and educational products the Eameses created for IBM, but was also important because of the opportunity to use Charles and Ray's vision and sensibility to gain insights for the future of the company. In his office, Charles had a tie line, a direct phone link throughout much of IBM.[1] As with their other key corporate relationships—for example, with Herman Miller, Inc., and Polaroid—Charles believed one always had to be able to work with both the person at the top and the person on the front line to achieve the best results for all concerned.

It was most likely in the context of such a discussion that Watson mentioned the upcoming dinner. Charles suggested: wouldn't it be nice to create a special gift for the laureates in honor of the occasion? Watson agreed and asked what Charles had in mind. Charles suggested a simple deck of cards that could be made of images related to Sir Isaac Newton.[2] Perhaps something along the lines of the House of Cards, simple and elegant. After all, beyond the obvious connection between the father of classical physics and the Nobel laureates, the Eames Office had just created an exhibition about Newton that had recently opened at the IBM Exhibition Center.

This was typical of the fractal nature of the Eames Office—each project and idea seemed to evolve into another. Each iteration offered another opportunity to hone the material tighter and tighter and get to its essence. Such iterations were sometimes transformations as well. In exploring each project, new connections and reconnections of and to ideas

Clamps holding individual decks of Newton Cards so that gold leaf could be applied to the edges

21

Top: selection of images from the Newton Cards. Bottom: Phylis Morrison, Ray, Michael Ripps, Dick Donges, and another staff member in the midst of the Newton Deck charette

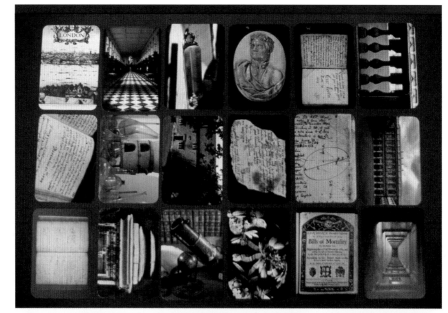

were made. Because the Newton exhibition had opened during the holiday season, Charles and Ray supplemented it with an additional textural layer of early English Christmas decorations, a fun and joyous connection to Sir Isaac's date of birth (Christmas Day).[3] Charles and Ray always had a highly refined sense of occasion.

IBM was then at the height of its corporate power. IBM *was* computers. Back in 1914, Tom Watson Sr. had joined the company that became International Business Machines Corporation and built it into the leading maker of custom-built tabulation machines for business and government. IBM became involved with electronic computers toward the end of World War II, and afterward Tom Watson Jr. had the vision to take the company in that direction. Today, the computer as a fixture of our lives seems inevitable, and IBM is no longer at the center of that world, but in the 1950s IBM was one of the first companies to recognize that future and take steps to make it happen.[4]

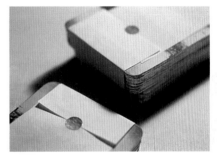

Two Newton Decks showing the Eames Office's attention to presentation

Watson surrounded himself with impressive folks and Eliot Noyes was among them. Noyes had been a curator of design at the Museum of Modern Art and an early champion of Charles's work at the time of the Organic Furniture competition. He and Charles first met in Grand Rapids in early 1941, when Noyes, Charles, and Eero Saarinen were working with the Heywood-Wakefield Furniture Company on the actual manufacture of the Organic Furniture.[5] During the war, Noyes and Watson served on the same bomber crew. Later, when Noyes was put in charge of design at IBM, Charles and Ray sent him a copy of *A Communications Primer*, their film introducing and explaining recent developments in communications theory. Though Charles and Ray graciously referred to this as an IBM-sponsored film, in fact Charles and Ray had made it on their own. Noyes and Watson saw the power not only of the film and its ideas, but also of the people who created it. Soon, Charles and Ray Eames become two of IBM's key consultants. Eventually, Charles was one of the few non-IBM employees invited to speak to the Corporate Management Committee, which dispensed billions of dollars of research money within the company over many decades.[6] Watson wanted the Eameses' thinking to be part of that process. But the special relationship allowed for gracious touches, for support of smaller things—and that was important, too.

The Newton Cards would be a perfect gift for the Nobel laureates, just right for the occasion. When, exactly, was the dinner? In four days.[7]

Instantly the Eames Office went into overdrive. As Alex Funke, an Eames Office staff member, recalls, "there are moments that glow in the memory, and one of them is doing these cards."[8] Everyone was pressed into service to get the decks out. And the fact that

23

everyone knew to put other projects aside and focus on the mission reflected a part of the way the office worked. There was not really a formal chain of command, or if there was, it had short links. Instead of staff meetings, there were informal gatherings driven by the need of each project. Charles set the mission in motion by discussing it with the people he need-ed to pull it off (and whoever else happened to be around—"close to the muzzle,"[9] accord-ing to some). Jehane Burns Kuhn remembers, "Charles came and talked to me about this, and he talked about it in an indirect way, and [at first] I didn't understand that this was something that was truly imminent and that [there was] some cost attached to [it], and so I said something indicating some skepticism or difficulty. . . . I should have known better: [when] Charles comes to see one in one's corner at one's desk and starts talking about something you'd better assume it—this is a real issue."[10]

The outlines of the task became clear. The images had to be selected from those Charles had already taken in England. With the Eameses, photography was part of the design process, a way of discovering and exploring. There were thousands of images taken for the Newton exhibition, but they had already been pared down to the ones used in the show, so this was where the selection process started. Of course, it is possible that previously unse-lected (rejected would be too strong a word) images were considered, but Charles and Ray had a deep respect for effort that had gone before. It was not a matter of avoiding work, but rather of avoiding the pitfalls of pursuing novelty for its own sake. Charles often advised, "innovate as a last resort"—ironic because Charles and Ray became known for the fresh-ness, invention, and, yes, innovation of their work. But to them such qualities were only a means to an end, not an end in itself. The danger of any innovation was the chance of losing the wisdom that had gone into the development of the idea to that point.

A timeline was worked out that would get staff member Randy Walker and the cards to the airport on the last flight from Los Angeles to New York before the dinner. Twenty-six of Charles's images were selected; Charles, Ray, and the team worked out the specifics; and the Eames Office moved into action. Bill Tondreau started printing each of the 12 sets of 26 cards by hand in the Eames Office color print laboratory.[11] Randy Walker began building a special wooden box to hold the decks. Ray was working with the ribbon treatment. Etsu Garfias and Hap Johnson in the front office were applying a print of marbled paper[12] to the back of each card. John Neuhart was embossing an ellipse containing Newton's signature onto each box. Someone else was applying the gold leaf to the edges. Mike Ripps, then editing a movie, was put to work cutting radiuses on the cards.[13] Literally "everyone in the office . . . really got involved, hands-on," Dick Donges remembers. "It was a hectic one, went home and slept for a couple of days."[14]

The remarkable thing was that every step of the process was done in-house. All those different kinds of work were possible under the roof at 901 Washington Boulevard, the home of the Eames Office for more than 30 years. "901" (as it was generally known) was very unspectacular from the outside—nothing but an old bus garage. But inside there was a complete, fully functioning workshop, separate black-and-white and color photo labs, a film shooting stage, archives and archivists, production areas, flexible spaces, a kitchen, dining area, picnic area, projection room, screening room, spectacular library, aquariums, and more. There were very few projects that, soup to nuts, the Eames Office could not design and fabricate within its own walls—and even those things it chose to send out for completion could be extensively mocked up first. As Gordon Ashby, a designer who worked at the

Charles at 901 with some treatments of the IBM logo as it appeared in one of their films

office (and once mocked up an entire building lobby within its walls), once said, "901 was Charles's instrument—and he knew exactly how to play it."[15]

Today we call this kind of capability "desktop publishing" and associate it with the tools of the digital age, but by the 1950s, Charles and Ray Eames had figured out a way to make this kind of work unprecious in the best sense. Making a movie or stills or an exhibition did not require special gearing up: you could just do it. And even if the task required a new skill, the Eames Office would rather learn how to do it themselves than send it out. This was true not only of production, but of the intellectual content as well. Sometimes this seemed labor-intensive, or just plain crazy, but Charles saw that the ultimate efficiency was in maximizing the number of times one could go through a process. In project after project, the hands-on process, the ability to do something over and over until it was right, was the key. It also paid off regularly with specific projects, such as the Newton Cards. It may be that this self-reliance, a sort of proto-desktop publishing capability, is one of the reasons the Eames work continues to resonate today.

So everyone was pressed into service, and all other work stopped. The time got tighter and tighter. Finally, as Alex Funke recalls, the last pieces were coming together when someone yelled, "'We've got to take the picture.' '[He's] got to go to the airport.' 'Take the picture.'"[16] They got the decks out the door and to the plane and made the deadline and took the picture—there were always pictures at the office. Randy Walker got to New York with the decks, and by the time of the dinner a deck awaited each of the laureates, who still treasure them today.[17] With hindsight, that moment may have been a kind of high-water mark, before a shift away—not only at IBM, but in corporate America—from such special touches. When Watson was at the helm, that kind of detail would be important—but soon that would not be the case. Back at 901, the Eames Office returned to its rhythms, with the satisfaction and pleasure of once more having pulled off the impossible.

# CHAPTER 3

# Lotas

In 1958, Charles and Ray Eames were invited by Prime Minister Jawaharlal Nehru to visit India, experience the country, and advise the Indian government on how that nation might address a feeling that "the general quality of things had been in recent years deteriorating. . . . They wanted some plan by which India itself could attack that problem of deterioration of quality."[1] Perhaps just as important was a clear subtext: how might Nehru deal with the forces of westernization tempting and pressing against his land, take advantage of some of the worthwhile benefits of modernization, and at the same time preserve the Indian culture? At the end of their stay, the Eameses were given the task of preparing a report, one that might include the possibility of an institute of design. Ultimately, this document would be known as the India Report.

Charles and Ray spent almost six months traveling all over the country and experiencing many different cultures.[2] They started in the north and made their way to the southernmost point of the subcontinent.[3] They ultimately made a number of different recommendations. On westernization, they essentially suggested that with literally thousands of different cultures, why would India need to look outside to yet another one? For example, regarding computers, they felt strongly that India should not buy a computer from IBM (this I am sure did not particularly endear them to IBM, but it is unlikely Charles and Ray gave that issue much thought). Instead, they suggested, India would be far better off building one from scratch—"from cardboard" if necessary.[4] Why, especially considering that such a computer would not be nearly as "good" as any IBM model on the shelf?

In the Eameses' reasoning, that was precisely the point. The mistakes made and thus the lessons learned from the miserable first tries would be India's, and the country might internalize the knowledge and build from these trials and errors. In essence, the Eameses were suggesting that a whole nation adopt its own learn-by-doing process. It is too much to suggest that they shaped the nation, because this sort of self-reliance undoubtedly resonated with Prime Minister Nehru who, among other achievements, was a founder of the Non-Aligned Movement.[*] Although IBM surely sold some computers to India at some point,

Part of the *India* 3-screen slide show. Photograph taken by Charles around the time of the India Report (1958)

* A bloc of developing nations determined to take a third path between America and the Soviet Union during the Cold War

Photo of boy
from *India* slide
show, possibly
taken at the
time of the
Eameses' visit to
the home of the
potter described
by Haku Shah

it is worth noting that India's stature today as a computing power is clearly based on the internally developed skills of its people, not on the fact that they bought some machines from a multinational corporation.

The experience of developing the India Report stayed with Charles and Ray all their lives, and the friendships they made there were lifelong. Haku Shah, a curator and preserver of traditional culture, remembering when Charles spent a morning photographing a potter in a remote village, wrote of the intensity of Charles's attention to and focus on the task at hand: "I took Charles only for ten minutes to this poor family who was residing there for the last 45 years. No body would SEE-CARE- SHOW APATHY to this FAMILY but I thought that

Charles would Love [them] and he did. He forgot that he is on the road and forgot that he was interacting with an ordinary poor neg-lected family. He thought that here is: A lovely family, in a cradle a child is there and the mother is singing lullaby. With bare minimum material a hut is created, temporary yet liveable, Charles took a photo of the Grandfather carrying the Child, I was thinking what is he getting in this photo?"[5]

Later, Charles and Ray sent Haku Shah copies of the photos taken in the potter's hut. "When the prints arrived the photograph was great, The meeting of TWO HANDS . . . Aesthetic beauty of the human being - Pleasure of seeing, Experiencing the growth of 7 months and 70 years together. Only Charles can see and share within a fraction of a second."[6] Those particular prints were lost in a flood in Haku's home in Ahmedabad, but the originals, and thousands of other photographs from this trip, are now in the Eames archives at the Library of Congress. Haku Shah eventually visited the United States many times, stay-ing in Los Angeles with the Eameses. During a stay with Charles's daughter, Lucia, and her family, he created an elaborate rice drawing on their hardwood floor as a thank-you gift.

There are many threads that weave their way through the Eameses' work over the years. Some are people; some are special companies; some are museums; some are philosophies. However one reckons those threads, India would have to be included. The connection between the Eameses and India was deep and mutual. At a gathering of friends right after Ray died, writer and artist Jan Steward remembered "the first time when I asked Ray what she thought was the most beautiful music of India. And she said probably the train whistles in the desert in Rajasthan [state]."[7] The Eames Office worked on a number of other projects connected to India over the years, including the films *2ⁿ* and *Banana Leaf* and the three-screen slide show *India*.

In 1955, the Eameses helped their friend Alexander Girard install an exhibition called *Textiles and Ornamental Arts of India*. In a tribute to Charles after his death, Pupul

Jayakar, the Indian curator of the exhibition, described her encounter with Charles at the museum: "A tall square-shouldered figure with a closely cropped head and the deeply penetrating eyes of the seer, he gazed intently at the fabrics, the pots, the enamel inlays and the squat earth-rooted animal forms, touching, lingering, shifting an object, pinning up a mirrored skirt, every movement precise, contained, eloquent. We met and for hours talked of India, of its craftsmen and the traditions that sustained them; he questioned me on the land, the people, the poverty and the affluence, the values, the philosophy, the environment that had sustained an ancient culture and the impact of the new technologies, the revolution in communications. He was eager to know what was happening to the psyche of a nation suddenly thrust into the turmoil of twentieth-century technology and its products."[8]

Charles and Ray made a film of the 1955 exhibition. When Jayakar came to 901 Washington Boulevard to record the narration, the mutual education continued. A couple of years later, it was Jayakar who suggested to Nehru that the Eameses be invited to India. At the end of their travels within India, it was time to present the conclusions to the Minister of Industries. In attendance at the meeting were the Minister, assorted officials, the Eameses, and a representative of the Ford Foundation, which had paid for the trip. Also present was Jayakar, who later described the meeting as unforgettable: The others "expected a project report on a product design institute which could service small industry; Charles Eames started quoting from the *Baghvad Gita*, spoke of values, standards of life, and the major revolution in communications. The Minister was puzzled and asked questions related to industrial design, while Charles continued projecting his insights on the Indian scene. There was utter chaos of communications. Later we had to convince the Minister and the Ford Foundation that behind the philosophy lay a hard core of technological data and thought, and that there would be a technological framework that would provide the research, service, and training in the field of design that was essential for small industrial production."[9] This ability to back abstract ideals with pragmatics was a hallmark of the Eames approach.

One of the specific recommendations of the Eameses' India Report was the creation of a National Institute of Design (NID), which was eventually built in Ahmedabad, long a center for the arts and today a home to a showcase of important twentieth-century architecture.* The Eameses traveled to the NID regularly to visit and teach and were regarded as spiritual godparents of the institute. Both Charles and Ray spoke at the NID within a year of their respective deaths. For them, ongoing time at the NID allowed them to meaningfully interact with and even contribute to a different society. For the students at NID, conversations with the Eameses became a highlight of their educational lives.

Charles and Ray felt that one of the key problems facing modern society—in America and throughout the world—was how to deal with the incredible array of choices

* Le Corbusier buildings are there as well as Louis Kahn's Institute of Public Administration building.

now possible. Charles described a manifestation in the United States this way: "California, and particularly Los Angeles, is a very special example. If it were as good a lesson as it is an example, it would be especially helpful. . . . People in large numbers from many different cultures came together to form a community—leaving all their traditions, social mores, inherited land responsibilities and restraints behind. The form the community has taken is more a product of its freedoms than of its restraints, and the result is frightening. . . . A very large community has been forced to make many decisions large and small—without the restraining effects of a common cultural tradition, or limitations that come with isolation, or social responsibilities of long-standing or a lore of materials and their appropriate use."[10] In India, the challenge was similar and over time even some of the choices faced were the same, but the cultural tools available were quite different.

Opposite: images of India taken by Charles during the development of the India Report (circa 1958)

After Nehru's death in 1964, the Eames Office was asked to design an exhibition eventually called *Nehru: The Man and His India*. Rather than designing it in the United States and shipping it to India, as the initial proposal suggested, the Eameses insisted that it be done with the help of students at the newly opened NID. Specifically, though the over-all issues and approach were structured at the Eames Office in California, the physical exhi-bition and much of the content were designed and made in India. How did the process work? Charles or Ray or both were at the NID for virtually all of the three-month process. And, extremely important, the Eames Office sent a few seasoned staffers (Bob Staples, Deborah Sussman, and others) with some essential resources—particularly for photography —to work with the students and staff of the NID. Designer Alexander Girard, a close Eames friend and collaborator, also worked on this project.[11] The practical experience of the Eames Office group in creating exhibitions was essential.

The Nehru show opened in New York in 1965, traveled to Los Angeles and London, and is still on view in Delhi. Designing with all the scheduled shipping in mind required a typically Eamesian blend of elegance and practicality. After all, much of the show's structure was held in place with a simple bamboo frame—very light and very Indian. Such lightweight framing needed a counterweight to keep the installation stable, but the amount of weight required would make shipping costs prohibitive. The solution? Sandbags that could be filled up at each venue and then emptied before shipping the structure to the next venue.

The most important part of the story behind the Nehru exhibition, however, is that when Charles and Ray were put in the position of *being* IBM—that is, of being the external vendor from whom a complete solution (and a good one) could be purchased—they insisted on the same path they had recommended to India. In a small but important way, they ensured that India's learning took place within its own borders so that the knowledge stayed there as well. This is yet another thread in the Eames story. They always sought to

LOTAS

31

Top: two lotas
from the Eames
slide show *Lota*.
Bottom: a small
lota from the
Eames slide
show *India*

understand a project's constraints as deeply as possible, and in this case that meant redefining the problem. Although the word "constraint" sounds restrictive, even paradoxical, to Charles and Ray it was a responsibility. Ray called this "keeping track of the big idea."[12]

The India Report closed with a discussion of the lota, a vessel used throughout India for carrying water. The lota seems to have gained significance during the Eameses' time in India, becoming an almost talismanic metaphor for them. Charles cited it frequently when discussing the design process because, while the lota had evolved to a point of shape and function universally seen as successful, "How would one go about designing a lota? First one would have to shut out all preconceived ideas on the subject and then consider factor after factor: the optimum amount of liquid to be fetched, carried, poured and stored in a prescribed set of circumstances. The size and strength and gender of the hands (if hands) that would manipulate it." The list of qualities to consider contained 18 other factors—from heat transfer and tactility to taste and cost in terms of work—before concluding with, "How does it feel?"[13]

But, of course, no one had ever made anything like this list before designing a lota, "because no one [person] made the lota."[14] And, even if one person had made such a list, he or she would never have gotten it right the first time. The lota was designed across the passage of time by a million smaller, unselfconscious choices. Another way to consider the qualities Charles and Ray found compelling is to imagine the lota's evolution continuing today (as of course it does). Imagine, for example, that someone took a lota and embellished it with an elaborate pair of handles, a pair of handles that everyone in the village—or even the region—agreed were the most beautiful they had ever seen. Well, unless those handles added to the function of the lota, chances are that in a few generations (probably a few years) very few—if any—lotas would still have the handles. But imagine instead that another person made a change to the lota that improved its function; in this case, within a couple of generations that change would likely be seen in every lota in the village or region—perhaps even in the country.

The Eameses cherished such examples of unselfconscious design because it resonated so well with their own philosophy and approach. A key reason for the timelessness of the Eames designs may in fact be that they were not merely attracted to traditional art (as indeed were many creators of the twentieth century) but went a step further and developed a way of designing that echoed in an unpretentious way the traditional processes they respected. What, a reader new to the Eames work might ask, does a lota have to do with an icon of modern furniture? The connection may lie less in the product than in the process behind the evolution of the Eames chair.

# CHAPTER 4

# Eames Chairs: A 30-Year Flash (Part I)

Charles was once asked, "Did you think of the Eames chair in a flash?" He replied, "Yes, sort of a 30-year flash."[1] And when he said that, it had indeed been over 30 years since he and Eero Saarinen had won first prize in the 1940 Organic Furniture competition at the Museum of Modern Art (MoMA)—or, tracing roots, even longer if you start with his earliest seating, the pews in Helena, Arkansas, with armrests in gentle curves. But Charles's remark clearly expresses something more important than specifics: his fundamental belief in design as a process, rather than a single outcome—a process that's never really over. One of the Eames Office's last projects, abandoned after Charles's death, was a timeline and exhibition on invention. It may well have been abandoned anyway had Charles lived longer, since he was already frustrated with it. He came to feel that the more one explored a famous invention—photography, computing, whatever—it was virtually impossible to pin down a single moment.[2] The Eameses' own 30-year flash is a perfect example. In the film *Design Q&A* (1969), Charles is asked, "Is design a creation of an individual?" He responds, "No, because to be realistic one must always acknowledge those who have gone before."[3] Though, interestingly, in a sense, what Charles and Ray ultimately developed was a way of creating whereby, after a time, they themselves became the ones who had gone before.

The 30-year flash began with the Kleinhans chair, which Charles Eames and Eero Saarinen designed for the Kleinhans Music Hall in 1939 and achieves a certain kind of completeness with Charles and Ray's design of the fiberglass chair in the early 1950s. However, as late as the early 1970s, the Eameses were still exploring related ideas, such as the Two Piece Secretarial chair (this accounts for the 30 years). This evolution is a perfect example of the design process as it worked at the Eames Office: the feeling that, rather than a single moment of inspiration, there was a constant working out of each issue one by one, a kind of learning by doing until a solution was revealed. The solution then became the starting point for the next part of the journey. In project after project, Charles and Ray practiced this philosophy; viewed in this way, the length and breadth of their careers trace nothing more (or less) than the logical extension of that design process into a way of life. In a way, this flash

Molded-plywood airplane parts at 901 (circa 1944)

becomes a metaphor for the way Charles and Ray approached design. If this was their way of working, then unquestionably it bore its earliest full fruit through the furniture.

By 1939, Charles Eames was 32 years old and head of the design department at the Cranbrook Academy of Art, located just outside of Detroit. He had been there for a year or so, having practiced architecture in St. Louis for most of the decade. He had become good friends with Eero Saarinen, who was a junior partner in the architecture office of his father, Eliel Saarinen. Charles also worked on projects in the Saarinen office from time to time. At that time, Eliel Saarinen, who was also the head of the Cranbrook Academy of Art, was designing the Kleinhans Music Hall in Buffalo, New York. Saarinen Sr. was the architect of the building, and Charles and Eero designed the seating.[4]

They designed a number of different pieces, including the armchair on page 38. They determined the single striking curve for the seat by doing some research, using an array of dowels to trace the shape of the human bottom and find the curve for the most comfortable support. Although these chairs were not mass-produced for the consumer market, one can see the possibility inherent in the design. The Kleinhans chair represents an important point in Charles's career because it was the first expression of his notion of wringing a solution from a single piece of material—a single-shell chair. From a materials standpoint, however, the chair was still essentially a curved slab design with no complex curves. It was more in the vein of the chairs of Alvar Aalto.

The chairs were installed and well received. They had been made in a modest quantity, but because it was a small run, the manufacture was essentially custom manufacture in volume. But Charles and Eero must have begun to reflect both on the restrictions and possibilities available to them. Therefore, in 1940, when MoMA announced the competition *Organic Designs In Home Furnishings*, Charles and Eero leapt at the chance. The competition, organized by Eliot Noyes, the director of design at MoMA, sprang from the desire to see design evolve organically from many of the changes taking place in society. His brief for it put the matter this way: "In the field of home furnishings there has been no outstanding design developments in recent years. A new way of living is developing, however, and this requires a fresh approach to the design problems and a new expression. An adequate solution which takes into consideration the present social, economic, technical and esthetic trends is largely lacking."[5] Noyes's brief went on to point out that the young designers who might conceivably address these issues worked at a considerable disadvantage: "they have no opportunity to form the contacts with industry which would enable them to have their designs produced."[6]

The Organic Furniture competition intended to address this problem in an unusual way. A number of manufacturers agreed to produce the prize-winning designs and a consortium of retailers (initially led only by Bloomingdale's in New York) agreed to sell them. In other words, the winner of the competition would have guaranteed distribution.[7] It is worth noting here that it would be extremely difficult to get such a competition organized today—a museum in tandem with manufacturers—because of perhaps valid concerns of conflict of interest. And yet this manufacturing dimension was absolutely key to the Organic Furniture competition's success.[*]

The contest drew 585 entries, captivated minds around the country, and was nowhere received more enthusiastically than at Cranbrook.[8] The combination of practicality and modern form was naturally irresistible to almost anyone at Cranbrook. No less than five teams from Cranbrook put together entries to the competition.[9] The Arts and Crafts influence there suggested to everyone the potential common ground between mass production and works of quality. This was a natural evolution for Charles and Eero (who loved competitions) as a way to continue their ideas through their entries. From Charles's experience with designing furniture for the houses he did in St. Louis, he knew the effort involved in designing a single physical chair. The Organic Furniture competition offered a great chance to address that issue and actually gain hands-on experience in the chair's manufacture.

Charles and Eero's design went considerably further than the Kleinhans chair. Instead of being a simple curve balanced gently on a structure, it was now an array of curves. Upholstery hid any flaws in the woodworkmanship, which made the smoothness of the forms and their unusual connection more striking. The designers hoped to make the shell's compound curves as uniform as possible and to create them in the wood itself rather than concealed offstage by the fabric. Such details could undoubtedly be resolved at the manufacturing stage if they would be so lucky as to win.

By the end of the fall term, Ray Kaiser (soon to be Ray Eames) was on the scene at Cranbrook, auditing classes in weaving. Ray helped some with the final presentation drawings, though the designs themselves were already complete. On these early chairs—to use her own words—Ray "was like a hand,"[10] one of a number of people around the school who enthusiastically pitched in. It was around this time that she and Charles began their personal relationship as well. In light of future work, it was undoubtedly invaluable for her to observe the process firsthand because in the end it was this group of designs and specifically this technique that would become the jumping-off point for Charles and Ray's own experiments. Another student involved was Don Albinson, who later worked at the Eames Office and worked on the important prototyping of the Eames furniture. He remembers Charles asking anyone in hailing distance to try out the chair.[11] Charles would watch carefully to see how people reacted to and experienced the chairs. In the end, Charles and Eero settled on five chairs, two sofas or lounges, two tables, and some case goods.[12]

The first six years of the flash, showing the pursuit of the mass-produced molded-plywood single-shell chair with complex curves, from left to right: Eames-Saarinen Kleinhans Chair (1939); Eames-Saarinen Organic Chair (1941); Eames molded-plywood sculpture (1942); Eames molded-plywood splint (1942)

The entry, including drawings and photographs of the scale models, went off to New York, leaving behind the exhausted entrants. Life at Cranbrook returned to normal, and Ray returned to New York as she and Charles contemplated their future. At the end of January 1941, the announcement came. Charles and Eero had won in two categories: chairs and case goods. Though the form of the Organic chair is its most arresting visual aspect and a mass-production challenge, the judges cited another innovation as well: the use of a flexible leg mount to provide a kind of springy feel.[13] But now the real adventure began because, in only eight months' time, MoMA would be having an exhibition of the award-winning pieces—in production. Now the Eames-Saarinen team had to deliver and so far they had only plans and a few models. Even so, their models and Charles's photographs had been so persuasive that people asked if they already had full-blown chairs—which, of course, they did not.[14]

To begin, they asked Albinson to make a full-scale plaster mock-up of one of the chairs. In fact, Albinson and another student, Jill Mitchell, went on Charles's payroll—both commented years later about being Charles's first employees.[15] Though there had been others in St. Louis, for the journey that began at Cranbrook they were absolutely right. Albinson recalls that Charles and Eero first used a patented technique originally intended only for a detail of a wooden tray. In larger applications like the chairs, this technique turned out to have considerable problems.[16] Another idea that they tested was using cycle weld, an automotive technology, to join the steel in the legs to the chair. Charles clamped a sample of wood and steel with the cycle weld and put it in his oven. The wood was reduced to charcoal (and was not great for the oven), showing the limits of that solution: the wood and the metal could not be heated the same way at the same time.[17]

The chair mock-up was taking longer than expected, while tables and case goods proved to be less of a problem. A contract for the tables and case goods was signed in April 1941, and they were ultimately manufactured by the Red Lion Furniture Company in Pennsylvania. But the chairs were a different matter. That same April the first wooden shell was finally created—to no one's satisfaction.[18] The manufacturers were getting anxious. In

July, Paul Posser at the Heywood-Wakefield Furniture Company said, "we're only doing it as a favor to the stores and the museum."[19] By then Charles and Ray had married and moved to California, while Eero was distracted by other projects such as his Defense Housing. A frustrated Charles wrote to Eliot Noyes, "I suppose Eero has told you of our finally getting around to some cast-iron dies. It makes me sick that we didn't insist on giving it a trial months ago."[20] In other words, there were more problems with the actual tooling. Indeed, each individual chair shell required a great deal of work in all sorts of ways. After the molding process, the wood was splintered, which necessitated the unsatisfactory concealment with fabric. In other words, the Organic chair, intended as an expression of the potential of mass production, had, as Ray later noted, "become a handmade object" after all.[21]

Perhaps Noyes summarized the problems of production and cost best in a letter to Alfred Barr, director of MoMA: "On the armchair and the reclining chair," he wrote, "the curves of the back were so complicated that it was not found possible at this point to get sufficiently finished surfaces to expose the wood. Therefore fabric has been applied to all the backs except the little dining chair. . . . The excitement of sitting in them is not going to be a middle-class thrill at this point because the prices are something terrific [too high]."[22] In fact, Bloomingdale's emerged as something of a hero in this story when it reduced its usual 100 percent markup to 10 percent. But even then the price was still too high to create "a middle-class thrill."[23] The shell alone cost $6 or $7.[24]

The Organic Furniture exhibition opened at MoMA in September 1941. A limited number of chairs had been successfully produced through the combined efforts of Charles, Eero, MoMA, and the manufacturer. Tight on money, Charles and Ray missed the opening— "the fireworks" as Charles wrote in a letter.[25] The verdict on the program was a mixed positive: on the one hand, good works were created and new designers were discovered and given meaningful experience with manufacturers; on the other hand, mass production was not achieved in any meaningful sense for the Eames-Saarinen shell chairs. The exhibition itself offered an interesting allegory. Noyes exhibited a traditional easy chair in a barred

Some finished molded-plywood furniture of 1945 to 1946, from left to right: Circular Table Wood, Lounge Chair Wood, folding screen, and Dining Chair Wood

cage like King Kong (there was a Gargantua poster behind it). The label, like one found at a zoo or natural history museum, read, "*Cathedra Gargantua*, genus Americanus. Weight when fully matured, 60 pounds. Habitat, the American Home. Devours little children, pencils, fountain pens, bracelets, clips, earrings, scissors, hairpins and other small flora and fauna of the domestic jungle. Is rapidly becoming extinct."[26]

If extinction of traditional furniture was imminent, it would not be at the hands of the modern chairs in the exhibition room, but it might come through their descendants. Charles had clearly learned that if you were designing for mass production, you had to discover how to make the tooling—not just the end product—yourself. This was a profound realization, one that dovetailed naturally with his gift for hands-on design and engineering. But it was deeper than that, because Charles must have recognized that design for mass production was a new animal. All of the dissatisfactions of the finished chairs were a result of not understanding the limitations of the process when he and Eero had designed the chairs. Charles later recalled, "We were setting out to, really, I would say [put] the Frank Lloyd Wright theory, at least my own version of it, to work—and it may have turned out looking more Miesian than Frank Lloyd Wright, but nevertheless it's one's own interpretation."[27] He continued, "The Organic show was more a kind of a statement of principle."[28] From a design standpoint, their key conceptual breakthrough was that they moved the plywood material away from the Aaltoesque slab in the Kleinhans to a shell concept. Charles and Ray would now have to find a way for this material to make a complex curve. As he said later of all the furniture on this path, "We wanted to make the best for the most for the least. It sounds a little pompous now, but at the time it was a perfectly legitimate way to approach things."[29] If the Organic chairs turned out to be essentially a statement of principle, it would take Charles and Ray five years to make the first pragmatic statement about production, and a full ten years to make it completely.

On January 8, 1942, less than a year after the announcement of the competition winners and a month after the attack on Pearl Harbor, Eliot Noyes wrote to Charles in frustration, "the whole project seems to be dribbling off into nothing because of [war] priority pressure; no more rubber, no more plywood."[30] Noyes was right, but only as far as it went, because the war that was presently bringing the Organic project to a merciful end would also end up being the testing ground for Charles and Ray's attempts to learn the right lessons. Charles and Eero had brought it this far. Now they parted ways (Eero bowed out to pursue more immediate projects on his docket; this parting was in the friendliest of fashions and there were many more adventures ahead in work and in play), and Charles, now partnered with his new bride, Ray, took the ball and ran with it.

Charles and Ray's move to Los Angeles meant not only a new city and a new life, but also a new way of understanding design and creation. This time, Charles would learn how to make it before he decided what it looked like. In other words, the design of the Eames chairs would not be some sort of "pure" expression of form for its own sake but rather something, in a way, even more distilled: an expression of the effort to determine and meet specific needs of materials, manufacture, and comfort. The design would take its form from that process.

In an apartment complex designed by modernist architect Richard Neutra in the Westwood section of Los Angeles, not far from UCLA, Charles and Ray dived into the challenge. Ray described it this way: "The problems [had become] obvious: [the organic chair] could not be manufactured the way it was meant to be, as a mass-produced object. . . . So the simple idea was to try to find out, what would make it a mass-produced object."[31] In other words, they needed to learn how to mass-produce molded plywood in compound curves in order to get the single-piece shell made. The form would come from that.

In the spare room of the apartment, they began to work on a device they eventually called the "Kazam! machine," named not for any strange noise but for its sense of magic, as with the special boxes Charles made for his daughter, Lucia.[32] This machine allowed them to mold plywood themselves. It had a curving plaster mold with energy-guzzling electrical coils running through it. Charles long remembered the terror of climbing a power pole by their apartment to poach enough electricity from the transformer to run the Kazam! machine, and the growing conviction he would electrocute himself. Fortunately he survived.[33] They created their plywood in the molding process by laying a sheet of the veneer (a thin plane of wood—the "ply" in plywood) in the form and then putting a layer of glue on the wood, and then repeating the process, usually between 5 and 11 times. (In the Organic chair, the wood was created by laying strips of veneer, not a whole sheet, into the desired form.)[34] A bicycle pump was used to inflate a rubber balloon after the Kazam! had been clamped tightly shut and push the wood against the form, giving it shape.

As they developed the Kazam! machine, Charles and Ray began to explore what it

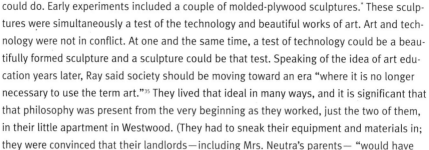

\* These molded-ply-wood sculptures (see page 38) are different from the ones Ray carved from splints. Though beautiful, the splint sculptures do not concern us here because they are not part of the direct lineage of the chairs.

could do. Early experiments included a couple of molded-plywood sculptures.* These sculptures were simultaneously a test of the technology and beautiful works of art. Art and technology were not in conflict. At one and the same time, a test of technology could be a beautifully formed sculpture and a sculpture could be that test. Speaking of the idea of art education years later, Ray said society should be moving toward an era "where it is no longer necessary to use the term art."[35] They lived that ideal in many ways, and it is significant that that philosophy was present from the very beginning as they worked, just the two of them, in their little apartment in Westwood. (They had to sneak their equipment and materials in; they were convinced that their landlords—including Mrs. Neutra's parents— "would have had a heart attack,"[36] to quote Ray, had they seen all the materials.)

Two copies of the taller sculpture are still in existence, but there may have been more—a subtle but important reminder of the sculpture's role as a test of the production process. Though at times credited just to Ray, these sculptures were, in fact, the work of both of them, as was much of the later furniture, which was often credited just to Charles. They also made many different one-piece molded shells, testing the limits of the technology and material.

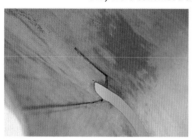

Detail of the molded-ply-wood pilot seat, showing the corner hole and cuts in the wood that relieve pressure to permit molding

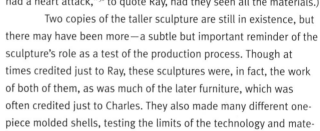

rial. Some splinter in one way or another; others have a slit or hole cut by the Eameses in them. These breaks, whether put in manually or happening naturally, all relieved the tension created by forming a single-piece shell with compound curves.

Charles and Ray continued to refine an idea that became a pillar of their design process: the "honest," or unselfconscious, use of materials. In other words, if a chair was made of molded plywood, it should show the molded plywood, not try to conceal it, and honor the plywood's inherent qualities. In a way, the notion is similar to the credo "form follows function," but the use of the term "honest" not only injects an ethical dimension but also acknowledges a human and subjective one, suggesting that there may be more than one path to a given design choice. As they sought an honest use of plywood, Charles and Ray were coming up against the incontrovertible experience ("fact" is the wrong word) that plywood did not want to be a single-piece molded shell.

As America geared up for war in earnest, all technologies were turned to the war effort. Dr. Wendell Scott, a friend of Charles's from St. Louis who was stationed in San Diego, came to Los Angeles and in a casual conversation mentioned a problem they were having in the medical corps. Braced in the regulation metal splints, the legs of wounded servicemen were ending up in worse shape after being carried than they were with a makeshift one. The reason was that the metal unfortunately amplified any vibrations from the stretcher bearers.[37] Immediately, Charles and Ray began to explore the possibility of using the molded plywood to solve this problem.

Soon after, they developed their molded-plywood splint. It conformed to the shape of the human leg,[†] giving support through natural form. It also was an extremely honest use of materials, wedding the Eames understanding of the limits of the material to the functional needs of the splint. Hold this beautiful object in your hand sometime if you can—they still appear in flea markets and vintage stores. Symmetrical holes relieve the stress of the bent plywood, but also give the medic a place to thread bandages and wrappings. The splints represent a perfect example of utilizing to advantage what the Eameses called the constraints of a particular design problem. Recognizing and working within these *constraints* was always key to their design process. It was not always easy.

Referring to the Japanese bomb scares,[‡] Charles commented ruefully about the frustration they felt: "And I remember, we'd—some dreary nights I'd go home, I'd say, 'You know, I—God, dear God, I don't want any bombs to particularly drop on Los Angeles or the United States, or any place, but if one must drop, wouldn't it be nice if it hit right in the middle of our plant!' The problems there had gotten to be fairly great."[38] And it was not always simply a matter of the obvious design issues—there were problems of financing, which ultimately led to partnerships with John Entenza and Colonel Evans of Evans Products.[39]

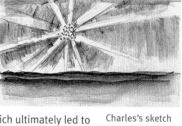

Charles's sketch of anti-aircraft fire over Los Angeles in a letter to Lucia, 1942

In the end, the best guess is that 150,000 of the splints were made and used. As a product and an experience, it was ultimately far more satisfactory than the Organic furniture. The Eameses, evolving into the Eames Office and the Molded Plywood Division of Evans Products, had developed and nurtured a fabrication process and even built the actual tooling that made the splints. This key development was a natural extension of their thinking. Charles and Ray realized that they had to earn the right to control the design and that the coin of the realm was not a contract but an understanding of the process.

The splints led to more wartime molded-plywood work, including a nose cone and other parts for the CG-16 glider (Flying Flatcar) in 1943. Look closely at the Eameses' pilot seat for another plane, a Vultee. In some ways, it solves the problem of the shell that was posed by the Organic chair: it is a single-piece plywood shell, but in order to make the material work, it had holes in the corners, and the veneer had to be applied unevenly. You can't just put a stack of veneers on top of one another and mold them. They must have cuts and other details that make it possible to create the curvature. In the pilot seat, the result is a single piece of plywood, but not the elegant form Charles and Ray were searching for. The pilot seat rather remarkably synthesizes the years of work to that date and provides a road map of the problems facing the single-shell solution.

† Charles's leg was the model. This process was extremely painful when he ripped all the hairs out of his leg removing the cast.

‡ Japanese U-boats shelled Santa Barbara in late 1941.

43

Right: Kazam!
machine in the
Eameses' Neutra
apartment in
Westwood,
California. Note
the wires for
heating in the
plaster and the
bicycle pump at
the lower right.

Something else was happening, too. Although the military is not the same as a consumer market, it is still a market. And making something that people actually needed was immensely more satisfying than the simple statement of principle that the Organic chair embodied. On a practical level, the splints led to self-sustaining rather than obligatory production. Charles and Ray were beginning to strike what would become their characteristic balance of idealistic vision and realistic implementation.

In 1945, as the sense grew that the war was coming to a close, the Eames Office, now two years old and some 15 people strong (including the folks manufacturing the splints), turned its attention back to furniture. With the important experience of the war years behind them, Charles and Ray pushed harder than ever. If there were a way to make a single-piece shell of molded plywood in complex curves, the Eames Office would find it. The office began working toward introducing the furniture at a December 1945 show at the Barclay Hotel.

Meanwhile, on the design front, Charles and Ray and the office staff were pushing— and pushing—the limits of the material. What was the honest use of molded plywood? Could it be a single-piece shell in complex curves? The cast of characters for the Barclay Hotel show was beginning to take shape in Charles's mind, but the headliners (meaning the single-piece shells) were not ready. Legs developed that used the curved wood. Three-legged chairs with metal legs, case goods, and tables, but always the frustration of the shell. Each time a split was necessary to make the curve work. In the end, they abandoned the idea of a single-piece shell and instead broke it into two parts: a seat and a back. They had finally uncovered the honest use of molded plywood. The LCW, the chair that resulted in 1945, is now an icon of American design. *Time* magazine called it "the chair of the century."[40] Did Charles and Ray regret the five years of work spent trying to make it one piece? On the contrary: about a different project, Charles said, "This way we know we have the right answer."[41]

Design historian Donald Albrecht has called the LCW a "brilliant failure."[42] Not because it wasn't a popular and critical triumph, but because the Eameses hadn't yet achieved the task they had set for themselves. And although the LCW launched Charles and Ray's careers, especially when Herman Miller, Inc., began distributing and then manufacturing it, Charles might well have agreed.

Despite so many steps in this journey, we are still only partway through this flash. The Eameses were, after all, trying to make a single-piece shell chair with complex curves, and a very low-cost one at that. They were still five years and two completely different materials away from their goal.

# CHAPTER 5

# A Good Learner

In mulling over the worlds of Charles and Ray Eames, from the Newton Cards through the lota to the Eameses' own lota in the form of the single-piece shell chair they pursued, one cannot escape the conclusion that conceiving, directing, and creating such a diverse body of work would require not only a profound vision but also a rich life experience. In retrospect, Charles's life experience leading up to the founding of the Eames Office, from his youth in St. Louis through his time at Cranbrook, is a story of accumulating exactly what he would eventually need—a deep understanding of materials as well as broad experiences in work, skills, lifestyles, and society. Though he did not have what anyone would call an easy childhood, his early years—and the curiosity, responsibility, and drive with which he engaged them—ultimately provided unique opportunities and hands-on experience. Charles, though often called a Renaissance man, was actually somewhat more akin to a Benjamin Franklin or a Thomas Jefferson, a kind of New World philosopher in the eighteenth-century mold. In fact, as one retraces Charles's journey, one can see a particular quality in him that he and Ray later found important in their study of Franklin and Jefferson as people. Like them, Charles was always a very good learner.[1]

Charles Eames was born in the twentieth century; his father was born in the nineteenth; and his father's father in the eighteenth. As Charles himself said dryly, "it made for a reasonably wide spread."[2] Many writers have contrasted in the Eameses' work the twentieth-century modernism with what they see as the nineteenth-century clutter. It may have something to do with the fact that the designer Charles Eames seems to have crafted and grasped so many of the essential qualities of twentieth-century America—from the physicality of new materials to the consequences and nature of the communications revolution. In a related way, his father, Charles Ormand Eames Sr., was profoundly affected by two of the most powerful facts of nineteenth-century America: the Civil War and the railroads. And as a result, these forces were extremely present in what Charles described as "largely a nineteenth-century upbringing."[3]

In the mid-1700s, Henry Eames embarked from County Limerick, Ireland. He was

Charles at the Laclede Steel Mill, early 1920s

47

Charles Eames Sr., sketched by Charles Eames Jr. (1918)

not a resident of Limerick, but departed from there for New England with the evangelist Charles Wesley. A couple of generations later Charles Ormand Eames Sr. was born in upstate New York, near Lake Champlain. At some point in the boy's youth, the family moved to the Chicago area.

In September 1864, at the age of 15, Charles Sr. became a soldier in the Union Army. He was part of the Chicago Board of Trade Battery, an artillery unit created in 1862 in response to a call for volunteers from President Abraham Lincoln.[4] A story has been passed down through the family of his being involved with reconnaissance even before then and, because of his youth, attracting little attention as he crossed enemy lines. When at last a soldier, Charles Sr. became his unit's fife player. To modern ears that may sound relatively safe, but in Civil War battle, the fife player and drummer boy were positioned near the young man who carried a unit's colors (a spot that tended to draw a good deal of enemy fire). Charles Sr. first saw action with the Chicago Battery shortly before the Battle of Kennesaw Mountain, famous for General William T. Sherman's order: "Hold the fort. I am coming." At the end of the war several soldiers from the Chicago Battery, including Charles Sr., were with the Michigan Fourth Cavalry in May 1865, when they captured Jefferson Davis, the president of the Confederacy, wearing his wife's cape as he tried to escape.

The Union Army's successful military effort joined and then evolved into the spectacular enterprise of the transcontinental railroad, binding, as historian Stephen Ambrose argues, the East and West with steel as the North and South had been bound by blood.[5] For several decades, the railroads complemented St. Louis's prime location on the Mississippi and made the city a critical hub of the industrial United States. (From 1870 to 1910, St. Louis was the fourth largest U.S. city.) After the Civil War, Charles Eames Sr. worked for the Pinkerton Detective Agency and later became the head of security for the Missouri Pacific Railroad. One of his perches for observing traffic was a steel-mesh cage high above the huge central vault of the St. Louis Union Station, through which all passengers needed to pass. From there he watched their movements, keeping an eye open for trouble in general, but particularly for lawmen who had notified him that they would be passing through with prisoners in custody.

Charles Sr. was frequently exposed to danger—no safe desk job for him. Years later his son, Charles Jr., would clearly remember the standing rule of instant obedience: if his father said do something, the boy had to do it instantly—no questions asked. Why? Because his father might be telling him to avoid a bullet and there would be no second chances.[6] Or as Charles recalled his father's words, "there may be a case where I can't afford to raise my voice; it might scare the rattlesnake."[7] Under her pillow Charles's mother kept a gun that her husband had taught her how to shoot with skill.[8]

For good or ill, at the end of the nineteenth century St. Louis was not as far from the frontier as its residents liked to pretend it was. Some of Charles Sr.'s original reports survive, and one particular incident in 1892 captures the flavor of his life as chief special agent and a feeling for what the young Charles grew up hearing about. After a train holdup near Coffeyville, Kansas, the suspects escaped into the Indian Territory (now Oklahoma). Because a badge of any kind would have "frightened away the game," Special Agent Eames engaged a white horse thief and a half-black, half–American Indian petty criminal named Cherokee Bill to help him find the four train robbers. Eventually, Eames and his scouts tracked down the outlaws at a remote ranch where another confederate had joined the fugitives to prepare for a string of bank robberies. At that point, Special Agent Eames and a handful of marshals rode several miles to the hideout. They even walked the last mile on stockinged feet for stealth, but it turned out one of their scouts had already poisoned the guard dogs. Special Agent Eames recalled what happened after he and the marshals rushed the door: "The next moment we were all upstairs. The outlaws were all in bed but had their clothes on and their revolvers and Winchesters in bed with them. Jack Turner and George Brown were in the bed farthest from the stairs while [the remaining three] were together in the other bed. Turner and Brown began shooting through the bedclothes and were promptly silenced. Three of the largest marshals jumped on the bed nearest the stairs and held the men occupying that bed so that they could not use their guns. We soon had irons on these three men and found that Jack Turner was shot through the heart and was dead while George Brown was fatally wounded. Securing a farmer's wagon we made the tedious journey to Venita where as soon as possible we took a train to Fort Smith and turned prisoners over to the U.S. authorities."[9]

Ten years later, in 1902, this same man, Charles Ormand Eames Sr. married Marie Adele Celine Lambert, a bride thirty years younger than himself. Celine (as she called herself) was part of the Aubuchon and Chomeau lines, families with deep local roots. Her forebears, who were already in the St. Louis area in 1764 when the French founded it as a trad-

ing city, continued to be productive community members as the city blossomed into a key commercial node on the Mississippi (her cousin Henri Chomeau, as county surveyor for St. Louis, helped lay out its "broad streets and magnificent distances"[10]). At various times St. Louis was claimed or coveted by France, Spain, England, and the United States, finally coming under the U.S. flag in 1804, after the Louisiana Purchase. But suggestive of the city's French character and persistent influence, Marie Celine's mother, Marie Adele Aubuchon (born in 1852) did not speak English until she started public grade school.[11] This was true of her sisters and cousins as well, the women who would eventually help Marie Celine raise her children. Strong women were the norm in this family, arguably underscored by a matri-

lineal tradition, represented by Marie's birth name in full: Marie Celine Adele Pauline Lambert. For six generations, the eldest daughter was always given the name Adele. Indeed, Marie Celine and Charles Sr.'s firstborn was Adele Eames (and Adele Eames Franks's daughter is also named Adele—yes, it can get a little complicated.)

Though the Aubuchon family had deep roots in St. Louis, Marie Celine's father, Pierre, had come to the United States relatively recently from the French portion of Alsace-Lorraine. When Germany captured Alsace in 1848, many French families sought to save their surviving sons from being drafted into the German Army by sending them to the United States. Marie Celine Lambert's father had four brothers, each of whom had been injured in European wars and one of whom had emigrated to St. Louis. Pierre's mother sent Pierre, her youngest, to live with that brother. There is no record that she ever saw either son again. After the months-long voyage across the Atlantic and up the river from New Orleans, the young boy was deposited by a sailboat on the west bank of the Mississippi with only the name of his brother pinned to his lapel. Pierre waited near where Lewis and Clark had stood more than four decades earlier and on the spot where Charles and Ray's dear friend Eero Saarinen would eventually place the Gateway Arch (and indeed a spot for which Pierre's grandson Charles and his wife, Ray, would design an unbuilt Jefferson Expansion Memorial). His brother found him and eventually got Pierre a job at the Restaurant Porcher, in the old Lucas Mansion at Eighth and Olive in downtown St Louis [12]

Pierre Lambert worked there for 15 years, eventually owning it after the Porcher family moved back to France. Family life revolved around the Porcher, noted for its hospitality and elegance and for a time being the home of the governor.[13] It also had a certain flair. In 1874, after the famous engineer James Eads completed the beautiful, elegant wrought-iron bridge that still spans the river, the restaurant created special menus in honor of the occasion. Yet for the people of this New/Old World community, a celebratory token like that was done naturally, rather than preciously. Eventually, Pierre Lambert met and married Marie Adele Aubuchon. They had three daughters: the youngest, Marie Celine, was born in 1879. Her family neither wealthy nor poor, she was born in the heart of St. Louis's Golden Age. Marie Celine was said to be so beautiful that men would turn in the street to look at her. Surviving photographs support this but do not convey her elegance and strength. Charles called her "the iron fist in the velvet glove,"[14] and her granddaughter remembered her as "warm and caring, very bright and loving."[15] It is not known exactly how Charles Eames Sr. and Marie Celine Lambert met, but a year after their 1902 marriage, Mrs. Charles Eames gave birth to a daughter, and, four years later, a son.

On June 17, 1907, Charles Ormand Eames Jr. was born in St. Louis, Missouri. One of his earliest memories was of his mother and father stopping in the middle of a piano-flute duet to step outside and look at Halley's Comet. The fact that they would do so told the three-year-old boy that something special had happened.[16] Indeed, in the mind of the child it was the musical interruption rather than the comet that secured the memory. Around the same age he contracted diphtheria. A small human-interest piece appeared in the local newspaper about his concern that Santa Claus would not be able to come down the chimney that Christmas because his house was quarantined. Young Charles asked his father to use his Secret Service training to determine if there were any red quarantine letters on the roof that might scare off Santa. Fortunately, the report came back negative.[17] This was the first time Charles Eames Jr. "made the papers."

Apart from the diphtheria and some typical childhood illnesses, Charles was a healthy boy with a loving sister, Adele, four years his senior. When Charles Sr. had to relocate with his family for work-related reasons, their migrations took them briefly to Brooklyn, New York. It was there that Charles Jr.'s father held him up to see the survivors of the Titanic as they docked, finally arriving in Manhattan after the tragedy; this was another memory that would stay with him the rest of his life.[18] The Eames family returned to St. Louis in time for Charles to attend kindergarten at Farragut Elementary School in North St. Louis, near the former site of the 1904 World's Fair. The kindergarten used the Froebel method of teaching, which involved blocks in primary and essential shapes as early teaching tools.*[19]

Young Charles was an extremely curious child and an avid reader of labels and instructions, especially those of patent medicines—printed in 15 to 20 languages. Charles would try to figure out each language by comparing, say, the Japanese and Italian words with the English ones.[20] It was like having the Rosetta stone on every bottle. His cousin, Celine, remembered that his gift for drawing seemed to be part of his persona from an early age.[21] Charles himself did not give credit to the school's art classes—in fact, he remembered himself and the other students referring to the weekly floral still-life assignments as "painting flags."[22]

* Frank Lloyd Wright was also raised with this technique as a child.

A GOOD LEARNER

51

A trio of clippings from an Eames family scrapbook (far left is from 1910; the others are from 1925)

Charles Sr. was a frequent public speaker and seems to have used lantern slides to illustrate these talks. His job often took him away from home for long periods of time and he would write home regularly to keep in touch. In 1914, though, when Charles Jr. was eight years old, the family's worst fears were realized: Charles Sr., while pursuing a criminal in the railyard behind the main station in Roanoke, Virginia, surprised the suspect, who turned and shot him. Charles Sr. never fully recovered from his injuries and had to retire from service. In the last years of his life, he wrote detective stories that capture some of the flavor of his life as a detective. Appearing in the *St. Louis Globe Democrat* and other publications, his stories have such dramatic titles as "The Talking Cane," "The Fruits of Crime," and "The End of the Trail."[23]

Charles Jr. later reflected that after the Froebel years he still "fared pretty well" as far as his elementary schooling was concerned. He felt he was fortunate that there was always at least one teacher each year who stuck to the basics, taking both their subjects and "their pleasures seriously."[24] Though he was applying that potent Eamesian phrase in retrospect, it is clear he felt the sensibility at the time. However, the young Charles could not apply his full capabilities to his schoolwork because his father's injury meant that he now had to help support the family. He got his first job at Upton Cody's, a printing and envelope shop in downtown St. Louis, not far from Eads Bridge. Salary? Four dollars a week, including Saturdays. This was quite a demanding schedule for a boy of 10 who was still in school.

The printing presses at Cody's had no safety guards—"you had to damn well get your hands out of the way. . . . I succeeded in keeping all my fingers, which was learning something."[25] Charles was not being mistreated (the wages and working conditions were typical of the era), but his situation gives some sense of the tight family budget: "to save a nickel a day with which I could then buy some soda water instead of drinking that hot water that came up in the building, I used to ride downtown on a streetcar." It was the Cass Avenue line, but he was not inside the streetcar. "We used to call it 'bumpering' a car out. . . . I had to fight the competition to climb on the bumper on the back of the streetcar." Even after he had fought his way onto the bumper, he was not necessarily safe: there were still the conductors to contend with. One of them caught Charles and started beating the boy's fingers with a ticket punch to make him lose his grip. "I fell off of the streetcar on to the cobblestones . . . and broke a rib, which still sort of sticks out in a funny way. Everyone thought I was killed but I thought they were going to put me in the penitentiary, so I managed to get the hell out of there."[26] He didn't tell his mother until after the rib had awkwardly healed itself.[27] Eventually, work at Cody's gave way to a job at Hyke and Ebler Grocers and then to a job working for the druggist Ernest Niemoller in North St. Louis.

At the end of February 1921, Charles Sr. succumbed to his wounds from the 1914 shootout in Virginia. The emotional impact of his death must have been profound, but Charles Jr. rarely talked about this time in any detail. Fifty years later, in relating what he called an "autobiography of situation" during one of his Norton Lectures at Harvard, he recalled, "my father died and the instruction reading paid off when I got to be browsing into boxes of photographic chemicals, plates, a Corona four- or five-by-seven with a rapid rectilinear lens, and everything . . . and soon I was . . . mixing emulsions and photographing on wet plates. I did it for a year before I discovered that Eastman had already invented film and this wasn't necessary. . . . This led to a sort of sequence of events, that completely spared me from adolescence. I don't know whether it's a good thing or a bad. I wouldn't want to risk it myself."[28] As he spoke of his father's death, there was no glibness or apparent suppressed emotion in his voice, but rather the precision of acknowledging a milestone too important to ignore but too private to discuss in detail. Instead the audience was left with a tantalizing connection—that this time of sadness in Charles's life had led him to photography, a tool that would become one key to the rest of his life and work.

Though Charles spoke ruefully of his unnecessary travails in the darkroom, it is impossible to imagine that he really regretted that time, because only in that way could he have thoroughly learned the precise technical underpinnings of photography. In a sense, it was ontogeny recapitulating phylogeny. How many other photographers (particularly those who were not at it full-time) of the latter half of the twentieth century had ever painstakingly made glass-plate negatives? Even in his teen years, Charles was already informally developing the learn-by-doing approach that he would later perfect at the Eames Office. Unfortunately, none of these early Eames images are known to exist.

Charles Sr.'s death had a radical impact on Charles Jr.'s family's life and lifestyle. While never wealthy, the family had been well provided for. With Charles Sr. now gone, the family had to economize and Charles Jr. had to do still more. "I was told I was a man and they didn't let me forget it,"[29] he said later. Though Marie Celine received a lifelong Civil War widow's pension of $30 per month, it was not enough, and she moved in with her sisters. At

the same time, Charles's sister Adele began bringing in money by working in the St. Louis city playgrounds in a program aimed at helping troubled youths.* Charles admired his sister's efforts, saying that "she had a real knack for working with real tough kids . . . some of them were real gangsters."[30]

Charles later declared, "I was raised by my mother, sister, and two aunts that . . . were still at the time reliving the [1904] World's Fair in St. Louis, and I couldn't wish any young man a better raising situation."[31] His mother's combination of stoicism, tolerance, and wisdom kept them all together. "I lived in a family where the women were very strong . . . as in many French families." Charles noted, "I am used to having strong women around."[32]

Though French Catholic families tended to be considered conservative, Charles remarked that "for a family who was, you know, super middle class respectable, [mine was] not in any way puritanical, both from a standpoint of drinking and wine and even attitude towards sex. . . . My mother was the motherly type of all time. And so were the French aunts. [And] it was my grandmother that used to think that if a young boy didn't have a glass of claret with his soup, that something was going to happen to his blood. And the neighbors would be horrified if their son had come to lunch and was given wine with his soup!"[33]

When Charles turned 14 in 1921, he entered Yeatman High School, where he excelled.† He was a captain of the football team and stood out in track as well. One friend remembered Charles racing in a 220-yard dash with his shoe loosening but running as hard as he could and finishing without the shoe.[34] Though Charles still had a job, there were out-of-town adventures too. In 1923, he took a train trip to visit cousins in Kansas and wrote his mother that "we gigged a lot frogs and ate them."[35] But such quintessential midwestern experiences were counterbalanced by others much darker, some in the steel mill where he worked when not at school. Years later he would say, "if you can imagine the labor and racial conditions [in that part of Illinois]. There would be blacks just murdered for the slightest—without any provocation."[36]

He became president of the senior class and contributed drawings to the yearbook. Drawing, drawing, always drawing. Charles also did well in mathematics. He did not claim too much for his math prowess, but instead pointed out that the teacher tended not to have a target beyond being "gratified you had a certain understanding. . . . However, that gratification is already something and you get interested. You got a feeling that there was a certain basis of pleasure in it."[37] (The value of that "certain basis" may have reverberated years later in the creation of the Eames exhibition *Mathematica*.)

Charles worked at the Laclede Steel Company in Venice, Illinois, all through his years at Yeatman High School. The job, which came about through his neighbor, Walter

* Adele later married a minister, Vincent Franks, and continued to be active in community and education programs. Known for her tolerance, high spirits, and candor, she founded a school through one of her husband's churches but eventually resigned from it because of its failure to desegregate.

† Yeatman High School was destroyed by a tornado in the 1930s.

Opposite: A bookplate by Charles for his niece Adele Franks. This page, top: this 1931 Christmas card by Charles gives a sense of the key landmarks of this era for the Eames family. This page, bottom: a lithograph by Charles shows a classic vista of the Eads Bridge on the Mississippi.

Kurtz, was a step up for Charles in two respects. Initially, it was simply that the pay and work hours were significantly better—40 cents an hour from 6 a.m. to 6 p.m. all week during the summer and on weekends during the school year. But more importantly, his employers discovered that Charles could draw. And so, while still in high school at Laclede, "I would be put on patterns and some vague engineering work and then I would make drawings," Charles said. "I would draw a lot and then I had been sort of introduced to the idea of architecture and because of this combination of experience and things, which was a little bit in advance of what would normally be expected, I was given a scholarship to the university— an architectural scholarship."[38]

As high school drew to a close, Charles was voted "most likely to succeed" and gave the valedictory. He headed to Washington University in St. Louis. The folks at Laclede hoped that he would return to the steel mill after college and, with his degree complementing the credibility he had from working in the shop, help the line workers understand and accept new technologies. It was an intriguing idea, but Charles had become captivated by architecture and wanted to pursue it as a profession. With a generous letter of recommendation from the owners of Laclede, Charles got a job designing lighting fixtures for the Edwin Guth Lighting Company. For Charles, Guth provided "an interesting transition" to architecture.[39] By the time he started his college studies in the fall of 1925, Charles had also begun a part-time job at Trueblood and Graf, a local architectural firm in St. Louis that had designed Union Station, where his father had worked. One of Charles's first tasks at the firm was to sort the drawings of the station.[40] Trains seemed to weave their way through Charles's life in many ways, large and small.

Washington University is ensconced in a lovely campus in University City, just outside St. Louis and near its Forest Park, a marvelous urban park that anchors the western portion of the city. Charles always displayed a spectacular interplay of intellectual gifts and personal charm, with neither apparently suffering for the other, and college life was no exception. Early in his first year at Washington University, after being elected president of his class, Charles was involved with a fairly elaborate prank in which he was kidnapped and held for a day or two. The police must have regarded it as fairly benign, but it was overt enough to have been reported in the papers for a couple of days.[41] All ended well—for the moment. The School of Architecture was a classical Beaux Arts school where about 300 students were taught in the traditional fashion of much sketching and copying. The environment itself was intensely rich and included a glorious half-scale model of the Egyptian Temple at Karnak, which gave a visceral sense of space to the students taught within it.[42]

Several students in Charles's class went on to prominence. Charles Hellmuth became a founding partner of HOK, today one of the leading large international architecture firms. Izzy Millstone, a civil engineer who built many of the freeways and developments in the St. Louis area, remembered Charles as a skilled draftsman, but not necessarily at the top of the class. However, Charles stood head and shoulders above everyone else in the school when it came to an exercise known as an *esquisse*, in which students had to solve a design problem in a relatively short period of time (usually no more than a day). Millstone recalled that Charles's *esquisse* solutions were widely recognized as the quickest and (almost always) the best, displaying the most profound understanding of the problem. Seventy years later this fact was still a vivid memory for Millstone.[43]

When Charles and Ray's friend Saul Steinberg learned Charles had no diploma, he made one for Charles. Look as close as you can and you will find no real letters.

Despite the demanding work schedule of his youth, or perhaps because of it, in college Charles seemed determined to enjoy the experience. For a while he stayed with his great uncle Henri Chomeau and his widowed daughter, Adele Starbird, later a prominent St. Louis writer. In a short essay titled "Devonair Charlie," which Starbird wrote after receiving a copy of the Eames book *A Computer Perspective* from Charles in 1973, she admitted that she had misjudged him at the time: "I knew he had great creative ability and talent, but I feared he might be defeated by his own facility, charm and good looks. I had seen it happen in others." It seems as though she had good reason for concern, for she observed another side of the *esquisse* that appeared so effortless to Izzy Millstone. To her, Charles was "entirely a free spirit," and she recognized in him what she called the family vice of procrastination. When he had a serious assignment, he would sometimes ask her, hopefully, "'Cousin, is there anything I can do for you this evening?' I recognized the symptom. 'Do you have an *esquisse* to do?' 'Well, yes,' he admitted. Then I brewed a pot of strong tea for him to take to his room, knowing that he would work until five in the morning."[44]

Professor Lawrence Hill, who taught Charles's history and elements class, had a passion for history combined with an unshakable belief in the principles of a Beaux Arts education. Charles considered him "one of the greatest teachers I ever had."[45] Professor Valenti made a different impression, living "the kind of mysterious domestic life in which you would never—the relationship was never clear. It was very mysterious, very interesting and exotic. He [also] made [the] Italian renaissance really come to life. He was a full professor that kind of enters into a plot with his students and in that way sort of gets them to work and do interesting things."[46]

Outside of school, Charles was quite intrigued by the work of Frank Lloyd Wright.

* He was briefly married (for a matter of days) in high school, but the marriage was annulled.

Jehane Burns Kuhn, who worked with Charles on the Norton Lectures at Harvard, points out, "Charles always said that as an architect he'd been very much influenced by Frank Lloyd Wright, not so much in terms of forms as in terms of some of the things that Wright had written about relationship between buildings and the land and buildings and the way people live."[47] He also saw that Wright understood architectural history even if the resulting work was not traditional. But Washington University's architecture program had no use for Wright. Charles could not understand why the school could not find a common ground there. As he would so many times, particularly when it came to the conventional labels given to various ideas, Charles saw the deeper connections between two things in apparent conflict.

Charles Eames was not calling for an overthrow of the school's Beaux Arts order, and indeed none of Charles's buildings feel "Wrightian" in any literal way, but Charles was arguing in essence that Wright was a fact and an important figure and thus deserved study. As he pushed to have Wright included somewhere in the curriculum, the message was clearly given to Charles to back down on this point. He did not and, in 1927, after just four semesters, Charles was asked to leave the university, kicked out for what Professor Hill later told him was being "prematurely interested and concerned with Frank Lloyd Wright."[48] "His views were too modern"[49] was noted in another report log. Later, Charles and Lawrence Hill became good friends, and Charles ultimately received an honorary degree from Washington University.

But such literal vindication was very much in the future as Charles weighed his options. Though he had just been thrown out of the prestigious local university, the good news was that the economy was booming and his skills as a draftsman were well recognized. Issues of modernism as a recognizable idea remained important to him. Ironically, in 1928, the Washington University student newspaper reported that Charles won a couple of competitions for a bandstand and a park pavilion "in the modern manner."[50] (Unfortunately, little more is known about them; they were never built and no drawings are known to survive.) Architecture was not the only area of exploration for Charles; he built his own lithography press and a pottery kiln as well.[51] Again, in retrospect, he was accumulating still more of the skills that would enable him to understand materials in the deep way his later work would require. And something else was happening: by the end of 1928, he was engaged to be married.*

Catherine Dewey Woermann was two years older than Charles and a fellow architecture student at Washington University. A Vassar graduate, she was the first woman in the graduate architecture program at Washington University. She was the daughter of Lucia Coyle Dewey and Frederick Christian Woermann, two solid members of the St. Louis German community. Frederick Woermann was a distinguished alumnus of Washington University and

an extremely successful civil engineer. Among his constructions were meatpacking plants, chapels, hospitals, and the aviary at the St. Louis Zoo. Although Catherine was regarded as talented and intelligent, the world that Lucia and Frederick Woermann raised her in did not envision too many roles for women beyond that of a traditional upper-middle-class wife. This ultimately contributed to a domestic situation that, in the end, may have pleased no one.

Catherine and Charles's courtship was quite intense, and very much over the objections of one of the men who had thrown Charles out of school. Dean Ferrand, a friend of the bride's father, assured Frederick Woermann that Charles would never amount to anything.[52] Nevertheless, Charles and Catherine were married on June 7, 1929. From Charles's mother, Catherine received a beautiful rose-gold pendant that Charles's father had designed. From Catherine's parents, the newlyweds received a honeymoon in Europe. By spending most of their savings as well, the young couple was able to prolong the trip into the fall, during which time they saw classical and medieval architecture in places like Rome and Siena, as well as work by such modernists as Ludwig Mies van der Rohe, Le Corbusier, and Walter Gropius. Charles does not seem to have taken any photographs during the trip, but some of his sketches from it were published later.

The Eameses returned from their honeymoon to a much different America than the one they had left months earlier. The Depression began almost as soon as they got back: "I came back, I was broke, but everybody else was broke, too. . . . The only thing to do then [was] to go into practice."[53] Indeed, Charles opened his own architectural office with Charles Gray, whom he had met at Trueblood and Graf. Later, Walter Pauley joined as a partner. Charles later commented about this venture on his own, "Going into practice of architecture in 1930 is really something. And it's the greatest thing that could happen, because you practice architecture and you have to do everything. And we did some little churches, we did some houses and residences, and if there was sculpture to do, you carved the sculpture. If there was a mural to paint, you painted the mural. We designed vestments, we designed

Above left to right: Charles and Catherine (1928); Lucia reading the comics, photographed by Charles (circa 1940); Charles and Lucia (1932)

59

lighting fixtures and residences, rugs, carving . . . and you helped build the building."[54] But, as the Depression began, business was very slow. Even the churches were still a few years away in October 1930, when Charles's only child, Lucia Dewey Eames, was born.

In the first year or so, Eames and Gray designed at least one complete building: a house for Engineering Professor Ernest Sweetzer. The firm also supervised the renovation of the Pilgrim Congregational Church, where Charles and Catherine had been married. Charles designed the lighting fixtures and some beautiful abstract, modernist details. As Gray, Eames, and Pauley, the firm designed two more residences in 1933, one of which has a bit of a modernist feel, the so-called Mason Road house. A recent owner said of it, "It is the only house I have ever owned where everything is in the right place." It's easy to believe that Charles would have regarded that as high praise.[55]

Independently, Charles designed the sets for some productions of the municipal opera in Forest Park. Lucia remembers "that it was fun to go with him backstage during the day and onto the huge outdoor stage, which was built around two magnificent [living] trees."[56] He painted as well, did small graphics projects for family, and worked with Emil Frei, the legendary stained-glass window designer. He even danced a soft-shoe number in the opera's chorus.

Outside of St. Louis, Charles measured buildings for Roosevelt's Work Progress Administration, including the cathedral in New Orleans. He fondly remembered these times — including weekends spent listening to Lyle Saxon, Roark Bradford, and Tennessee Williams — in the Norton lectures: "if you talk to anybody that lived through that period — where they were painting a mural in the post office or whatnot — why their voice will quiver and . . ."[57] and then, as he often did, Charles let his voice trail off evocatively. But after a time, that was no longer enough. He seemed to be chafing at something within himself, within the circumstances, within the marriage, and within the nature of his practice. It was one dimension of a malaise that infected their circle deeply, to the point that many folks were treating it with alcohol. As another St. Louis architect said of the Depression era, "It wasn't just stockbrokers who were jumping out of windows."[58] In the end Charles said, "I went to Mexico because while we were struggling along . . . because now this was like '32, '33. . . . And finally you want to get drunk every night."[59] And this was a vicious circle he had no intention of joining.

So, in 1933, Charles did something drastic, something without much of a plan, but something that ultimately may have been as important as the other skills he had gathered by this time: He moved his wife and daughter in with her parents — establishing, in effect, a trial separation from Catherine. Then, after they were safely ensconced, he went to Mexico with just 75 cents in his pocket, promising to return, but not knowing or saying exactly when.[60]

Top: a painting by Charles of the Municipal Opera (1932). Inset: detail of back of picture. Bottom: stained-glass door by Charles at Pilgrim Congregational Church in St. Louis (1931)

# CHAPTER 6

# Painting in the Broadest Sense

The differences in Charles's and Ray's upbringings were significant: economically, geographically, and simply from the standpoint of their respective genders, including the sheer breadth of work and life experience they were exposed to before the time they met. Nevertheless, the similarities they shared as young spirits may be significant as well: both lost their fathers before they were adults, both eventually left their hometowns behind, and both had a love for and exposure to theater and film. Perhaps most important, Charles and Ray were both extremely and truly curious about the world around them. Their voracious thirst for knowledge and openness to experience meant that, when they ultimately joined forces, their collective past was tremendously rich.

Self-portrait by Ray Kaiser, age 16

Because Ray's parents died relatively young (neither reached age 60), little survives today of their family lore. Alexander Kaiser, Ray's father, was the youngest son of Maurice and Henrietta Kaiser, whose own parents had been among the relatively early Jewish settlers of the then-frontier town of Stockton, California.[1] Founded in 1849, Stockton is located in the lush Central Valley, and the Kaiser family was one of the early merchants in that town. Though 90 miles inland (by water), the port permits ocean going vessels to be loaded there. Henrietta, born in Germany in 1840, came to America as a young girl with her family, moving on to Stockton by 1861.[2] Henrietta and Maurice seem to have met in Stockton but possibly lived in other towns before returning to raise a family.

In any event, soon after the Kaisers' son Alexander was born in 1873, the family was living in Stockton. By 1889, Maurice Kaiser and a partner took over a general store called Granger's and renamed it Friedberger and Kaiser.[3] Six years later, when he was 22, Alexander went off on what seems to have been his first extended time away from home. The young Alexander had a flair for the theater, and at the age of 22 he went on a three-year tour as a "mesmerist," visiting towns all over the west "and exhibit[ing] his powers in mind-reading."[4] He spent a bit of time in vaudeville but, by around 1900, found himself back in Stockton working at his brother's jewelry store, known as "the little store with the big stock" (eventually his brother George and Mr. Friedberger's son took over the family business).

63

Alexander enjoyed the precision and craftmanship of working with jewelry, but his real passion was for the theater. Nevertheless, working there had at least one important result: it was there that he met his future wife, Edna May Burr, who clerked at the shop.[5]

It was a three-year courtship and, soon after they met, Alexander left his brother's employ to found his first theater in 1903. On November 23 of that year, he and some partners started the Stockton Novelty Theater which they built themselves. About this vaudeville theater, Alexander was quoted (in a tongue-in-cheek fashion) as saying, "I give 'em high-class junk and they eat it up!"[6]

Ray's mother, Edna May Burr, was a relative of the controversial U.S. vice president Aaron Burr,* and the lore of that family was rich with a feeling of an unfair treatment Burr received at the hands of history. A letter from Burr has been handed down from generation to generation of the family line.[7] When Ray lived in New York in the 1930s, for a time she used the initials R.A.B.K., the B standing for Burr, not Bearnice (which she dropped for a time).[8] Not much is known about the Burrs living in Stockton at that time. Edna did have a love for the theater, but what one of the newspapers said then is still true today: though Alexander was relatively well known around town, "his bride is not so well known, being of a retiring disposition."[9]

Edna May Burr

Edna and Alexander were married October 16, 1906, in a service presided over by the Rabbi Erlanger, "with the dignity and impressiveness that attends the matrimonial rites of the ancient faith in which he is a gifted teacher" (as the Stockton paper somewhat awkwardly put it).[10] Edna's sister, Dorothy, was the maid of honor. Apparently the couple was planning a secret wedding, but as the paper reported, that did not pan out: "Mr. Kaiser got cut his license after hours last night, hoping to get married and be on his wedding tour this morning before his friends learned of the facts, but it leaked out last night and this morning the two were showered with congratulations at every turn. But the end is not yet, wait until they get back."[11]

Though Edna and Alexander were married by a rabbi, Edna was Episcopalian, and raised her children in that faith. Religious labels would become less important to Ray as an adult, but as she was growing up she thought of herself as Episcopalian. One of the few times Ray's niece heard about the family's Jewish heritage was when she learned that Ray, as a high school graduate, had been rejected from at least one East Coast school as a result of it.[12] Alexander's parents, who eventually settled in San Francisco, were observant Jews. Ray had memories of their Chinese cook, who prepared incredibly delicious Jewish meals in her grandparents' San Francisco home.

When they were married, Edna was 19, Alexander, 33. On their return, they leased the house they were married in and set up housekeeping in Stockton, where their first child, Maurice, was born. In 1909, when a disastrous investment in potatoes led the Kaisers to lose just about everything, the trio moved to San Francisco so that Alexander could manage two theaters for another company.[13] It was here that their daughter, Elizabeth, was born in 1910. Then, one evening in April 1911, Alexander got an abrupt change of assignment from his boss: "Kaiser, you are going to Sacramento to-night to take charge of the Grand Theater for us."[14] And, like that, the family was headed to Sacramento, capital of the state of California. Sacramento at that time was a city of 45,000, one-tenth the size of San Francisco, which was the biggest city in the state. But because of its place at one end of the Transcontinental Railroad and its status as the state capital, Sacramento had shed (or at least had tried to) its frontier ways a little sooner than other cities of similar size had done. Not too long after his arrival, Alexander started the last theater he would build from the ground up: the Empress.

Alexander Kaiser in the 1920s

Ray was born in Sacramento on December 15, 1912. Her birth certificate bears the name Bearnice Alexandra Kaiser, but her older brother Maurice nicknamed her Ray-Ray when she was very little and the name stuck.[15] She changed her name legally to Ray when she was an adult. Right around this time, Elizabeth, the Kaisers' older daughter, died suddenly at the age of two. The sense in the family was that this tragic event led Alexander and Edna to be very protective of their surviving daughter.

Over the years, Alexander Kaiser worked with such disparate performers as Wyatt Earp, Al Jolson, and the Deiro Brothers (accordionists). Hundreds if not thousands of lesser-known acts passed through his theaters over the years. The ballerina Anna Pavlova performed for him in Stockton. Ray's mother and brother Maurice, then a baby, watched from the wings, and Pavlova kissed her brother during the curtain calls. Ray remembered her mother telling her that she "realized afterwards that [Pavlova] would take off her slippers and throw them away after each performance."[16] Alexander was always very proud of the fact that he was the first vaudeville manager to pay Al Jolson $100 a week.[17] Even after Alexander got out of the theatrical business, he and Jolson remained great friends and loved to go off fishing together. The outdoors in general and fishing in particular (he landed some fish of then-record size) were Alexander's passions. Though such "manly" activities tended to be shared with Maurice, who was also older, Ray spent time in the outdoors with her father too. At times, Ray would go "roughing it" and panning for gold with her uncle George. The nuggets of gold she found became lifelong treasures.[18]

Maurice, Ray's older brother, described their father as "like the Pied Piper . . . he always had candy and little magic tricks for the children, who followed him to and from the

theater. . . . Very magnetic and charming, but stern with his son, and very indulgent of his daughter."[19] And, in fact, Maurice commented that, understandably, "after the death of Elizabeth, everyone was very protective of Ray." As for their mother, Edna, Maurice said she was "everything a mother could ever be . . . warm, loving, caring . . . her job and hobby was her family."[20] Ray and Maurice remained quite close throughout their lives.

When Ray was five years old, her father, after 14 years in theater management, decided to move into "the department store field."[21] Perhaps this decision was based on a desire for a change of scene or the needs of a growing family. Unfortunately, it seems his new partners did not live up to his trust. A letter from Alexander's brother refers to "dismal rumors" about the partners.[22] So, in 1919, Alexander Kaiser returned to the theatrical trade, this time running "the first Loew's theater on the Coast," called the State Theater. Given that Ray would go on to make films, it may be significant that this theater was a combination motion picture–vaudeville house. The opening show acts reflected the mix: *Madam Peacock*, a melodrama written by and starring Alla Nazimova; *One Week*, a Buster Keaton short; and steel-guitar soloist Sam Naoni.[23]

Maurice Kaiser at West Point, circa 1930

It was probably not long after this time that Ray began to study ballet. Ray described her teacher, Leila Maple, a former member of the Russian ballet, as "a marvelous woman, who was beautiful and strong and strict—all the great things in a teacher. The underlying element, early on, besides the influence of my parents and [that] of teachers at school that had been impressive at an early age, was the sense of discipline and devotion [she instilled]—being able to accomplish something."[24]

The movie theater and a stint running the 1920 State Fair were Alexander Kaiser's last professional achievements in the theatrical world. He left theater behind for good and embarked on a new career with the California State Life Insurance Company. In this line of work he seemed to have found a kind of calling. He was remarkably successful, being a leading producer for the company for over 100 straight months. One of his friends had an interesting insight, observing that some of the other very successful salespeople in this line had also made a late career shift.[25] Whether consciously or unconsciously, it is hard to imagine that Ray did not learn from her father's example that the skills gained in one field could be transferred in the deepest sense to another field.

Alexander's career change was a good move for the family's finances, and Ray was considered relatively wealthy by her friends. Ray's friend Barney Reese recalled their girlhood together. Near the high school, "there was a tearoom across the street, Betty's Tearoom. And it was excellent, excellent food. And it was expensive. Ray could eat there every day. And Ray did."[26] There were also many social clubs, like the Manana or Jinx clubs. "We all belonged to a high school club together, and we'd go to those. In those days, when you had a meeting on a Saturday afternoon, you dressed up. And the hostess—actually the mother—always had a marvelous, virtually a luncheon for the girls to nibble on and so forth. Unheard of today, but in those days, why they made quite a—it was quite a process to go and it was an entertainment." Reese continued: "There was everything about Ray to know that . . . she wasn't, to me, a faultfinder, looking for what's wrong with the world."[27]

It could be hot in the Central Valley of California, as one of Ray's schoolmates remembered: "In those days, you stayed over [at a friend's house]. And Sacramento's hot nights, and no air conditioning—and you'd take some ice up and put it up on your bed, but then we finally figured out: go swimming . . . at night."[28] But it was a safe place: "You could take the streetcar downtown at eight o'clock at night to go to the movie, and come home at eleven by yourself, and you could meet people there and—safe as all getout. . . . We had our home never locked—there was no key."[29]

Although Ray was an active participant in the Sacramento social scene, when she joined the high school art club she dived into her art projects with fervor. Her notebooks are filled with sketches. It is noteworthy that at roughly the same ages, Charles and Ray were both learning about drawing and about representation as a key function of drawing. Eventually, they would both learn to transcend the limitations of their times, but first they mastered the conventions.

Barney Reese remembered her mother saying that Ray, an avid reader, was a good influence on her daughter. "So many doors were opened in my mind that Mother felt it was Ray who had enriched my life with the art and her different interests."[30] Ray was somewhat heavyset in high school. Her friends worried about her because "she just didn't appeal to the boys. That's all it was. But she was never downcast, any of that. Like: 'Poor me, I'm a little mouse and I never been out with a boy.' None of that. She was always her same old self, and I loved her laughter. Her laughter was terrific. [She was] short, and [it was] her structure, that's all. But we girls, we who loved her so, and I was so glad that Charles saw this gem that had so much to offer."[31] Another good friend of Ray's, Marion Russell, was "a beautiful blonde" who would regale her friends with tales of her dates. Barney remembered the sight of Marion and Ray walking together: "the two of them were the cutest things you've ever seen, because they both had . . . rumble seat coats. They looked like brown bears."[32]

When Ray was in her early teens, her parents' marriage had its ups and downs, but ultimately Edna and Alexander were able to work things out. Ray said later that her "parents were absolutely extraordinary, the more I realize it. I never knew it at the time: the quality of enjoyment of games and toys."[33] The enjoyment included the natural world as well: "My

Sketches by Ray Kaiser from the 1920s, from left to right: a house in Sacramento (possibly the Kaiser house); sketch from class; "Holiday Greetings"

father loved being in nature, and we would go out in the country when we were small. Sunday meant going—he just liked the idea of being in nature. Even Sunday school was not as valuable [to him] as being in nature."[34]

Edna and Alexander's successful reconciliation only must have made things more ironic and excruciating when suddenly, at the age of 56, Alexander had a heart attack. He and Maurice had been fishing the clear blue waters of Lake Tahoe in California's Sierra Nevada mountains. The outing was planned as their last fishing trip before Maurice went off to West Point. Despite the chest pains, Alexander insisted on rowing to shore and, further, that his son head off to West Point as scheduled.[35] Alexander died in San Francisco on July 8, 1929. Although the family had been well off, Alexander's sudden death, coupled with the stock market crash a few months later, put the family in a difficult financial position. Nevertheless, there was enough money to go around, and throughout the Depression the Kaiser family was well-off (by the standards of the time) but not wealthy. The trusts that Alexander had set up supported Ray, Maurice, and Edna through the 1930s.

Maurice Kaiser ultimately graduated from West Point and went on to pursue a distinguished career in the military. He achieved the rank of colonel and was ultimately director and secretary of the standing group, NATO. But he was always most proud of his wartime duty in Europe and his command of the 16th Armored Group, Camp Irwin, in California. (Charles and Ray visited him there a number of times.)

The year 1931 was one of transitions for Ray. In February, she graduated from Sacramento High School, and then attended Sacramento Junior College. She began applying to East Coast schools in preparation for a move that summer to Manhattan. Ray and her mother wanted to be closer to Maurice at West Point. Ray was accepted to May Friend Bennett School in Millbrook, New York (about 90 miles up the Hudson River Valley from New York City, not far from Poughkeepsie and West Point), and began classes there in the fall of 1931. Her mother, Edna Kaiser, lived on East 63rd Street in Manhattan at the time.

Ray remembered her two years at Bennett fondly. The setting was marvelous. She wrote of her frustration of facing finals and a term paper while a glorious spring was all around her: "But the country is *Gorgeous* now and I can't bear to miss a minute of it. There are all kinds of birds about and flowers and shades of yellow and green. It's all too beautiful." At the time, some friends were visiting her mother in Manhattan and she tried to persuade Edna to bring them up: "I want the Nathans to see it *terribly*."[36] The italicized words in the quotes are Ray's; the tone of voice, phrasing, and the passion to share the beauty with someone else—all would be familiar to anyone who knew her decades later.

In 1933, Ray moved to Manhattan. While she had enjoyed the opportunities to visit New York City from Bennett, after her graduation she became truly immersed in the culture of the city. She considered going to Cooper Union to study engineering. Around that time, Helen Donnelly, a friend from Bennett, was a key player in the effort to bring the painter Hans Hofmann to the United States from the deteriorating situation in Europe. He taught first at the Art Student's League and then at his own school. Ray signed up for Hofmann's first classes. "He was marvelous. It was a great part of my life—a great experience. It meant a great deal to me. I worked with him for six years. It was like working with him, it wasn't as most classes are considered today, I think. It just went on and on."[37] And it was a lot of work.

But work and play were intertwined. Ray remembered seeing Chaplin's *Modern Times* with Hofmann. "I've never laughed more. He laughed so, we were just in stitches from it all. No one could enjoy anything more than he, but as far as his teaching, it was structure and relationships, and color as structure."[38] For some, Hofmann had a reputation of being about fixing things in boxes, but Ray adamantly disagreed: "He didn't close anything, he opened everything and made it possible to see wholly, I think, as we do see: we don't see a line, we see a line and both sides of the line. . . . I don't know of anyone else who was as able to relate the experience of life to a canvas, to a format."[39] The idea of structure as something that could free you to see things still more richly was an important common ground Ray would eventually share with Charles.

Ben Baldwin, who joined the Hofmann classes in 1936, remembered that "[Hofmann] was very fond of [Ray] and very fond of her work. But, it was very different from everybody else's in the class. There was nobody doing anything like what she was doing."[40] Ray remembered the specificity of Hofmann's comments: rather than saying that they had done right or wrong, he would try to help the individual students achieve their own ideas.[41] Baldwin recalled a particularly striking Hofmann technique: he "would come in and look at what we were doing and very often we were working in charcoal from a model and he would take a razor blade and slice the thing in lots of different pieces and move it all around, with thumbtacks, so that it had a much more spatial relationship."[42] Hofmann was also noted for the precision with which he posed his models, sometimes taking up to

**Statue**
*Of Liberty*
**Beckons**

WEST LEFT BEHIND—Miss Ray Kaiser, who sailed to her home in New York after visiting friends at Sacramento.

an hour to set a single pose.

Ray's nickname was Buddha in the Hofmann circles and she adopted it gracefully. Her classmates at the Hofmann school included Lee Krasner, Wilfred Zogbaum, and Robert de Niro, among others. Interestingly, many of Hofmann's students were not planning to become painters at all. Baldwin described Ray this way: "she was always, you know, on point. She was always . . . she was like a Gaston Lachaise, sort of bursting with enthusiasm about everything, particularly when it was that big [indicating size of a dime with forefinger and thumb]."[43] Summers in the 1930s were mostly spent in Massachusetts. Hofmann had a studio in Provincetown, on Cape Cod. The students piled into Helen's old Rolls Royce and drove up there from Manhattan.

From time to time Ray took trips to see Maurice and his young family. Maurice's son, James Kaiser, remembered his aunt's visits vividly: when "I was very young, Ray brought a new dimension, for me, to nature and to the mundane. For example, she taught me to sew on buttons—a skill I use even today. They stay on, too! Bees, flowers, fish, bushes and butterflies were shown to be more than they appeared. She seemed, to a kid of three or four or five, to bring a magical quality to things in life. I don't think she ever 'played' with me, but she was sort of a fascinating fairy godmother type."[44] James's sister, Midge, echoed that thought: "She never treated me like a child, but like a colleague that she wanted to learn from. She would come right into my world and would take me into hers."[45] This way of engaging children as equals was another quality that Ray and her future husband would share.

Though she no longer thought of Sacramento as her home, Ray visited a couple of times during the six years she lived in New York. Barney Reese remembered a dance during one of Ray's visits back: "It was some kind of a club dance. So when Ray came—and in those days, why, all the boys wore suits and the girls wore silken dresses and so forth. . . . And of course she hadn't brought a party dress, she didn't know about that, and we said, 'Oh, come on, you have to come.' And she wore her nightgown, which had spaghetti straps, and it looked just like a party dress that today's girl would wear, exactly the same, and . . . no one knew it was her nightgown, you see. And she wore it with all the aplomb of her cocktail dress. So that was stamped in my memory forever: how to cover any emergency, why, Ray could do it well. And she had a good time."[46]

Ray's letters to her mother during the 1930s are filled with reports of luncheons, diet concerns, friends seen, clothing styles, and driving safety tips ("Mother, for my sake . . . stop at the first sign of rain"[47]), among other topics. The correspondence has the charm and poignance typical of mothers and daughters of that era. One 1936 letter offers "this weight business is really getting me down."[48] Another from that year was written from Ray's first plane flight "just to tell you that flying is indeed the great experience I have heard it to be, [including] the glory of the clouds as seen from above." Ray continued, describing a casualness of schedule unfamiliar to us today, that there was the "unexpected fun of a landing at 7 P.M. at Cartertown, Pennsylvania, to let off a couple of passengers." Ray also entreated, "please believe I appreciate

every single thing you've done."[49] Taken together, the letters remind one of how important the closeness between mother and daughter must have been for both of them: in a way they *were* their family. And they were somewhat rootless: the man of the family, Maurice, was married and on the usual military nomadic trail; Sacramento was no longer home; and, economically, they had only the trusts, which were sufficient but not lavish and in the hands of distant bankers.

In addition to the news and the pleasure of gossip, two other dimensions of these letters emerge. One is Ray's powers of observation. Her descriptions of her friends' clothing are almost Chandleresque in their precision, as is her 1939 account from a train ride—the Orange Blossom Special—from Florida to New York: "At Union Station in Washington, I saw something really thrilling—a very handsome man in his thirties—striding along with his chin high and by him—a Seeing-Eye dog! I just can't believe he was blind except that I watched him put on the

* Seeing-Eye dogs were first introduced in the United States in 1929, and so were not yet a common sight at the time Ray was writing.

† Philip Barry is best known today for his play *The Philadelphia Story*, the basis of the movie of the same name.

dog's leash at another stop and it was really wonderful—his whole air was one of self-confidence and he was very well groomed and cheerful—you just couldn't pity him."* [50]

Throughout her life, Ray was very aware of her cultural milieu, and the letters convey this too. When she came to New York, she seemed determined to absorb as many different cultural experiences as she could. But more than that, she was thinking about what she saw from a critical perspective. Another letter to her mother reads almost like a capsule review: "Saw the Philip Barry† show *Here Come the Clowns*. It was so good, totally unlike his first efforts such as *Holiday* or *Animal Kingdom*—here he really attempts something and while isn't completely successful due to lack of clarity of one character only, still the attempt is far more interesting than his other successful comedies. . . . Eddie Dowling plays the lead and does it very well. Madge Evans. Doris Dudley. (Daughter who played the daughter in Ina Claire's *End of Summer* by S. N. Behrman with Osgood Perkins as the psychoanalyst, remember?)"[51] Ray and her mother had seen *End of Summer* together three years earlier. The next month she wrote her mother that she had found the book that Barry based the show on: "The book clears up several points or at least shows me just where he went off."[52] In another letter, she wrote "We also listened to Orson Welles' broadcast 'Mutiny on the Bounty' . . . very well done," and in another, "Saw Hitchcock's *The Lady Vanishes*. Top notch, of course."[53] In yet another, she tells about going with her friend June Carter to see Cole Porter's *Leave It to Me*, *Lohengrin* at the Met, the U.S. premiere of Paul Hindemith's *Sonata for Four Hands*, and so on.[54] Also during this period Ray studied dance with Martha Graham.

Ray's memory and attention to nuance—both of which would become part of the rhythm of the Eames Office later on—are here in the letters as well: "I bought a wooden spoon and two little white china dishes (35 cents for 2) for ice box use. They are made of that old white china that isn't used anymore. When I asked what they were, the 'Authority' of the shop was asked—he said they were old soap dishes which they brought up for the Ritz ages ago to use as *hors d'oeuvres* dishes!"[55]

But what the letters only hint at is Ray's passion for painting, and the hours she spent at the easel each day, whether with Hofmann or on her own in her studio. In one letter, she writes about returning to the studio where she is "loving having a painting in front of me all of the time."[56] One cannot see the notebooks she filled, the canvases she adorned, or the sketches she made. There are realistic bouquets of flowers that she painted at Provincetown, as well as abstractions of human form. Still others seem to be in the style of Miro or Picasso, while there are many biomorphic forms that seem more uniquely hers. Some compositions hold together better than others, but in all these paintings one senses an artist trying to be rigorous and structured with a medium that to the uninitiated might seem to have an unalloyed free form.

In 1936, the same year a young architect named Ben Baldwin joined Hofmann's classes, the American Abstract Artists (A.A.A.) group was founded. This group coalesced around the notion that U.S. abstract painters and sculptors were being ignored by the mainstream museum community. About half of the group's initial members were Hofmann students, and in some ways the group evolved into the abstract expressionist movement.[57] In the first five years, artists such as Josef Albers, Lee Krasner, George McNeil, Lillian Kiesler, Laszlo Moholy-Nagy, and Fernand Leger exhibited in the group's annual shows. And although they were not formally members, it was a measure of the robustness of the alliance and the validity of the essential idea that Ray encountered people like Piet Mondrian and Arshile Gorky through it. At one point she traveled to New Jersey's Newark Airport with Gorky to see his now-legendary murals.[58]

The A.A.A. was literally an organization more than a stylistic movement, in the sense that beyond some general commonalities there was no prescribed official style. Instead, there was a specific goal: to find a place (both physically and intellectually) in the artistic community where these works could be valued. There were scheduled meetings, and Ray was a frequent participant in them. But as the enterprise of the A.A.A. developed, Ray and Ben Baldwin began exploring a couple of projects, wherein Ray would paint a mural for one of Ben's architectural projects. She seemed to relish the interplay of the aesthetic and the pragmatic.[59] She was also developing a strong interest in architecture at this time, and there also seemed to be a greater and greater disconnect between the breadth of her interests and the focusing of her own talents exclusively on painting. But also by this time, one personal issue in particular loomed large for Ray.

By about 1938, her mother was feeling ill and had to move to St. Petersburg, Florida, for health reasons. The idea was that Edna could be relatively close to Maurice, who was stationed at Fort Benning, Georgia. Ray traveled to help her mother set up housekeeping, which took some time. Ray's friend, Lee Krasner, wrote her, "Are you painting or is that a painful topic?"[60] Eventually, Ray did make it back to New York, but that Edna knew what Ray had missed is clear. In fact, Ray tried to reassure her in a letter after her return to New York: "As far as 'stagnating in St. Pete' goes, mother, I wouldn't have missed it for anything. Don't feel that way please. I really don't believe we've ever had such a grand Christmas, do you?"[61]

In January 1939, Ray's classes with Hofmann resumed. It was a new crowd at Hofmann's studio: "the gang of Bauhaus students now studying with Hofmann have everything to learn but at least appreciate Hofmann."[62] By this time, her friend, Mercedes Carles, was working for Fernand Leger, the French painter. Ray and Mercedes were out shopping when they ran into Leger: he "bought us cocktails. It was very exciting but annoying too as I could understand him but couldn't speak as he refuses to speak English."[63] Another time

Ray was walking down Broadway with her friend Jane Carter past the St. James Theater, just as the opening night of Maurice Evans's production of *Henry IV* was letting out. They saw critic Robert Benchley rush out "to meet his deadline I suppose" and Orson Welles too— "looking like the wrath of God." Then they poked their heads inside the theater and happened to see Evans himself, still in makeup, giving a curtain speech.[64] A Saturday in May found Ray in Valentine's Gallery looking at Picasso's *Guernica* mural—"remember the one in the magazine I had in St. Pete?" The gallery is "far too small but also shown are the drawings and paintings which are equally terrific."[65]

One day Jane Carter came with Ray to a Hofmann lecture and then joined the gang for lunch—Hofmann, Mercedes Carles, Lee Krasner, Wilfred Zogbaum, Arshile Gorky, and Georgio Cavallon. Jane "thought it very Bohemian,"[66] Ray wrote. Her letters have that Bohemian feeling: names that are now names to conjure with are part of the landscape, not handled with kid gloves, but very much appreciated. Some (like Krasner) were friends, some (like Gorky) were acquaintances, others (like Welles) were creators of work she admired or was aware of; but all were voraciously observed and noted by Ray. In retrospect, she was truly taking in her time, this era; she was gathering the information she would need to take her own work to the transcendent place she knew it could go.

In March 1939, Ben Baldwin was back in New York. Ray, Ben, and others of the Hofmann gang went to the opening of the A.A.A. show at the Riverside Museum. "It was exhausting—about 400 pictures—room after room and two floors!"[67] Ray wrote. She and Baldwin discussed a project to be done in California, but as Ray said, "it is very unsatisfactory not being able to confer except through the mail." The *New York Times* review was "not good, but certainly better than last year."[68] Nevertheless, frustration was building inside Ray in regards to her situation in New York.

In the fall of 1939, Ray went to Florida to be with her ailing mother. She was still in touch with her friend Ben Baldwin: they discussed a proposed mural for a house of his in Alabama. But around this time she had heard back from "Mrs. Swift," a collector in California. She articulated frustration in a letter: "Did I tell you that Mrs. Swift (from S.F.) was amazed at the Miro influence in my mural—I am still raging—when I think of the limitations of the medium, paint, purpose and everything. How could it possibly turn out other than it did?"[69]

The point for Ray was that what had been perceived as a deliberate stylistic choice was not mimicry but the application of a rigorous set of principles to the material. In other words, given the nature of painting, if you apply certain principles, the work is always going to turn out a certain way. Ray was not copying Miro but turned out to have taken a journey that produced similar results. The difference was one of process, and it was extremely

Two paintings
by Ray. Left:
Untitled (circa
1939). Inset: *to
Hofmann Love
from Buddha*
(circa 1941)

important to Ray. But it suggested profound limitations to the medium, particularly in the way she intended to explore it. It also strongly implied that she was hungry for new ways to apply the disciplines she had learned.

About 40 years later, a young woman came up to Ray and asked, "Mrs. Eames, how did it feel to give up your painting?" Ray replied, "I never gave up painting, I just changed my palette."[70] Though it is clear she was considering such a change, it is equally clear that the change did not occur until she traveled to the Cranbrook Academy of Art, just outside Detroit.

Ray nursed her mother until the end. Edna May Kaiser died of cancer in the spring of 1940. Ray closed up the house in Florida and, at the suggestion of Ben Baldwin, applied to Cranbrook. While her six years of study with Hofmann had been extraordinary, Ray seems to have sensed that it was now time to put some new hues into her palette.

*Chapel in a mountain village near Saltillo.*

# A St. Louisan's Mexican Diary—in Water Colors

### Each Picture Made by Charles O. Eames
### Is a Personal Memento Recalling a Fiesta, a Fine Dinner or a Night in Jail.

**By a Member of the Post-Dispatch Sunday Magazine Staff**

SOME travelers record their wanderings with much writing in notebooks, with snapshots or souvenir postcards or towels from resplendent but unwatchful hotels. Charles O. Eames, St. Louis architect, painted pictures which serve as a diary of his ramblings in Mexico. In the azure of cloudless skies, the buff of sun-baked adobe, the green of distant hills, the red and yellow of bright serapes and the purple of evening shadows on chapel walls, he set down vividly the impressions of a traveler sensitive to the beauties of a strange land.

Each picture is a memento of a personal experience. A water color of a market place in Monterrey recalls the day Eames spent in jail for painting it. A view of a little mountain church reminds him of the simple, kindly people who worshiped there and their hospitality to him. A street scene in Saltillo brings back the sounds of fiesta and the fragrance of frijoles and pan dulce. Some of the paintings merely record, of course, occasions when the artist was delighted by a fine harmony of line or mass or a striking arrangement of color in something he saw; but these occasions are important personal experiences to the artist. Three of the water colors—pages from the painter's "Mexican diary"—are reproduced on this page.

Eames, who studied architecture at Washington University, drove down to Mexico in a flivver last fall. He had very little money with him and knew no Spanish, but he suddenly had decided he wanted to see something of the country south of the Rio Grande, and he was young enough to be confident he would get along all right. He did get along pretty well—barring a couple of arrests. He returned not long ago with his supply of oil and water color paintings, a number of which he has since sold; a small collection of native artifacts of artistic and archeological value, including a wand used in the black magic of ancient Toltecs, and recollections of a grand time.

The architect confined his travels to the northern states of Coahuila, Nuevo Leon and San Luis Potosi. Part of the time he lived with people of the peon class, eating and sleeping in their lowly houses, often repaying their hospitality by making pictures of them. Once he was the honored guest of a mountain village, having won the friendship of the villager by repainting a statue of St. Peter in their chapel. A fiesta was held in celebration of the event and stolid-faced peons thanked him with tears running down their cheeks.

Two arrests were less pleasant incidents of his sojourn in Mexico. The one at Monterrey came about, as he understood it, because some citizen thought that in painting a small market place the artist was trying to give an unfavorable impression of the town.

In Linares, State of Nuevo Leon, he spent a couple of nights in the town jug. It appears he had a book containing fine pictures of Mexican archeological treasures, and certain minor officials thought the book put their country in a bad light—as a place of low culture. Again an American Consul procured his release—and he was allowed to keep the book.

Since returning to the United States, Eames has exhibited his Mexican paintings at Norfolk, Virginia, and a showing is planned for them in New York next winter.

*A market place in Monterrey. Eames was arrested for painting this.*

*Former residence of bishops and street scene in Monterrey.*

# CHAPTER 7

# From Mexico to Cranbrook

Julian Blaustein, a thoughtful and pragmatic man and a successful film producer in Los Angeles, was a close friend and confidante of Charles and Ray's, close enough that Charles actually considered bringing him into the office as a kind of line producer in the 1970s. During an interview, Blaustein paused for a moment and then said quietly,

> [Charles] knew who he was. And that's a tough assignment right there. I don't know about you, but I think as you go through life you'll suddenly become aware that not many people know who they are, what they are about. Are in touch with themselves. Maybe I'm wrong, but I know I find it very difficult among the people I know to find many who can answer that, who can live up to that criteria of personal behavior. I think Charles knew who he was.[1]

If this is true, and Charles's life and work suggest that it is, then the key pivot of his journey toward self-understanding may well be the time that Charles spent in Mexico in 1933 and 1934. The trip itself was quite dramatic, but the internal journey was even more so. From that time forward, the drifting of the early 1930s was gone and the energy seemed to be building to a kind of reinvention of himself. When he returned he was no longer mired in the frustrations of St. Louis but instead seemed to be seeking a way to transcend them and to take himself to a new level. This is not to say that Mexico was a magic bullet for Charles, but rather that it was the beginning of a process of taking stock of and ultimately changing his approach and situation in life.

In 1933, Charles had left St. Louis for Mexico with little more than an instinct that the trip might help. He spent about eight or ten months[2] in Mexico, and his daughter, Lucia, remembers missing him intensely. To the very young child, there was an impression of great adventure, but she had no conscious awareness of the pressure Catherine and Charles's marriage was under. Charles's return was joyful. Lucia long remembered her father returning with boxes of colorful folk art, fabric, papier-mâché dolls, and a metal cane with a small knob on the top that formed the head of Satan with two very sharp and pointy horns on the

When Charles returned from Mexico there was an exhibition of his paintings at the St. Louis Art Museum, and they were featured in the full-color section of the newspaper.

77

Still from the
Eames film *Day
of the Dead*
(1957), made
more than 20
years after
Charles's first
trip to Mexico

sides.[3] A friend felt sure Charles had "been eating up . . . the visual culture of Mexico, the colors and the textures, and all the material things that one has there to see."[4] Charles would frequently allude to his Mexican experience in conversation with others at the architecture firm he formed upon his return.

For Charles, the trip to Mexico was a mixture of highs and lows. He traveled mostly in the Mexican state of San Luis Potosí and to the city of Monterrey, sometimes venturing deep into rural areas. He described driving a very old Ford to the end of a road, and then taking horses from there, and eventually traveling on foot to some even more remote villages.[5] He fed himself by trading manual labor and, quite often, his sketches and paintings

for food. This was not as reliable as he might have hoped because he said there were times when he was very hungry and "often . . . nearly starved."[6] He painted churches and vistas, and after his return the St. Louis Art Museum mounted a show of his paintings, some of which were also reproduced in the color rotogravure section of the *St. Louis Post-Dispatch*.[7] Basically, he said, he was on his "own, in a relatively hostile environment—because, you know, any environment is hostile when you haven't any money and you don't speak the language."[8] And yet, Charles's friendly nature and genial spirit served him well there, and more than one colleague would later note how comfortable he was in experiencing other cultures on their own terms, something he likely learned during his time in Mexico.

In one town, Charles was actually thrown in jail overnight because he had brought with him a book on pre-Columbian art. The Mexican police explained to him that that "primitive" dimension of Mexico's history was insulting to its people[9] (which is ironic now because Mexico has since come to recognize this heritage as a great source of strength and pride). The rats in the jail formed a particularly vivid memory for him. Another close call for Charles was being rounded up with the citizens of a village for an involuntary smallpox vaccination and watching the dirty needle get closer and closer as it was used over and over. He got the shot and, fortunately, he and the other recipients were lucky not to have suffered anything worse than a sore arm.[10]

There is an unfinished Eames film called *Banana Leaf*, based on a kind of parable that Charles developed in his talks. Abridged, the story goes a little like this:

In India, those without and the lowest in caste, eat very often off of a banana leaf. And those a little bit up the scale, eat off of a sort of low-fired ceramic dish. And a little bit higher, why, they have a glaze on a thing they call a 'tali.' And there get to be some fairly elegant glazed talis, but it graduates to a brass tali, and a bell-bronze tali is absolutely marvelous, it has a sort of a ring to it. And then things get to be a little questionable. Silver-plated talis and solid silver talis, and I suppose some nut has had a gold tali, but I've never seen one. But you can go beyond that and the guys that have not only means, but a certain amount of knowledge and understanding, go the next step and they eat off of a banana leaf.

Charles continues with a remark that shows his blend of realism and ideals:

I'm not prepared to say that the banana leaf that one eats off of is the same as the other eats off of, but it's that process that has happened within the man that changes the banana leaf.[11]

Perhaps it was this "process that . . . happen[s] within the man"—or something like it—that Charles was referring to when he said the most important thing he learned from his time in Mexico was that "at least, damn it, you're not afraid to be broke!"[12] And so he decided at that point not to "take any . . . job—the objective of which you don't agree with." He continued: "and this has all kinds of advantages to it. It means that any work you attack . . . you can bring your whole experience to it. You can bring your whole self to it; you don't bring any half experiences. It also means that you don't take a job that you know is wrong, but you take it as a stepping stone. That's no good. It . . . leads to all kinds of bad habits."[13] And unlike some Depression survivors (though many of Charles's experiences during this era underscored the importance of thrift), he did not choose later on to hoard money but to spend it on good work in the here and now

Charles had the ability and the desire to look at an issue or an experience like the Mexico trip from many sides at once. He could consider it in a lighthearted way (like the time he found himself in a bullring as a matador[14]), in a positive light (learning how to survive on literally almost nothing), or with a genuine chill (as when he said it was like he "had been through an almost fatal illness,"[15] perhaps in reference to that dirty needle). The Mexico trip, and indeed his whole way of life before and after it, would have been ripe for such mulling and exploration. He clearly began not only to reassess his situations but also to challenge the assumptions behind them. It would take time to implement these new, higher standards to his satisfaction. He also took another, very tantalizing, lesson from the trip: "[I] would never be suckered into a mistake I did not make myself."[16]

After Mexico, Charles started a new architectural firm with Robert Walsh, an acquaintance. Though Eames and Walsh designed a number of houses, Charles later felt that the most important aspect of the firm's work was the experience rather than the designs. But others valued the work differently: Huson Jackson, who heard about an apprentice position at Eames and Walsh, said "I was advised—in fact, my neighbor who was employing me at the time said, 'You'll find [Eames and Walsh] the most creative office, the most interesting office'—he was thinking really of the most interesting architect to work with in the city—'and it's an opportunity you should take.' " Jackson arrived to find an office dedicated to the art of architecture. "I felt this, of course, very much in the intensity of the design effort that went into the projects that we were doing then."[17] Bob Walsh was a quiet man; some felt that his passion was really music. Jackson saw the partnership this way: Walsh was the "technical architect who could help to bring the thing through in a solid way, and the flashes of inspiration came more from Charlie."[18] He also recalled Charles spending a lot of time in the library. Alice Meyer, who commissioned the firm to design the Meyer House and was Walsh's sister-in-law, remembered the partnership similarly: "Charles was the imaginative designer, and Bob was a more practical man as I remember."[19]

Jackson remembers the office fondly. He was the only employee besides the two partners. "It was a very flavorful office, I can tell you—and sometimes a little raunchy in flavor." He laughed. "There always was lots of joking, and there was lots of good humor, and one of the things that amazed me was [Charles's] fluency with the language, his ability to compose poems. There was a guitar in the office, and there was music at times, and sort of spontaneous poetry, and some of it limerick style. I remember once, we used to order in sandwiches at lunch, and one day [Charles] just picked up the guitar and composed a poem—the order in the form of a poem. Incredible! His talent, visual and verbal as well, was a definite eye-opener for me."[20] Sometimes the partners' children were on the scene as well. Charles took Lucia to a meeting with a client who was a Jesuit priest. After a tour and a discussion of the project, they joined several other priests for lunch. At one point the talk was a bit over Lucia's head (she was six or seven at the time) and Charles quipped, "don't confuse my issue,"[21] a remark that provoked a round of hearty laughter.

On the marital front, however, things were not so great for Charles and Catherine. Perhaps the most poignant measure of their marriage is that in all my interviews with those who knew them (as well as in all my reading of contemporary correspondence), I have not encountered anyone who commented even casually that the union was a happy one. It seems to have been a tough go from the start. The times were extremely stressful, of course, but Catherine and Charles were never really a great fit. Neither their dispositions nor their aspirations were well matched. Though by upbringing they shared a respect for Old World protocols, as time went on Charles's free spirit and restless mind caused him to have less in common with Catherine's somewhat constrictive social circles and her often forbidding St. Louis society remove and distance. And perhaps the ease with which her architectural interests were left behind disappointed Charles. Huson Jackson remembered once remarking on the paradox that there was a fair number of female architecture undergraduates at Washington University but no female architects. Where did they go? Charles replied, "They marry architects."[22] The common ground of a Beaux Arts education may, in fact, have been too traditional for a new kind of partnership.

For Catherine Woermann Eames's part, she was born 50 years too early. She proved herself to be an able administrator as well as a shrewd investor later in life, and she had an obvious inclination toward architecture. It is hard to imagine anyone more perfectly suited to be a successor to her father in the Woermann Construction Company, but Frederick Woermann, a good and generous man in many ways, could not conceive of a daughter running the family business. (His two sons had died in infancy.) If Woermann had felt differently, perhaps it could have been an interesting partnership for Charles and Catherine, considering that Woermann Construction built the Sweetzer house and some of the other houses as well. But even had that happened, there was something about Charles's trajectory that made leaving St. Louis inevitable, and something about hers that made such a move impossible.

Home life, of course, was not all subtext. Charles and Catherine's marriage lasted about 11 years before their final separation, and there were plenty of good times in the household as they both tried to make it work. Lucia remembers that when they lived out in the country, Charles painted in bold letters over the door a quote from Thoreau: "He who saws his own wood is twice warm."[23] And in the spring, when the weather made the roads more easily passable for friends to visit, her parents "gave a gala party for which my father created very large, fanciful masks for the trees at the edge of the woods near the house."[24] There was also something for the kids. A number of their friends were also part of the Paint-and-Putter Club (a group of local painters) and some were active in the local art scene. At one party, they all painted "beautiful hard-boiled eggs to be hidden in great numbers for the children's hunt and to paint marvelous designs on hollow, blown eggs that were strung on raffia for the ladies."[25]

Lucia also recalls how much her father loved the comics (a fact later reflected in the Eames film, *Comics of the Fifties*). He had especially loved *Little Nemo* as a child, and so, with his daughter "on Sundays," she remembered, "[we] spread out the wonderful full-page full-color spreads to intently read together: among others, *Prince Valiant*, *Terry and the Pirates*, *Toonerville Trolley*, Rube Goldberg's elaborate, fanciful, and logical contraptions, the *Katzenjammer Kids*, *Flash Gordon* (whose episodes the Meyer cousins and I enthusiastically played out when our families got together), Al Capp's *L'il Abner* and then *Dick Tracy*."[26] When Charles visited Lucia's first-grade class at the two-room Rock Hill School around Halloween, he "spotted the string of orange construction-paper pumpkins stretched above the window . . . each by a different child but identically and carefully traced . . . and immediately [he] courteously but firmly explained to the teacher that in the future I was to do my

own work and not trace someone else's."[27] Like many other stories, it shows Charles's understanding of issues both of appropriateness and mass production.

The Eames and Walsh office designed a number of buildings during its roughly three years of operation: small houses, two churches, and the Meyer House, which was a huge commission for its time. It is particularly striking that none of Charles's commissions immediately before or after his trip to Mexico allowed him to pursue the modernist ideas so evident in his school competitions. Of course, this is old news to architects, but judging from his later, more expansive definition of architecture, this fact must have struck a nerve. Three projects leap out: a model house for the *St. Louis Post-Dispatch*, St. Mary's Church in

Helena, Arkansas, and the Meyer House. The first project was part of a program that, like the Case Study program later on, attempted to empower potential homeowners by asking architects to design "ideal small homes." To save money, the architects went with a pitched roof because they felt it "required only one-story construction instead of two," though this "more or less eliminated the possibility of a thoroughly modern house."[28] In this case, the solution proposed was a French-style townhouse, but the fact that they favored the primary need (economy) over the secondary one (modernism) is revealing. Eames and Walsh chose brick as the primary material because it was plentiful and of high quality in the area. As the *Post-Dispatch* writer observed, after these two choices "the house developed more or less naturally along French lines."[29] The same concept was echoed later in Charles's assessment of the work of Richard Neutra: that his most profound contribution was the honing of his residential architecture plans to their essence over a lifetime of work.[30]

St. Mary's Church is very important for a number of reasons. On a career level, it was published by Howard Meyer in *Architectural Forum*. It also seems to be the project that first attracted the awareness of Eliel Saarinen. The church impressed Alice Meyer[31] (no relation to Howard) as well and convinced her to commission the firm for her own house.

But St. Mary's is also simply a beautiful church. It has a very mittel-European sensibility; Eames and Walsh crafted a true gem. The project was the passion of the church pastor, the charismatic and committed Father Thomas Martin, who traveled to St. Louis from Helena hoping to find an architect to build a great church—the best possible church for his congregation on a limited budget (of course). The reputation of Eames and Walsh undoubtedly helped him find the firm. The church they created has a simple, honest feel from the outside, sustained as one enters through a vaulted door and views the handsome brickwork. The church is approached from the east, the Mississippi River a scant mile behind. Inside, the high expanse of space envelops you. A dramatic mural rises behind the distant altar, including the six Old Testament prophets who foretold the birth of Christ. Painter Charles Quest, who created the mural, wrote that Eames "decorated the large ceiling beams with appropriate religious symbols [and] kept the brick interior very simple and austere like many of the early church buildings."[32] Stained-glass windows flank you from a distance as you walk down the aisle, the sun giving the southern windows an afternoon glow. Dangling from the ceiling in a line are spherical brass lighting fixtures that Charles designed; they appear to change as you move. As you walk toward the altar, you see the moon and the stars in the lamps, but as you return, after communion, you see the sun—literally seeing the light. Charles also designed the pews and the cabinetwork. The pews may have been Charles's first experience with producing furniture in volume, though he had earlier designed and produced lighting and other pieces.

The church was built by Vaslau and Oldrich Kesl, a local father-and-son team.[33] The Kesls could trace back centuries of an unbroken lineage of builders and artisans in Vaslau's native Czechoslovakia. Oldrich's children remember how suspicious the senior Kesls were of a big-city architect coming down from St. Louis. But in the end they all got along famously. What really impressed Oldrich was Charles's attention to detail, including the way all the brickwork had been carefully worked out in the plans.[34] To use Charles and Ray's later quote, "the details are not the details, the details make the product."

Charles involved other artists he knew from St. Louis. Emil Frei was responsible for the stained glass windows, and Sheila Burlingame made a small sculpture for the front of the church. Quest created the murals in a style that deliberately evoked the early Byzantine churches and conveyed a broad allegorical scope. The church was well received and continues to be embraced by the community today. In addition to *Architectural Forum*, it was published in the *St. Louis Post-Dispatch*, where Alice Meyer saw it when she and her husband, John Meyer, were thinking about building a house.[35] (She likely would have seen it anyway—in addition to the connection to Walsh, Catherine Eames was an old friend.)

The Meyer House was Eames and Walsh's biggest project in St. Louis. Though the churches were larger in size, their construction was far simpler and posed fewer challenges than the Meyer House. The multiacre property is in what remains an exclusive area of St. Louis called Huntleigh Woods, not far from Alice Meyer's parents' house. Completed in 1938, the Meyer House is from an earlier era, not so much in style as in function. With a large family and a desire to entertain houseguests in the nineteenth-century style of allowing whole families to routinely stay the night, the Meyers required numerous servants to run the operation.[*36]

Alice Meyer's parents were aghast at how long the design process was taking, as Eames and Walsh searched for the best solution. One set of drawings was scrapped, and so

* Today this poses a challenge for the preservation of this beautiful and important house, because even the most well-off no longer live this way.

Detail of Meyer
House brick-
work. Charles
asked Alice
Meyer what her
favorite piece of
music was, then
commissioned
these carved
bricks.

the architects began anew.[37] It was during the design of this house that Charles and Eliel Saarinen began their connection. After seeing the pictures of St. Mary's Church, Saarinen wrote Charles a note, initiating contact.[38] Charles traveled to the Cranbrook Academy of Art in Bloomfield Hills, Michigan, at least once during the building of the Meyer House.[39] Saarinen saw the plans and made some suggestions that were taken — like simplifying some of the shell alcoves into cleaner bays. When asked if Saarinen had "consulted" on the house, Alice Meyer corrected the term as being a little strong.[40] A letter from Charles to Eliel confirms a sense that there was but one formal session of critique. But Cranbrook was part of the complete Meyer home in a number of ways. Eliel's wife, Loja Saarinen, designed some curtains and a rug. And Carl Milles, the great Swedish sculptor in residence at Cranbrook, allowed the Meyers to buy a casting of one of the heads from his fountain, *The Meeting of the Waters*.[41]

Charles designed a set of comfortable chairs and a table for the Meyer House, as well as various fixtures, including a mirror and a chandelier. The chairs were custom built by John Rausch, a St. Louis woodworker and cabinetmaker. Charles seems to have been struck by the effort that went into one chair with this kind of custom-manufacturing process. As with some of the other homes, the Meyer House was built by the Woermann Construction Company. It is said to be the first house in St. Louis with aluminum windows and the first to have a poured-concrete second floor.[42]

The finished house is full of treasures. In it Charles seems to have been exploring curves: a circular library/study opens off a landing on the main stairwell, while a set of nested curves relate the back terrace and its view of the gardens to the echoing form of the dining room. Other kinds of treasures mean even more to those who know the work that would follow: the deliberately exposed steel beams in the basement foreshadow the Eames House, and the curve of the custom-made aluminum railing presages the later furniture. Funny little narrative bricks built into the house itself have something in common with the exterior photographic panel of the Eames House. Ceiling sconces are lined with a Japanese rice paper for a subtle lighting effect. "I don't know where Charlie found that," said Alice Meyer later.[43]

The Meyer House was apparently a lovely house to live in as well. The family remembers it fondly, moving out only after John Meyer's untimely death. But for Charles, ultimately, there was a great deal of frustration in this project. He learned a lot about the forces arrayed against satisfactory expression of an architect's intent. It was also a difficult time financially. In the summer of 1937, after the groundbreaking on the Meyer House, Catherine wrote to Charles's sister that the overhead of the office was eating up any profits (likely due in part to the prolonged development of the design). Making matters worse, the

lease on their own home would expire in August, and they weren't sure if they would be able to afford to renew it.[44]

Charles began working in the evenings for Emil Frei, designing stained-glass windows, to support himself, his family, and the office. Being a little girl at the time, Lucia remembered the Frei workshop fondly. She has written that "Charles and Emil would let me explore [the] Frei workshop: a treasure trove of *tessera* and sheets of glass—glorious colors from soft shades to jewel brilliance held in and against richly worn wooden draws, chests, and tables; mock-ups, drawings; small mosaic panels. And then we would follow the tantalizing wisps of cooking aromas upstairs to Mother Frei's kitchen to eat *saurbrauten*, *leibkuchen*, *springerleis* . . . or whatever the treasures of her table of that day."[45] At home around this time, trying to cheer Lucia up before an imminent tonsillectomy, Charles "moved me to the living room couch and cajoled me into a happier mood by painting on the wall above me a hilarious scene of angel and devil collecting and funneling—presumably my—blood through a great contraption."[46] He knew his audience: it worked.

During the construction of the Meyer House, Eliel Saarinen suggested that Charles consider coming to Cranbrook. Charles's exact initial response is not known, but in January of 1938, Charles wrote to Saarinen that the Meyer House "has just been completed and, as

85

Seven details of the Meyer House, clockwise from top left: library in the round; detail of aluminum arm railing; grate; aluminum door handle; aluminum windows; door knocker; light fixture in library

at the end of each job, I have the craving to be able to start over—better prepared and with a clearer conception. Then I think of Cranbrook." Eliel's invitation to Cranbrook was just what Charles needed. Or more accurately, it could be what Charles needed. On a practical level, he asked "if there is a chance of obtaining a fellowship [scholarship]."[47] Later, he recalled that he also told Saarinen, "I'd like the fellowship if I could come and not really produce any work in the sense of work on a project, but if I could go up and just—just plain read for a year. And in a sense what it was was an attempt or a desire to make up what I had lost in the academic world . . . just wishing I had the time to . . . the idea of living in a library for a year."[48] Saarinen agreed to both the financial aid and, just as important, the approach. As Charles headed to Cranbrook, he seemed to know that this was close to his last—and possibly his best—chance to fundamentally change his approach to architecture and indeed his approach to the world. Having mastered many basic skills in his St. Louis practice, Charles was now ready to transcend them. In his requisite application to the school, Charles called architecture the "most vital of the creative arts . . . closely related to the social, cultural, and economic aspects of our civilization."[49] And though he always saw architecture broadly, he would say later that it wasn't until Cranbrook, that "I had any conception of what a 'concept' was."[50]

Today Cranbrook Academy of Art is a part of the Cranbrook Educational Community in Bloomfield Hills, Michigan. The school was founded by George Booth, a wealthy Detroit publisher, as a contribution to the "common good." That may sound a little vague, but it reflects the power of Cranbrook as an institution that grew organically from a feeling rather than a specific plan. In 1908, George and Ellen Booth moved into Cranbrook House, a structure they had commissioned from architect Albert Kahn on a 120-acre property. They always wished to have a public dimension to their property, and the first such institution was the Bloomfield Hills School in 1922. Around that time, one of the Booths' sons suggested that they speak with Eliel Saarinen, his professor at the University of Michigan. Saarinen was a great Finnish architect who had achieved international stature with his second-place design in the Chicago Tribune Tower competition in 1920, which had led to an invitation to teach in Ann Arbor, Michigan.[51]

Saarinen's first formal involvement with Cranbrook was in 1925, and he lived and worked there until his death in 1950. He designed the Cranbrook School, Art Museum, Academy of Art, and Science Museum. Gregory Wittkopp subtitled his book on Cranbrook's Saarinen House (designed by Eliel for himself and Loja) *A Total Work of Art*,[52] but the same phrase could easily be applied to the whole Cranbrook grounds and experience.

It was into this world that Charles arrived in September 1938. He was alone again, Catherine and Lucia having stayed behind in St. Louis—another separation. Formally,

Charles was part of the Architecture and Urban Planning program. His studio mates were Ben Baldwin (Ray Eames's friend from the Hofmann studio), Harry Weese (future designer of the Washington, D.C., mass-transit system), and Ralph Rapson (a future Case Study architect with a Minneapolis-based practice). They shared a common space at the Cranbrook Academy of Art, but both Eliel and Charles stuck to their bargain, and Charles initially spent a great deal of time in the library. It was a treasured period that later led Charles to remark, "those who know of Rembrandt early [in life] are cheated of the pleasure of discovery."[53] When Rapson was asked if he had ever observed the interplay of an Eliel critique of one of Charles's projects, he replied bemusedly, "Charles was almost never in his studio, which

was rather strange. But he spent all of his time in the ceramics studio, in the weaving studio, in the metal shop, photography . . . in these other allied studios. And he was obviously preparing himself for that wonderful, rich, and varied kind of practice that he had. He went well beyond architecture per se."[54] Rapson also remembered Charles's special interest in photography: "he spent a lot of time in the darkroom, 'cause he [said], 'That's where the control is.'"[55]

Though photography was well known to Charles, it does not seem to have been a part of his St. Louis practice (perhaps for economic reasons), but he emphatically reconnected with it at Cranbrook. Rapson recalled a lot of touch-football games on the Cranbrook lawns, with Charles at times participating but also taking pictures—and then sometimes puckishly blowing them up huge. These dramatic, grainy action shots would at times mortify their subjects by immortalizing the instant of an undignified landing.[56] Later on, Charles mentioned in a letter about photographing the potter Maija Grotell's hands for an exhibit, "I took a series of damn good photos of Maija's hands and had them blown up way to hell and gone for the exhibit as potting tools."[57] This was using scale in a different way—to emphasize that Grotell's hands were themselves her tools.

At Cranbrook, Charles met Eero Saarinen. Eero, born in Finland and a bit younger than Charles, was Eliel's son and an instructor at Cranbrook. Like Charles, he had studied architecture at a school that favored the Beaux Arts style—Yale in his case—but he had made it through the other side and graduated. The writer Allan Temko says, "the splendor of Saarinen's drawings [at Yale] shows how his energetic genius enlivened even an academic idiom."[58] After college, Eero had traveled for a couple of years in Europe, returning to join his father's firm as junior partner (though it was renamed Saarinen and Saarinen).

Charles and Eero became fast friends and, indeed, lifelong friends. Eero was probably Charles's closest friend in the world, both professionally and personally. Eero loved competitions in design and elsewhere (he had won his first when he was 12: a Swedish matchstick design competition).[59] Rapson remembered Eero sneering at the football games until being persuaded to join one and then enjoying the competition so much he couldn't get enough of the game.

After a few months of recharging himself with reading, Charles gradually began to be drawn into the Saarinen and Saarinen firm. "By that time, there were interesting things to be done in [Eliel] Saarinen's own office," as Charles said, and he eventually worked there part-time. By the end of the school year, Eliel "asked me to form—what the school had not had, was a design department. And so I sort of put together a design department."[60] Charles and Eero were friends but also, on some level, competitors, if only because they were both up-and-coming architects. Charles had more experience, but Eero was a partner in a world-renowned firm. The challenge for Eero was that it was still his father's firm.

Charles and Eero worked together designing the 1939 Cranbrook faculty exhibition. Charles made an exquisite model, which, in its extraordinary detail, calls to mind some of the models the Eames Office would eventually make for its own films and exhibitions. In addition to teaching, Charles was working on the design for a vast basin for the Milles fountain entitled *The Meeting of the Waters*, which was to be installed in front of St. Louis's Union Station. He traveled to Minnesota to select the granite for the installation.[61] An allegory of the marriage between the Mississippi and Missouri rivers, which join a few miles north of the city, the fountain has 19 human figures, all, in a classical style, nudes. Charles's concerns about his hometown's provincialism were not helped when City Councilman Hubert Hoeflinger complained, "I've been to a lot of weddings but I never saw one where everybody was naked."[62] Charles and Milles were close—Milles would even sometimes cut Charles's hair.[*][63]

It is tempting to judge Eero's thinking at this time by the large-scale and passionately analytical curvilinear forms of his later work, but those had not yet been much expressed, so what connected Charles and Eero aesthetically at this point was not simply the futures we see in hindsight, but their more immediate pasts. And what connected them in the case of the furniture for the Kleinhans Music Hall was the fact that designing those chairs was architecture on a scale at which they both could exert a real impact on its form within the elegant, rectilinear monumentality of the Saarinen and Saarinen Office. Eero always acknowledged his father's influence on his work, and it is probably fair to say that the emergence of Eero as the firm's leading voice did not start until after World War II and was not really complete until, ironically, 1947. Ironic, because 1947 was the year that Eliel and Eero submitted separate entries to the Jefferson Westward Expansion Memorial Competition—what became Eero's St. Louis Arch. Indeed, initially the Saarinen office thought the victory telegram was for Eliel.[64]

So, on the Kleinhans furniture, Charles and Eero were not just collaborators, but co-

* Fifty years later, the only story of this time that Catherine shared with me was a memory of driving Milles from Michigan to the opening in a rainstorm with the windshield wipers off—because Milles was getting dizzy from them. She was sure she was going to crash.

FROM MEXICO TO CRANBROOK

89

conspirators exploring the curved form on a smaller scale and perhaps beginning to get a handle on the potential of molding plywood. Alvar Aalto, the great Finnish designer and master of molded plywood, had spoken at Cranbrook in the late 30s and so the whole community was aware of the material and his work forming it into simple curves. Whether the idea of the single-shell chair had formulated itself before the Kleinhans project is unclear. It is clear, however, that it is partially expressed in the Kleinhans Chair. And it is easy to imagine that both Eero and Charles challenged each other to frame the Kleinhans problem in a more abstract and universal way. Indeed, both of the young men seem to have understood that a collaboration between two young, strong-willed architects, both still formulating their respective

approaches, could push them to do something better as a team than if each had worked alone.

But another project, also a competition, probably had a greater impact on the Eames process than anything else Charles would experience at Cranbrook (except of course meeting Ray). And that was the competition for the Smithsonian Gallery of Art. In this project, as in so many early ones, the process was more important for Charles's development than the design itself. Charles was from time to time asked why the Saarinen Office won so many competitions. What was their secret? Charles was always a bit unimpressed by quick fixes in general, but he also had a habit of answering even the most annoying question matter-of-factly. This is how he addressed the question at the Norton Lectures:

> This is the trick. I give it to you; you can use it. [The Saarinen Office] looked at the program and divided it in all the essential elements—which turned out to be about 30 some odd elements —and we proceeded methodically to make 100 studies of each element. And making, at the end of the time, 100 studies, we tried to get the solution for that particular element that suited the thing best, and then set that up as a standard below which we would not fall in the final scheme. Then we proceeded to break down all logical combinations of these elements . . . and this turned out to be quite a few. And we made 100 studies of all combinations of these elements, try[ing] to not erode the quality that we had gained in the best of the 100 of the single element. And took these elements, and began to then search for the logical combinations of the combinations.[65]

There were several more stages before they even considered a plan. Then there was: "study after study after study and on into the other aspects of the detail of the presentation. It went on—it was sort of a . . . a brutal thing."[66]

But they made the cut and got into the second round of the competition:

Now you have to start [again]; what do you do? We reorganized all elements but this time, with having a little bit more experience, chose the elements in a different way—still had about 26, 28, or 30 of them—and proceeded. We made 100 studies of every element. We took every logical group of elements and studied those together in a way that would not fall below, sort of, the standard that we had set. And went right on down the procedure. At the end of the time—before the second competition drawings went in—we really wept. It just looked so idiotically simple that we thought we'd blown the whole bit. And [the Saarinen Office] won the competition.[67]

Though the Smithsonian Gallery of Art was never built, the process, the importance, and the value of pushing and pushing until the heart of the problem was revealed, was something that stayed with Charles forever. He and Ray would create their own way of allowing each iteration to reveal the path to the essence. After all, it helped answer his own pre-Cranbrook "craving to be able to start over—better prepared and with a clearer conception."[68] Years later, Lucia Eames was with her father when someone said to him ingratiatingly, "Oh, Mr. Eames, you are such a genius." He replied, "Genius? Nothing—we just worked harder."[69]

FROM MEXICO TO CRANBROOK

91

CRANBROOK ACADEMY OF ART
BLOOMFIELD HILLS, MICHIGAN

ELIEL SAARINEN
PRESIDENT AND DIRECTOR
DEPARTMENT OF ARCHITECTURE AND DESIGN
RICHARD P. RASEMAN
EXECUTIVE SECRETARY

CARL MILLES
DIRECTOR DEPARTMENT OF SCULPTURE

ZOLTAN SEPESHY
DIRECTOR DEPARTMENT OF PAINTING

INTERMEDIATE SCHOOL STAFF
HARRY BERTOIA
CHARLES O. EAMES
MARSHALL FREDERICKS
MAIJA GROTELL
WALLACE MITCHELL
MARIANNE STRENGELL

Tuesday

Dear Miss Kaiser

I am 34 (almost)
years old, singel (again) and broke _
I love you very much and world
like to marry you very very soon *
I cannot promise to support us
very well - but if given the chance
will shure in hell try -

* soon means very soon

what is the size of
this finger ??

as soon as I get to that
hospital I will write "reams"
well little ones
love xxxxxxxxx Charlie

# CHAPTER 8

# Charles and Ray Eames

After her mother died of cancer in 1940, Ray closed the house in Florida where her mother had stayed and contemplated her own next move. Maurice, Ray's brother, was the only real family she had left. He was on his way to a military base in Lake Charles, Louisiana. He could—and would—be a source of comfort and strength for her, but Louisiana was no place for Ray to put down roots. Moving back to New York did not feel right to her either. She was frustrated with painting but still committed to her art. Increasingly intrigued by architecture, she wanted to understand it better. She had always been fascinated by structure, particularly in relationship to dance, but now she was interested in exploring it architecturally. Even Chicago suggested itself because Ludwig Mies van der Rohe was at the Illinois Institute of Technology. But in general, it seems that her feelings circled in on the idea of at least visiting California, where she was considering building a house.[1]

Ray's friend, Ben Baldwin, suggested that she go to Cranbrook. He had been there himself (and had been Charles's studiomate) and there was a lot going on—many people sensed that these were vintage years at Cranbrook.[2] Ben's sister, Kitty (Baldwin) Weese, recalled it a little differently, saying that her brother told Ray that there was an instructor at Cranbrook that she might find personally as well as intellectually interesting. To be clear, it was more tease than serious suggestion that Ray set her cap for Charles, but it is tantalizing. Ben did not remember it that way; he recalled suggesting that she come to Cranbrook. He also recalled an impression that things between Catherine and Charles were worse than ever.

During Charles's second school year at Cranbrook (1939–40), he was a faculty member. Catherine and Lucia joined him, and the family moved into the faculty housing at Cranbrook. Catherine took some ceramic and weaving classes and did her best to fit in, but she missed St. Louis. Lucia was thriving at the Brookside School. As the 1940–41 school year approached, and Charles was named head of the new Industrial Design Department, he was beginning to wonder how long he wanted to stay at Cranbrook.[3] Nevertheless, he committed to stay through the school year. One can only imagine the strangeness of the situa-

This letter, from Charles to Ray in late May 1941, tells its own story.

93

Lucia Eames at Cranbrook, photographed by her father, circa 1940

tion for Charles, and especially Catherine, as their marriage grew colder and colder in the smallish apartment on Academy Way. Charles's third school year at Cranbrook promised more of the same. Looking back at the summer of 1940, Charles's mother saw an edge in her daughter-in-law she hadn't seen before. She later wrote in a letter, "I know if she [Catherine] said divorce often to Charlie—it would be just like him to tell her to go on and get it."[4] In fact, it was Charles who would eventually ask for it.

Ray Kaiser applied to Cranbrook in August 1940 and was accepted a few days later. It is interesting to compare her application with Charles's of two years earlier. In the "prior experience" section, for example, Charles's application was filled in with his many various jobs, whereas Ray's was blank. She indicated her time at the Hofmann school and that was it.[5] It may have been that she was only planning to audit and thus felt no particular pressure to squeeze every little detail out of her recent past. But it does suggest how different the paths they had taken really were and how difficult it is to compare their work before their meeting side-by-side. For Ray, Cranbrook was a continuation of an ongoing art education wherein one's task was each day to put one's thoughts and ideas on paper and make them tangible. For Charles, Cranbrook was a much-needed opportunity to reassess and reapproach his chosen field after almost a decade of professional practice, where the only things that had a chance to be realized were the ones that were commissioned by other people (and it might be added, for money that would support his family). But what Charles and Ray had in common when they arrived (at their respective times) at Cranbrook was something far more basic and essential—the beginning of a feeling that the discipline in which they had trained would be most valuable to them as a structure.

About her time at Cranbrook, Ray said in 1980, "I was at Cranbrook for a very short time. . . . I only realized it the other day when I went back and everyone was expecting to hear a great deal about Cranbrook, and I counted the days and there were not very many."[6] She arrived at the beginning of the term, planning mostly to audit Marianne Strengell's weaving classes and soon after fell in with the design and architecture crowd. Other students at Cranbrook at the time included Don Albinson, Jill Mitchell, and Tony Rosenthal.[7]

As the semester started, Charles was champing at the bit. He found the design projects more satisfying than the teaching. His relationship with Catherine was just about at its breaking point. In fact, they were de facto separated during the summer of 1940, even before the beginning of the 1940–41 school year. Work at Cranbrook was becoming difficult for Charles. Although it was how he supported himself and his family, the actual job was beginning not to mean as much to him. By the standard of his lesson in Mexico, it was not that he no longer believed in Cranbrook but that he could no longer give all of himself to the teaching. There were other projects: he and Eero had started working on the designs for the Organic Furniture competition; Charles was designing a small studio for actress Irene Rich (it would be for her daughter, Frances, a sculptor at Cranbrook). He had visited the California site in the summer as well. Charles had also started a brand-new project in a whole new medium: film.

Charles began production on a film project for Cranbrook at this time. He never completed it, but the existing footage is fascinating. Charles seems to have considered the project to be two films, possibly three. The first, a Cranbrook documentary announced in the school's newsletter, was intended as a promotional film. The second, a vignette, was about ceramist Maija Grotell who headed the ceramics department at Cranbrook. The third, a fragment, may have been intended as a short on sculptor Marshall Fredericks. In several ways, the Maija Grotell footage is the most intriguing. First of all, Charles edited the film into a coherent sequence about the throwing and firing of a pot, and it is very likely the film was screened at the 1941 faculty show.[8] So, unlike the others, the vignette was completed. But also the Grotell film is very much like a certain subset of the later Eames films that are extremely good at giving the viewer a very specific direct experience. *Babbage* is this way, as is *Polyorchis Haplus*, among a number of others. Even in its style and some images, which are beautiful abstractions, the Grotell vignette suggests the later films. Throughout Charles's last year at Cranbrook, filmmaking was constantly on his mind.

Despite (or perhaps because of) the fact that they would live much of the rest of their lives surrounded by other people, Charles and Ray were two of the most private people imaginable. They were also always focused on the future and what was coming next. With their grandchildren they lived "in the moment," whether swinging on a rope swing, photographing a spiderweb, or enjoying a strawberry. Unfortunately, this has meant that many of the private events in their lives together, such as the precise moment they met and fell in love, were not recorded. But it did happen. It's just that the two people who really knew what happened are gone. Jill Mitchell, who was a second-year student in design that year, put it this way: Charles and Ray were "so discreet that one really wouldn't—one would only think of it in terms of the fact that they really shared interests."[9]

One of those first shared experiences took place at an in-school convention organized by Charles and Eero where all the departments presented their work and ideas to the rest of the students. Charles's design students had prepared an exhibition called *What Is Design?* and a record called the *Emperor's New Clothes*, which played under an empty display case. Mitchell remembered Charles and Ray working together on a mobile of ceramic and metal for the convention, describing their work as "certainly the most publicly shared

Right: A strip of
four photos from
a photo booth,
undated, likely
1940s

* Eero eventually
joined the OSS
and served in
Washington; Charles
filled out his
Selective Service
papers but was
never drafted.

experience. . . . I am sure that just their mutual interests were the things that attracted them
to each other."[10] But of the wrestling with the consequences, the treasuring of their intima-
cies, and the beginning of their life together, there are some glimpses.

Ray helped prepare the final drawings (along with other students) for the Organic
Furniture competition, and by the end of that time, Charles and Ray were hooked on one
another. And as Ray left for "home," which was really her friends' places in New York, in late
1940, she and Charles had to figure out what this all meant.

After Christmas, Ray was still in New York, and she and Charles corresponded regularly by mail and occasionally by phone calls. They had some confidantes at Cranbrook.
Charles wrote: "Nancy is kind and so brings up your name so I can mention it out loud."[11]
Later, in January 1941, he wrote quickly on a postcard, "Your window is dark when I go by at
night."[12] The record for this time is a little asymmetrical, consisting only of his letters to her,
because he burned her letters after he read them "as per our agreement."[13] (Ray seems to
have been particularly concerned, though clearly it was his still being married to Catherine
that made the situation so delicate.) Charles said of Ray's letters, "I take them off in some
secluded corner like a hound with a prize bone and have as wonderful a time."[14]

It was an all-around complicated year at the Cranbrook campus. In 1941, it is likely
that the people at Cranbrook were a little more aware than most Americans of the situation
in Europe. The strong Finnish contingent was following the Winter War (1939–44) with ago-
nized interest (the Soviet Union invaded Finland soon after Hitler invaded Poland). There
was even talk around the table of the Saarinen house as to whether Eero should return and
fight.[*15] Marianne Strengell's sister's ship was bombed in the early part of 1941.[16] World War II
was under way, but the United States was not yet immersed in it.

By February 1941 and against this background, Charles and Ray had committed to a
future together and to traveling to California in June. It was time for Charles to tell his wife
that he wanted a divorce. He told Catherine in early February he was "ending things."[17] The
conversation seems to have gone as well as could be expected, and he wrote Ray that
Catherine "agrees that wherever I have a home Lucia would be free to go and come."[18] She
later seemed to have second thoughts.

In the midst of all this came news of winning the Organic Furniture competition,
that key early milestone of the 30-year flash. Charles went to New York for the announcement, but Ray by now was with friends elsewhere.[19] She did not see him in New York at that
time; perhaps propriety would not let her. Fear and excitement must have been roiling in
both of them. They began planning for life after Cranbrook. All the existing letters of the
next few months orbit around arranging things for their trip to California. There would be
ups and downs and concerns, but this plan was at the center of it all. Ray began to wonder

what job to take, given that it would only be for a short time. Initially, this seemed to scare Charles: "after the past ten years it is only natural that I should feel a certain terror in helping find or suggesting possibilities of work for a woman close to me. It is just a slight condition and will not last and in fact is slipping away as soon as I said it, maybe that's all it needed so don't misunderstand it."[20]

Charles was true to his word. Soon after, he wrote that "if we could only be together we [might] think a bit more clearly."[21] In fact, one striking thing about the letters is how much a work partnership seems to have been implicit from the very start. (The precise mechanics being the province of the future). Theirs was clearly a meeting of minds as well as of hearts. In a February letter, Charles asked Ray, "Do you think that between the two of us we could write the scripts for and direct subjects like Modern Architecture in the US, sculpture in US, painting in US, Beauty in Useful Objects, if it's given the right slant it would have punch for the producer, public and us."[22] Not only does that last trio anticipate their later design diagram but notice, too, how filmmaking was part of the vision even before Charles and Ray began working on the furniture.

In mid-February of that year, Charles informed Richard Raseman, executive secretary at Cranbrook, of his decision not to return the next fall. Raseman was "touching" in comments about Charles's work at Cranbrook and even mounted a "stay at Cranbrook campaign."[23] Charles wrote to Ray, "What almost turned the tide" was the assurance that they could work together and that Ray would have a place at Cranbrook. "That we could be working close," he wrote, "and with each other means much you know." But Charles felt it was time to move on, though not without concern: "You won't be too shocked when you find how nasty the big world can be to little us? You've only seen me where I'm sort of 'all right'—really think now darling how will you feel when you are the only one that thinks I'm o.k." Nevertheless, by "all the commonsense laws I suppose it be the thing but [the] thought of coming back next fall would make me sick."[24] This was their first crucial choice as a couple, and one that Charles knew he was making for both of them. After Charles told Raseman he was leaving, he called Ray, as he noted in a letter: "when I told Richard (I would [leave Cranbrook]) I acted on what I instinctively felt was right—I did this before I got your letter so that you wouldn't feel responsible but I did want to hear your voice so I could confirm what I felt and thought you did—and it did."[25] In fact, "Actually over the phone I was afraid you would say, 'Yes, stay.'"[26] This decision-making process may be a harbinger of one motif in

97

their design careers—that is, of the right things being done for the right reasons.

The correspondence suggests that Charles must have reflected for some time that work would be an essential component of his future life and, therefore, that his life partner would need to be a work partner as well. However, this insight evolved during their time together, rather than being fully formulated beforehand. In Ray, Charles may have seen a woman for whom aesthetics and design were an essential part of her nature and thus a partnership might truly work on his new internal terms. For her part, the letters suggest that she saw in Charles a man who was not only as voracious as she was (perhaps even more so) in exploring various forms of expression, but also a man who was doing good, tangible things and planning even bigger ones. But overanalyzing a new romance, even that of one's grandparents, is a dicey game: they were also simply in love. Charles wrote Ray that "Lilly [Eero's wife] thinks you are beautiful too and is not one to be fooled about such things."[27] In another letter, "if only you get all the little thoughts I think between the lines, or do you?"[28] And in yet another, "Dear Ray, we will start off pretty damn broke and I wanted to hear you say it wouldn't make any difference."[29] Their design partnership was, from the start, an interesting and very human blend of collaboration and tradition.

However, in the spring of 1941, they had to face the pain and awkwardness of Charles's divorce, the pressure of the architecture and film projects, the endlessness of the problems with the Organic Furniture, and the practicalities of their move. "If I ever live through this spring, it is one charette after another and several at a time . . . the only thing that keeps me going is that it is all for us."[30] Ray never did get a job for the brief interim, and Charles wrote, "I guess the fact that you have been able to keep busy all this time without 'working' probably scares the hell out of me."[31]

There were also family reactions to contend with. Ray's brother, Maurice, was worried about Ray getting involved with "another artist,"[32] as he later put it. By now Charles's family knew. His mother even called him to ask what was going on. He said it was all for the best, but nothing more. Celine Eames wrote her son directly about her granddaughter: "[Lucia] is a complex little piece of humanity—and really so very much like you inside of her."[33] She wrote her sister that she was "dead inside," and continued, "I am devoted to Catherine and I am crushed when I think of Lucia for she will never be happy without Charlie."[34] As is often the case in the Eames story, design and life interweaved, though uniquely so at this point. In the same letter, Celine reported that Adele, Charles's sister, had been in New York and had seen the Organic Furniture show, even though the Museum of Modern Art guarded "the designs like the queen's jewels because they fear they will be copied by other manufacturers. I suppose Charlie's prize was $1,000.00. I suppose that is what Catherine will get her divorce with because he has never kept anything for himself."[35]

It was true enough. In March, Charles was served with divorce papers. "Grim is the procedure," wrote Charles, but "the domestic complications in living quarters have a slight farcical character."[36] There was at least one welcome break for Charles: a two-week train trip to California, primarily to pursue the never-built studio design for Irene Rich, was a great experience, though attempts to make contact with the Hollywood studios were not fruitful. One letter contains a beautiful rendering of the passage of time: images of the plains when he went to sleep and when he woke and again a few hours later. He had a facility with words, yes, but he was always creating images. On the way back, he met Ray's friend Helen Donnelly in Chicago; she quickly wrote Ray with her blessing: "a swell guy, one of the wisest young men I have met."[37]

On Charles's return, he faced more travails with the Organic Furniture. The manufacturing of the Case Goods was on track, but not the shell. Wrote Charles, "interesting, if trying."[38] There was another concern that both Charles and Ray recognized: they hadn't seen each other since December. Charles declared that "we must see each other soon: this business of becoming 'dream people' in each other's minds is no good."[39] They seem to have had a "conference," as they began to call it, in New York sometime in May, and they started zeroing in on a wedding date (sometime toward the middle of June) and place (Helen Donnelly's in Chicago). Maurice was still unimpressed by Charles on paper—he even wanted the prospective couple to visit Louisiana for his approval before the wedding (they did not). There was a lot of talk about pragmatics. Charles understood at least one key dimension of Los Angeles: "More about car, I wouldn't dare go out west without one because I think it would be bad for us not to form, at this time, a completely mobile unit."[40] Flexibility was always a favored Eames approach. Charles also encouraged Ray in her "packing, sorting and *weeding out.*"[* 41]

In May, the divorce was finalized,[†] and around May 30, Charles proposed to Ray in a letter, which is reproduced on page 92. She said yes. Soon the school year ended. "Lucia was very cute insisting I get my share of the loot from dividing the apartment."[42] The Organic Furniture was weighing heavily on Charles and Eero, perhaps especially on Charles because he had no other prospects of income. It was also already clear that the single-piece shell with the complex curve might be impossible with the proposed manufacturing process. Charles was treated for an ulcer, which his doctors told him came from "stress and overwork." "I could have told them that,"[43] he wrote to Ray.

On June 20, 1941, at Helen Donnelly's apartment in Chicago with Eero and Lilly Saarinen, Maurice Kaiser and his wife, and a few others in attendance, Charles Eames and Ray Kaiser became husband and wife. Eero Saarinen played an odd trick with the wedding cake. When the happy couple started to cut it, he protested: No, no, no, you have to cut this

* The pleading emphasis is his.

† Catherine leaves the story now and, so, a word of closure: she pursued a career in academia, eventually becoming associate dean of women at Washington University. She remarried in 1962 to C. Carter Lewis and lived in St. Louis until her death in 1996.

Above left: April
1942 *Arts and
Architecture*
cover designed
by Ray. Above
right: Ray and
Charles with
John Entenza on
the future site of
Case Study
Houses 8 and 9

way—the knife at one angle; then this way—the knife at another; now this. Eero instructed carefully, "Start at one edge, and you start in and cross . . . now get back, turn completely around and go back, and with a 30-degree angle 'til you meet the circumference of the cake, now turn 45 degrees and cross." Then he said, "Now let me . . . let me think. . . . Go halfway through the thing, bisect the angle that now faces you 'til you link the perimeter, come back at. . . ." Then, as Charles told the story, suddenly "[Eero] says, 'Oh, my God! It only applies to Finnish cakes!'"[44] Eero's antics make a little more sense if one knows that Charles and Ralph Rapson snuck into Eero's house the day of his wedding to Lilly and cut the legs off the bed, making for a comical beginning to the wedding night.[45]

On meeting Charles, Maurice was relieved, to say the least, and he and Charles were extremely close the rest of their lives. Surviving the wedding, the cake cutting, and the brotherly inspection, Charles and Ray Eames drove to California in a new Ford, owning not much more than that vehicle. Charles borrowed some money from Eero against the theoretical chair royalties, and he was grateful to Richard Raseman for issuing his last paycheck a little early. Barney Reese said that she and the rest of the gang in Sacramento didn't know about the wedding until afterward: "[Ray] didn't tell us she was having a romance. She just waited until it was a fact. And doesn't that sound like Ray? . . . She couldn't have been happier, and that was the best part."[46]

Charles and Ray arrived in Los Angeles on July 5, 1941.[47] It was 12 years to the day after her father's death had started Ray on a path out of California, and now she was back (and almost exactly 12 years to the day since Charles and Catherine's wedding). They weren't youngsters but they had a fresh start. They were thinking about movies, but not the usual Hollywood fare. They knew hardly anyone in Los Angeles, but that was just fine with them. They just didn't have much money. Architecture projects were few, and the studio for Irene Rich was not moving forward. There were more problems with the Organic Furniture, though the project was not dead yet (and, indeed, some examples were produced).

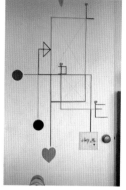

However, it was frustratingly clear to all that the Organic Chair would not achieve the competition's goal of low cost and would require a new effort.

During the first month or two, Charles and Ray lived at the Highland Hotel in Hollywood. Los Angeles was beginning to swell with what would become the wartime economy. The newlyweds began connecting with people almost immediately as they started to get the lay of the land. One connection was with John Entenza, publisher of *Arts and Architecture* magazine, who was said to have introduced Charles and Ray to Austria-born architect Richard Neutra, who in turn found them a spot in the Strathmore Apartments he had just built,[48] part-owned by his wife's parents. But there was an even more pressing need: work. Charles summarized the situation well in a letter to Eliot Noyes on September 2, 1941: "Here we are in Hollywood, right. After many weeks of searching for work with some gleaming future I finally gave up and two weeks ago started work with Metro Goldwyn Mayer [MGM]—all hope for the future is lost but I get a regular paycheck. Ray (the gal that was with me the night at your apt) and I have just moved into an apartment built by Neutra and it is much fun—like the shoemaker's shoeless children. We have no furniture (except some I have whipped up out of black iron pipe that would have won the 'competition with ease.' At least the poor people could afford it)."[49]

The 65 steep stairs heading to the Eameses' apartment made an impression on everyone. It is difficult to imagine anyone sneaking so much material up there during the night. They also impressed for another reason. Frances Bishop, a very early employee of the Eames Office, recalled how limber Ray was from her dancing lessons: "One thing I can remember about Ray was that she'd stand on one step, and she could bend down and put her hands flat on the one just below her. And she'd do that sometimes when we'd walk downstairs."[50] Bishop also remembered "polka lessons at UCLA . . . we used to go once a week and—Charlie, Ray and I. We had a lot of fun. She was great at it and he was pretty good. And I wasn't that bad either."[51]

In addition to the pipe furniture—mattress-ticking for cushions, so truly inexpensive—Charles and Ray ate their meals off laboratory equipment. Chemistry beakers and Pyrex dishes were part of their table service at the Strathmore Apartments in Westwood. There still exists a charming "to buy" list of the lab equipment to purchase. They spent eight years, the rest of the 1940s, in their Neutra-designed apartment. The delight they got from it is clear in a thank-you letter Charles wrote to Neutra just before they moved to their next abode: "The apartments you have developed here have given each the opportunity to develop his surroundings in the most expansive way, each feeling that he is living within his own garden and complete privacy."[52]

A print of the silhouette of a tumbleweed that Charles and Ray collected on their way to California

At MGM, Charles served in the art department, under the leadership of Cedric Gibbons. Charles was mainly a draftsman, doing architectural drawings for set design and the like. His first gig was designing the dressing rooms and the backstage area for *I Married an Angel*. He also did the hat-shop set for *Mrs. Miniver*. Larry Bachmann, the screenwriter, remembers his sister telling him he had to meet the guy who had done the most amazing drawing of a train. Bachmann and Charles hit it off and became lifelong friends.[53] MGM was not Charles's dream job, but there were rewards. He wrote Lucia of the pleasure of visiting a set where he watched Katherine Hepburn perform in *Woman of the Year*. She is "a joy to watch,"[54] he wrote. Another time he watched the crew as they tantalized Leo the Lion with a juicy steak to make him roar for the MGM logo.[55]

During their first two years in Los Angeles, Ray did some covers for *Arts and Architecture* and Charles wrote some articles for the magazine. Ray also continued with her painting, taking an ever-more essentialist approach, and her work was eventually exhibited in the Los Angeles Museum's third group show. At nights and on weekends, they began their experiments with the molded plywood. In June 1942, Charles and Ray tied up one last loose end from the Cranbrook era: a couple of hundred dollars he still owed the school. He paid it off, followed by a note written on a scrap of wood that said, "I have had to take a 'leave of absence' from MGM so Ray and I could devote all (and I mean all) our time to experiment for the navy."[56] After the experiments left the apartment, they opened offices in Westwood, then on Rose Avenue in Venice, and finally at 901.

In 1943, the Eames operation moved into 901 Washington Boulevard in Venice, its home for 45 years. Julian Blaustein remembered visiting the site with Charles before they moved in: "I kind of remember Charles taking me out to 901, saying 'I think this is what we'll do here.' And you know, I said I guess he knows what he's doing; it was an empty warehouse. And it just, that appealed to him enormously. 'Course you know what he did with it."[57]

Frances Bishop, who worked at the office then, remembered that it was a somewhat seedy, though strangely rural neighborhood, with field mice in the building. But Charles and Ray liked it, she said, "cause it was close to the beach. You know, we could just walk down there and have our lunch down there. . . . I remember the building; it was a big nothing. But after they got through with it, and all they did was put up a big 901, but that did it. And it was there for years and years."[58] Percy Harris, an MGM friend who was one of the first Eames Office employees (on the splints), remembered two 901 "recreations—flying kites and shooting the bow and arrow," the kites on Venice Beach and the archery inside the warehouse.[59]

In addition to the furniture work and the splints, there was some work done on the molded-plywood gliders. The Eames Office had nothing to do with the design of the aircraft itself, but rather with its implementation. The office gained important experience in the process, including the manufacture of a huge "blister" that formed the nosecone of the Flying Flatcar glider. The extraordinarily graceful object was 11 feet by 7 feet by 20 inches deep but weighed under 90 pounds. After the Eames Office team successfully manufactured it, it turned out the army had asked several other teams to try to do so and all of them failed. It was easy for Percy Harris to understand why: "The big one was the blisters of the airplane . . . because then I had to make the electric blanket, and [it] was terrible! Oh, I hated doing that because it was huge, and I had to stretch wires every quarter of an inch, and your hand got terribly cut. . . . It just cut through the gloves. And if you didn't do it properly, you'd short everything."[60]

Even unsuccessful endeavors could bear beautiful fruit. Said Frances Bishop: "I remember the stabilizers. And I remember having a Christmas party in that huge factory and they—and some of the defective stabilizers were left and they were hung from the ceiling, and I remember what they looked like, you know, they were rounded on one end and then they . . . flared out a little bit and of course, they were—it was just a rough thing. . . . But [Charles] saved them. And so then when you walked into this room, this huge factory—and that's where we had our Christmas party—they were hung from the ceiling and then there was a wire at the end of it and a little halo and they were hung on an angle, so it just looked like the room was full of angels flying. It was just beautiful!"[61] Another time, it was Ray who adapted the debris of the office: she made flower bouquets out of wood shavings.[62]

By this time Lucia joined them during summers and some other times. Charles and Ray had mounted a "Come to California" campaign, which had overcome the travel concerns of Catherine's mother. Alexander Knox, who would win an Oscar for playing Woodrow Wilson, and some of Charles and Ray's other new friends from Los Angeles had joined in the effort.

CHARLES AND RAY EAMES

103

Lucia helped and played at 901 most of the time. One summer, Charles and Ray rented a small beach cabin, where Ray gave Lucia and her summer visitors, Chrissie and Buddy Meyer, drawing lessons on the weekends.[63]

In addition to the aircraft work and the furniture, there were other projects and explorations at this time that would set the stage for many of the Eames Office's achievements over the following decades. In 1943, Charles published in *Architectural Forum* magazine a plan for a new kind of city hall.[64] John Entenza was involved in this project as well. In a sense, the plan took the Eames philosophy of connections (in the film *ECS* several years later, Charles intones simply, "the connections . . . the connections . . . the connections"[65]) and applied it to urban planning. "It should be impossible to think of the Juvenile Court without thinking in terms of the Children's Clinic without thinking in terms of a Board of Education."[66] The project was also an important bridge to the use of architecture to structure information (as would be seen later in the *Mathematica* exhibition and the *Aquarium* and *Metropolitan Overview* proposals, for example), but in this case the architecture was a metaphorical intermediary for the needs of the city as a social and political entity.

*Lecture 1*, a single-screen slide show that Charles first gave at Caltech in 1945, concerned "the relationship between design and the structure of the man-made and the natural world."[67] One can see clearly in it the gift for beautiful abstracted form that was yet another connection between Charles and Ray. But Charles was thinking about even more ambitious uses of visual media. Alexander Knox remembered how dazzling photography was to Charles. Knox met Charles and Ray through Percy Harris, when Charles was still working at MGM. They connected when Knox, an amateur cabinetmaker, needed some help with the details of fabrications. As always, Charles had a keen understanding of materials. Knox remembered Howard Hughes pressing to meet Charles and Ray regarding the Spruce Goose[68] (the largest plane ever built—and made completely of wood). Eventually, it is believed that a few folks from the office spent some time with the Hughes team giving pointers on molding plywood.

Knox also remembered discussing, in the late 1940s "a marvelous idea of how to play Shakespeare against translucent screens," something he and Charles were hoping to do at the Old Vic Theater in London with Tyrone Guthrie (the theater's artistic director): "Charlie said, 'Why can't we set up a few screens and these screens could be like the wings in the old theaters or they could be anywhere.'" The screens would have films as well as stills. They went so far as to shoot stills for a production of Hamlet. Knox's favorite was of the "classic scene of Hamlet. And Charlie had the brilliant idea of displaying the whole of the Renaissance—jewels, religion, fruit, silks, velvets, cut velvets, brilliant Bernini sculptures in gold and he did—we did a collection of fruit, a few exotic things." [All of this was intended to be projected behind the actors.] "And we picked up all the jewels Doris [Knox] had and [borrowed] all the jewels [from the actress] Geraldine Fitzgerald. [Then we put them on] a wooden tray that was decorated by Ray with red and green enamel so it looked like it was all fresh paint. So the jewels all got stained with that. It was a wonderful photograph of brilliance. . . . That was, I think, the best set. This was to be enlarged and it was to be directly behind the queen's bed. And it fits in with . . . some of the best lines of that—of that scene. . . . Anyway, the way of getting that into action in the theater was rather complicated but it worked. I mean it would have worked if it had ever been done. . . . There were many, many other scenes besides the Renaissance scene. The ghost scene, well that was a marvelous selection of the best gothic really." It was actually fairly worked out, but unfortunately, Guthrie left the Old Vic Theater before the plan could be pursued.[69]

Equipment for the manufacturing of the molded-plywood airplane parts— one can see here a tail stabilizer being formed.

Knox continued: "Charlie is the only director, really imaginative director I ever worked with except maybe Willie Wyler. And Charlie would have been brilliant at it. He could have caught the essence of a scene and done it in a way that would have improved the actor's job of getting the words across. I had a great deal of respect for Charlie's ability to catch on to what one meant."[70] There were other times when things took unexpected turns, according to Knox: "We used to go out to Chatsworth sometimes because I was very fond of the hills and we were going to shoot a bit of a film I wrote out there. And we stopped thinking about the film entirely in order to take some very close pictures of some ants in a little anthill at the top of one of those green hills."[71]

Another time, Alexander and Doris Knox had "a funny little alcove" they wanted to make into a dressing room. "I wondered how—what to do to make it look nice," Alexander recalled. "And Charlie said, 'Make a silver top on the dressing table,' and I said, 'How do you do that?' And he said, 'Well, it's fairly simple,' and he did it. He did a thing with silver foil on a piece of plywood and it was smooth and reflective. It was lovely."[72] Later, the fiberglass rocker was designed for Doris Knox, who was pregnant at the time, but the child *in utero* was walking by the time the design was actually completed.

These early projects and explorations were important harmonies for Charles and Ray, ones that would emerge more fully in the coming decades. They are critical to the Eames story because they provide an essential reminder that Charles and Ray's breadth of vision was with them from the start and was part of the coherent and exciting way they looked at the world. Furniture, photography, multimedia, and exhibitions were all part of the score from the beginning, but it was their journey toward a single-shell chair that provided the drumbeat of the 1940s for Charles and Ray.

# CHAPTER 9

# A 30-Year Flash (Part II)

In an interview in the 1980s, Ray was trying to explain something about the *Nehru* exhibition and she found herself explaining about the India Report and then Nehru's vision. Finally, she indicated good-natured exhaustion, and offered that "everything hangs on something else."[1]

In the 30-year flash, everything connects as well. The Organic Chair hangs on the Kleinhans Chair, the splint on the sculpture, the sculpture on the Organic Furniture, the LCW on it all. We resume this biography of the single-shell chair at the end of 1945. Part of that evolution is the transformation the plywood chair makes from compelling prototype and example into production, that in turn hangs on its reception by the marketplace. Everything hangs on something else.

The molded-plywood furniture had been well received at the 1945 showing at the Barclay Hotel in New York, so much so that Eliot Noyes at the Museum of Modern Art had invited Charles to have a show of his furniture at MoMA in March. Frances Bishop remembered, "We were awfully busy getting things ready."[2] The objects in the show would be the molded-plywood chairs and screen, the case goods, a tiltback chair where the whole chair kind of rocked back with you, switching your weight onto another back leg. There was also the molded-plywood elephant, children's chairs, and a lot of wonderful supporting material, including a rotating drum that treated a chair like a stone in a rock tumbler. The point? To show the visitor that these strange, airy-looking chairs were tough.

Evans Products was the manufacturer of the Eames furniture at that time. It is worth a moment here to detail the somewhat complicated series of companies that were involved with the Eames furniture during the 1940s. Charles and Ray were the core of design operations for what they thought of as the Office of Charles Eames at that time. Though she was always an important part of the partnership and was often at 901, at that point Ray was still painting regularly and often during the days. Although today we recognize that most of the things (like the sculptures) credited to Ray alone were in fact created by both Charles and Ray and most of those things credited to Charles alone (like the furniture) were designed by

Verla Shulman enjoying the fiberglass arm shell, end product of the flash

107

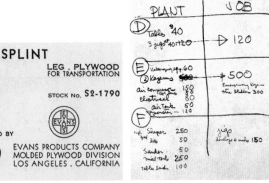

**1 SPLINT**

LEG . PLYWOOD
FOR TRANSPORTATION

STOCK No. **S2-1790**

MANUFACTURED BY

EVANS PRODUCTS COMPANY
MOLDED PLYWOOD DIVISION
LOS ANGELES . CALIFORNIA

From left to right: label for the molded-plywood splints; Charles's notes as he budgeted the production of the splints (note the line item for "2 Kazams"); a tumbler at the 1946 MoMA show that demonstrated the strength of these (to some) fragile-looking chairs

both Charles and Ray, at this point their transition to a full partnership was still in process. This partly explains the title of the show at MoMA—*Furniture by Charles Eames*. Nevertheless, the message of partnership clearly came through somewhere, somehow, because as early as September of 1946, R. Buckminster Fuller inscribed a copy of *Fluid Geography* "To Charles and Ray Eames, the delicate geography of whose way of creative living must have gladdened many hearts as it does mine."[3]

In order to manufacture the leg splints during the war using the Eames process, an entity was created around 1942 called the Plyformed Wood Company. Charles had left MGM, bringing Percy Harris, Griswald Raetze, and Gregory Ain with him to begin production on the splints. Harris remembered this time fondly, using "a plaster mold, and the wood was strapped to that and then put into the pressure. And I used to spread the glue and do all those sort of chores, which I enjoyed very much."[4] John Entenza was an investor in this company run and owned by Charles. This company could not handle the unique fiscal pressure of military contracts (specifically the long delays in payments) and, in 1943, Evans Products was contacted and they bought out the Plyformed Wood Company (and assumed the debts) which now became the Molded Plywood Division of Evans Products.[5] But, as Percy Harris says, for the folks there "it was always called the office."[6] Evans Products, a Michigan-based wood products company, was owned by Colonel Evans, an irascible character who respected Charles and granted him considerable leeway in the management of the production entity. There seems also to have been an understanding that after the war Charles's furniture would be produced by Evans. Colonel Evans died in 1945, which could not have been an opportune time for any company to make such a transition.

A lot was riding on the MoMA show at for the Eames Office. Don Albinson, who had been a pilot during World War II, came to Los Angeles in late 1945 or early 1946 to work with his old teacher and boss, Charles Eames (Don had been a student and worked on the Organic Chairs at Cranbrook). He had the distinct impression that this MoMA show would be the last thing that Evans Products would do for the Eames furniture. "It's my understanding that Charlie figured this would be it. He'd had his show and . . . and that would be it . . . The guys at Evans Products had gone about as far as they were going to go with this operation out there."[7] Charles's mother wrote her sister at the end of December 1945 that Charles was going to have a show at MoMA. She summarized the situation even more concisely, "[Charles] says if his furniture venture succeeds it will be fine, if not, terrible. So hope for his sake it will."[8]

* Interestingly the press focused a lot of attention on the tiltback chair, which, like the 3-legged chairs at the Barclay Hotel show, proved to be an idiosyncrasy that didn't survive.

Evans Products rarely marketed to consumers directly and at the time had become grossly overextended in another area of the company. The West Coast operation was a logical place to cut back. The 1946 MoMA show was in a sense the payment of a debt of honor by Evans Products to Charles. As far as Evans was concerned, only one thing went wrong: the show was a success.

The reviews were quite positive.* It was clearly this show and the products in it that launched the Eameses beyond the *succes d'estime* of the Organic Chairs. But even more important, other manufacturers and distributors were interested now. This was critical because Evans didn't really want to continue. Further, even if they had, they really had no idea how to reach a wider market. Charles felt he would be able to handle production, but needed help with distribution. Two companies expressed serious interest: Knoll and Herman Miller, Inc. Florence Schust Knoll was probably a little more on top of what the Eameses were up to through her own time at Cranbrook. She had married Hans Knoll (founder of the H.G. Knoll Furniture company) and in 1946 they were beginning their own partnership, a furniture company called Knoll Associates, known today simply as Knoll.

Herman Miller was interested because George Nelson, the head of Design for Herman Miller, brought D.J. DePree and Hugh DePree to the MOMA show. He told them, "this is the future of your company."[9] George Nelson was a great designer in his own right and became over the next years a good friend of Charles and Ray's but at the time he didn't know them. He also had veto power over other designer's work through his contract with Herman Miller, but as he told colleague Alfred Auerbach, "I wouldn't think of having them submit their designs to me."[10] It has to rank among the acts of simple integrity in design history that Nelson would bring the DePrees to the Eames work. After all, on some level, Eames could be perceived as competition for Nelson. And Nelson had only joined the firm a year before when DePree had been "impressed"[11] by Nelson's ideas of honest design. But Nelson recognized that his role as director of design required doing the best for the company—and he probably gave less thought to the issue than this paragraph, but it warrants noting.

Dirk Jann DePree was the owner and leader of Herman Miller, Inc., started in 1905 as the Star Furniture Company. DePree's father-in-law, Herman Miller, loaned DePree the money to buy the company in 1923 and D.J. named the firm in his honor. At that time, the

A 30-YEAR FLASH (PART II)

109

firm manufactured primarily reproduction colonial furniture. The depression hit the firm hard. In 1931, modernist Gilbert Rohde joined as director of design. Some people asked later why the firm took a chance on such modern designers as Rohde, Eames, Nelson, Isamu Noguchi and Alexander Girard. DePree replied that it wasn't a chance, "we had no other choice."[12] He also observed that "there was more integrity than in the traditional. Modern was giving more utility in less space at less cost in a given room."[13]

A few years after he and the Eameses had joined forces with Herman Miller, George Nelson described the firm this way: "It is a small company operating in a small town and by the owners . . . [that believes] What you make is important; Design is an integral part of the business; The product must be honest; There is a market for good design."[14] Herman Miller is still based in that small town (Zeeland, Michigan) in a very conservative part of the state. Dutch Reform remains the dominant faith of the area, and D.J. DePree was a pillar of his church. Charles and Ray were not particularly religious. But they found a deep, deep common ground with DePree on issues of integrity, quality, honest use of materials, and good design.

The Eameses' choice between Herman Miller and Knoll was an important and difficult one. Charles and Ray certainly respected Hans Knoll and knew and liked Florence from Cranbrook (she was "practically an adopted daughter of the Saarinens."[15]) But Ray pointed out that "Charles was drawn to the DePrees because he thought they were very straightforward, honest business people, as opposed to the Knoll idea of 'image' and 'international design.'"[16] She was not implying anything about the business integrity of Knoll (which is and was impeccable), but she was putting into business terms an Eames concern that "what works good is better than what looks good, because what works good lasts."[17] In other words, the people who had just designed the most revolutionary chair of the 20th century felt that they were better off with a company that took that approach as a given and put it in the marketplace as simply a good chair. They felt uncomfortable asking people to buy the chair as a landmark of international design or "design style," they wanted them to buy it because it was comfortable and worked. This is a key insight to the way Charles and Ray viewed things. You could (and indeed had to) compete on a practical level rather than a novelty level as with their sculpture, where the Eameses had seen no conflict between art and technology.

So the Eameses went with Herman Miller. DePree often talked about the time he and Charles formed a covenant on the shores of Lake Michigan. The follow-through was a bit more complicated than that because of the issues of manufacturing and the fact that the tooling was already in California. So for the first two or so years (1946–48), Herman Miller only marketed and distributed the furniture; in approximately 1948 they began the manufacturing as well. Initially the manufacturing was done right in the 901 space. "When we first started to make furniture," Charles explained, "why, we built the tools right in the office. It was an architect's or a design office . . . We built the tools. We also built the first 5,000 chairs that were made, right in the office. And we built the tools upon which the first 50,000 chairs were made and sent them out. And this is working, fighting out each little thing and each little problem—problems in rubber, problems in welding, right on the brink of disaster every minute. . . . Most of the answers were essentially architectural answers and they dealt and fell back necessarily upon constraints."[18]

It is important to remember that although the MoMA show was a success, not all the production details were worked out. In a sense, this kind of design show can be a blue-print for production—but, this time, unlike the follow-up to the Organic show, the Eameses experiments in the Neutra apartment, the splint production and all the other experiences meant that this time the Eames Office was on the right track. But that doesn't mean it was a smooth ride. They had hoped to use radio frequencies (in a process not dissimilar to a microwave) to attach the shockmounts (which hold the seat and back to the legs and other support), but in the end had to use a special kind of glue. Charles pushed the team very hard. Don Albinson remembers one crisis when "we had one horrible thing where Charlie had told them that . . . we could cook the finish on the plywood seats and backs when we were gluing them together. And it was true we could cook the finish on a plywood seat or back, maybe once out of every hundred tries, and then the other times. . . . We'd chisel it off. . . . We couldn't find a parting agent that we could put on that would ensure this thing would pop off. [So] Milton Driggs, who was a chemist, and I, we tried everything. . . . We had shoe polish. . . . We went through the stores, you know, lard, margarine. We tried—God, motor oil—everything imaginable." Albinson laughed. On Sunday night they found Saraseal (kind of a wax finish they had been using for something else), "And so Monday morning we got up, bleary eyed, and went to the shop, showed them, you know, with no problem at all, how nice this was molding and coating off and everything. We managed to survive that crisis."[19]

But there were more twists in the rollercoaster. In April of 1947, Evans Products, having secured the deal with Herman Miller, brought the tooling back to Grand Haven, Michigan to do the manufacturing there. From Evans management standpoint, though it was not good for the furniture, it was an important way to consolidate operations. Ultimately, however, the fit of a consumer product with the rest of Evans was not a good one. As Charles said, "they weren't particularly interested in furniture and Herman Miller sort of bought them out."[20] Herman Miller finally took over manufacturing rights in 1948 and has manufactured the Eames furniture to this day. The original tooling (of the 901 space) trav-eled again at that point from Grand Haven to Zeeland where it stayed.

* As a formal matter, the Molded Plywood Division of Evans Products ceased to exist around this time. It also later became an area of dispute with Entenza, who had invested in the Plyformed Wood Company, which Evans had bought out. When other dimensions of Eames work became successful, he felt he should participate. The matter was resolved acrimoniously in the early 1950s. Charles and Ray operated as a sole proprietorship for decades until formalizing as a partnership in the 1970s. In the early 1980s, Entenza and Ray broke bread together, beginning a reconciliation.

For the Eameses, 1947 was a complicated year. It had to have been a relief to not be responsible for the manufacturing, and yet the sudden distance posed issues of quality control.* The operations transfer also meant layoffs in the Eames Office because the staff that wore so many hats could not be covered by the manufacturing monies. Literally everyone was out of work. Somehow Charles and Ray managed to hold onto the building, but it was empty. The Eames operation was down to just the two of them again. Suggestively of where the future lay, although Evans Products no longer had an ongoing connection with the Eameses (aside from continuing to pay them a royalty), Herman Miller brought Charles on as a design consultant.

Don Albinson had been unemployed for a while when Charles and Ray began rehiring for the new endeavors. He recalls a brief time when, "I was then the only employee [of Charles and Ray's] . . . and we had this great big empty building, 901. And . . . we set up a target for a bow and arrow and we got a bow and arrows and we would target shoot inside the building. Got pretty good at it."[21] But the others were brought back as soon as possible: Milton Driggs, Frances Bishop, Jay Connor, Marion Overby and others as projects unfolded.

In a sense, then, the essence of the molded-plywood journey was over for the Eameses. A graph would show an intriguing symmetry, right down to the archery. They had started as a couple following up on the well-hidden promise of the Organic Furniture experience, evolved a design solution, expanded into a full-fledged manufacturing entity guiding a gifted team to break down design and technological hurdles and now they were alone. The Eames Office had extracted a million nuances from this substance: what it could do, how it stretched, how it finished, how it looked, how it mass produces, which woods worked, what plys, what glides, what shock mounts, and a raft of other things that became second nature to the group at the Eames Office. The design process had finally yielded a fairly complete and quite robust understanding of the constraints implied by plywood. Though they would continue to use the material in new products, the past six years had really been a crucible. Plywood could never make a single-piece shell in the way they had originally wanted. Some at the office even thought Charles had been "persuaded . . . to abandon the whole unified form."[22] But that was not the case at all. In fact, it was part of the Eameses genius that they never let go of the idea. Interestingly another Museum of Modern Art competition would provide the impetus to push the concept further.

In 1948, MoMA announced an "International Competition for Low-Cost Furniture Design" to encourage the design of "mass-produced furniture that is planned and executed to fit the needs of modern living, production and merchandising. " Designers were encouraged to partner with engineering teams. It was an open competition, but six teams got modest grants through MoMA, including a team partnering the Eames Office with the UCLA

A nice assemblage of various experiments (including those in metal) tried during the Low-Cost Furniture Competition. Note the stamped metal chair in the middle.

school of engineering. The idea that they collaborated on was a stamped metal chair.

But before exploring the issue of mass-production, what about mass consumption? Or to put it another way, "How do you design a chair for acceptance by another person?" Charles asked rhetorically. "By not thinking of what the other guy wants, but by coming to terms with the fact that while we may think we are different from other people in some ways and at some moments, the fact of the matter is that we're a hell of a lot more like each other than we are different, and we're certainly more like each other than we're like a tree or a stone. So then you relax back into the position of trying to satisfy yourself—except for a real trap, that is, what part of your self do you try to satisfy? The trap is that if you try to satisfy your idiosyncrasies, those little things on the surface, you're dead, because it is in those idiosyncrasies that you're different from other people. And in a sense, what gives a work of craft its personal style is usually where it failed to solve the problem, rather than where it solved it. What you try to do is satisfy your real gut instincts and work your way through your idiosyncrasies, as we have tried in the stuff we've done, the furniture or the ideas. You know, it's tough enough just trying to make the first step of understanding without trying to introduce our personality or trying to outguess what the other guy's thinking."[23]

For the new competition entry, the concept was fundamentally simple. It was a con-

Right: the mold
for the stamped
metal chairs and
the section of
the metal chair
that joined the
seat and back

tinued pursuit of the single-shell concept in a new material. The new arrow they had in their quiver, though, as a result of the plywood work, was a better understanding of how to understand a new material. What material? Charles observed in the entry, "Metal stamping is the technique synonymous with mass production in this country, yet 'acceptable' furniture in this material is noticeably absent."[24] In other words, car fenders, made of stamped metal, were objects (like the one-piece shell of the Eames's dreams) which made complex curves in a single piece, so why not use this technology to make a single piece chair shell? The Eames Office found out during the manufacturing process—the learn-by-doing approach again. The stamping work was actually done at the office, which was ironic because the UCLA group had a hydraulic press but it was rarely available. Fred Usher, who was there at the time, had a nuanced slip of the tongue, "it's just a progress—a process of . . . working it out."[25]

Major problems developed. First, the chair (at the least the shell for the side chair) was stamped in three pieces that needed to be welded together. Second, both aluminum and steel (the two metals being used) were cool to the seat. To compensate, there was an extremely fine layer of vinyl or neoprene (respectively) used to surface the metals. Though it solved the direct problem, it may also have served to flag a fundamental inelegance in the solution. But, as always, there was learning. Fred Usher remembered, "We would finally get to where we could manage these materials, which were all sort of new. That was one thing you couldn't really go out into industry and really get much help from, because they were new at it too, except for the neoprene which had been around for a while, quite a while."[26]

The most substantial problem was the stamping process itself, which was quite dramatic. The Eames Office built a stamping machine that was essentially a drop hammer. With its wooden tracks, Albinson says it "was a wooden—it was really like a guillotine,"[27] except with a cudgel not a blade. A 300-pound weight was lifted with a block and tackle to a height of about four or five feet above where the metal sheet was placed. (Part of the dead-weight was actually an old leg mold from the molded-plywood days—an extreme example of the office's commitment to iteration.) Under the metal sheet was the female of the form, cast in plaster; attached to the weight was the male of the form. The rope was cut and WHAM! As the metal began to find its shape, the neighborhood dishes would rattle. (Don Albinson says when there were complaints the Eames Office folks would blame it on an earthquake.)[28] Fred Usher remembers the real problem: "The Hydrocal plaster molds were thick and reinforced with Sisal and other materials. . . . Because of this use of them . . . they would just get smashed after two or three drops. But we did get these pieces made."[29] This was clearly not going to be an efficient way to make chairs—three chairs from one expensive mold.

Clearly there were other ways to form metal, but none of the options were sitting right for the Eameses. A big factor in that was the tooling, which was estimated to cost $80-100,000 in 1948 (over half a million dollars today). With the Herman Miller company earning less than a million dollars a year, that was unlikely. Even if hypothetically another manufacturer could be found, the tooling alone had the potential to make the chair unbelievably expensive. Worse, tooling that expensive would be limiting. What if you make a mistake? Or a change? The Eameses' process depended on the ability to take small steps, massage the results, and keep moving forward, always improving, iteration by iteration. Once you make a $100,000 dollar tool, however, it is very difficult to say, "The next one will be better, please throw it away." Charles and Ray saw no reason to give up that control and so began to look around at other materials.

In the meantime, the Eames Office submitted the plans for the metal chairs to MoMA and won second prize. The flash had taken an important step forward in form. An exhibition of winning work was announced for eight months later, and by the time it opened, next to the metal chair prototypes were some of the same shapes, but in a completely different material: fiberglass. Charles and Ray had arrived at the last of the materials in this part of the journey.

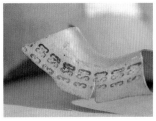

In late 1949, Sol Fingerhut and Irv Green of Zenith Plastics got a message from a Charles Eames about a new application for fiberglass. They remembered being fairly skeptical, a feeling that was not enhanced when they called back and the phone was answered with a phone number. "We were just kind of suspicious about the phone number answer." The men did eventually connect and arrange a meeting. When they arrived at 901, the exterior of the office was pretty suspect, and Charles was late. But then, Sol says, finally "the meeting that started off at two o'clock became an electric meeting: really, really intense. Ended up, I think, around seven o'clock that evening. Went over a whole range of different items. . . . And Charles was very concerned about two things: how to get the attachment, you know, to the base, and how to treat the edge of the chair shell. And we discussed that, and I knew that in order to get the rubber fastened properly, that the surface had to be cyclized by the developers."[30]

The first meeting was just three people, "Irv Green, myself and Charles. Period. The three of us. That was it." Sol continued," I can't recall all of it, but the meeting was controlled by Charles. He asked the questions, and the same questions in different ways, you know, different directions, to get satisfied in his own mind that this was, one, a viable alternate to the steel shell which he had in mind, and, two, were we the people that he felt that

he could work with? And so, if you understand that he was really directing the whole meeting, and the questions were always coming back in a different direction, a different way, as to. . . . What can be done? and Can this—how is this gonna be handled? And this and that, et cetera. I recall that it was an extremely long meeting."[31]

In this and other meetings Fingerhut remembers, "He was absolutely fantastic . . . in the way he would really, kind of, pick us up and carry us along with him in his discussions. This was his method: . . . in order to get us to maximize what we would do for him— for his project—he would have to really have us understand, the best that we could, what he was striving for."[32] In a conversation after our interview, Sol remarked to me that it was uncanny how Charles knew the right things to ask.[33]

It is significant that Charles was the only member of the office present at this critical meeting, because it really underscores how the design process worked for the Eameses. Just as Charles and Ray had figured out the essence of their molded-plywood process before they began making the splints and thus involving others, so too with the fiberglass chairs. Charles got the lay of the land concerning fiberglass in a very thorough way before unleashing the extremely talented and important members of the team on it. And, of course, that research was much deeper than a single meeting.

Larry Bachmann, a friend of Charles's from MGM, felt that Charles had his antenna out in an almost unique way. He remembered Charles mentioning to him British writer C.P. Snow's *Two Cultures* ideas—concerning the developing schism between science and the humanities— and he (Bachmann) finding it interesting and then moving on. Six months later the issue hit the mainstream like a hurricane. How did Charles always know?[34] This kind of early warning radar was also true of materials.

In the mid-1990s, as Craig Hodgetts and Ming Fung were developing their design of the exhibition *The Work of Charles and Ray Eames: A Legacy of Invention*, Hodgetts walked into the shop of John Wills, a noted fiberglass fabricator and boat builder. There, sitting on—not in—a trashcan kind of structure was something that looked a lot like an Eames fiberglass shell, and, of course, it was one.[35] And the story behind it relates to that ability Charles had to be aware of the right things, the useful things. In 1947, John Wills had developed a way to cure fiberglass at room temperature. This was an important development for the material, because it meant that heat and pressure were not necessary to create a fiberglass object (the radio domes that Zenith Plastics made in World War II used a solar cure that was not as reliable as one would hope). In fact, one of the first products Wills made this way was a prototype for the Skorpion Crosley car.

He recalled how Charles arrived "out of the blue"[36] in a beat-up Ford at his (Wills's) workshop in Arcadia, California, in 1948 or 1949. Charles had with him a craft paper mockup of the armshell and asked Wills to make a fiberglass shell of it. At that time, fiberglass technology did not permit making a female mold, only a male mold. In this technique, the paper version would be destroyed in the process of creating the fiberglass shell. One side, the outside, would be pretty crude, but the inside would be smooth. The charge: $25. Wills made two just in case. When Charles came back a week or so later, Charles looked at the fiberglass shells very carefully, circling them, sitting in them, taking them in. When he sat in it, the improvised base was a circular piece of corrugated metal from an agricultural feeder. When it came time to pay, Wills asked if he wanted both. Charles replied, "I can't really afford it—maybe some other time."[37] The one left behind remained there for almost half a century. After Hodgetts and Fung saw it, Wills donated it to the Henry Ford Museum.

*The chair that stayed on an ash can in John Wills's shop for over 40 years, seen in the exhibition The Work of Charles and Ray Eames: A Legacy of Invention*

A prototype is a piece that has the features of the final production piece—prototypes are the final stepping stones. In that sense, the Wills chair is not even really a prototype; it is, more accurately, a model of the idea of making the chair in fiberglass. It is a model in the "feeling-your-way sense." The hands-on process. Is it the right material? What happens if it is honest? No one else I spoke to from that era mentioned Charles's trip to John Wills's shop (though quite possibly someone knew of it). But either way, it is a nice documentation of something that often happened behind the scenes at the office: Charles seeking out his own understanding of a material or a project or an idea before delegating the exploration of what he felt were the richest veins of it. A theme throughout the Eames work is this sense that Charles and Ray never delegated understanding.

* The button or shock-mount is also used on some of the molded-plywood pieces too. It is a rubber disk with a washer in it. Glued to the fiberglass shell, it gives something for the legs to attach to with a screw.

Though the Wills chair is important, it was but one small step in the journey of actual production. Wills was not equipped for mass production in any event. But Charles now knew the questions to ask. Sol Fingerhut and Irv Green had really impressed Charles and he soon put them together with Herman Miller. Fingerhut and Green, in turn, persuaded their company to share the cost of the tooling with Herman Miller. Another revealing but important decision was made early on, which was to try to manufacture the armchair first. Herman Miller, Zenith, and the Eames Office all agreed that if one could make the more complicated armchair, the side shell would be a picnic.

As with the molded-plywood chairs, Charles and Ray were determined to let the design evolve from an understanding of the manufacturing process. Sol Fingerhut remembered this conversation, "For example, the parchment chair was translucent, and the button* [once] bonded on would show through. And Charles's answer was 'It's honest.' Because it's, you know, functional, it's there for a reason, it's there and it shows, you know, that's okay."[38]

Irv Green remembers a similar conversation with the very hands-on D.J. DePree. DePree had

In 1971, the
Eames Office
came out with the
two-piece plastic
chair—still will-
ing to explore the
issue of the shock
mounts.

come out to California, and was discussing the shockmount, "And it wasn't the small button [shockmount] you have today. It was a three inch button—we call it a button—a rubber with the steel molded inside. And I remember DJ saying, 'Gee, I could see the button.' And I said, 'Yeah, but it's honest.' And he turned to me quickly and said, 'Oh, you're learning the language.'"[39]

The idea of the honest use of materials doesn't mean the Eameses were pushovers. Irv Greene remembers, "And he had curious ideas such as putting a fiberglass rope in there

and so forth. And I guess—this is a long time ago—I said something to the effect that well, 'We can't do it.' And he turned to me with a little bit of a temper and said, 'Then we don't have a product. Forget it.' No. He wanted things done the way he wanted them. He didn't compromise that much. But he was pragmatic in the sense that [if we] absolutely couldn't do it, [it] changed some way."[40]

In addition to materials and engineering, the Eameses were also quite concerned with color. Green recalled, "They knew exactly what they wanted. They knew the colors exactly to the T. [They wanted] to select colors that would minimize the effect of discoloration due to the process itself. They also wanted the colors that would be neutral, that would work in different situations in interior decorating: the parchment, the greige and the elephant hide gray, which was really kind of a light black, a, you know, warm light black."[41] Sol remembers that process as an intense one. "So they ultimately had to come out. They came out to the plant and worked with me, I remember, two or three evenings until midnight. This was in Gardena. And hour after hour, just . . . just making samples—color samples of chairs to develop the colors. It was a tedious process, but it was very important to them that the color be right." In fact, "We molded chair after chair until they finally thought they had what they wanted, and then we put that one aside. And this was a long process, because they knew exactly what they wanted in the final color. But we couldn't get it exactly right; it was just an experimental approach."[42] Irv Green didn't work closely with Ray until the color process, but remembers her intensity on that issue. But color was important to Charles and Ray both. Green remembers that the elephant hide gray seemed to be the most frustrating and difficult to pull off. He finally said, "Well, why don't you mix up something and then we'll copy it," which they did. Forty years later Green vividly evoked Charles's "final statement before he made his own color. He said—you know, he used to use his hands a lot like this." In saying this,

Green made a gesture like trying to shape the air, "He was trying to like mold this thing. He said, 'What I really want is a black with feeling.'"[43]

The fiberglass armchair was at the MoMA show along side its metal ancestors and its sensual cousin, La Chaise. The design of the fiberglass chairs continued to evolve subtly from 1950 to 1953. The rope edge that was present in the early chairs was eliminated, in part to save cost. More designs were made that utilized the material, including an upholstered version that sprang from what might have become waste. As Sol said, "Charles could take those problems and turn them into a positive thing."[44] Since many structurally sound shells were being rejected solely for discoloration, they began to upholster them. Eventually these were so successful that Herman Miller began manufacturing shells just to be upholstered.

With this chair the Eameses had finally achieved their goal of low cost. Charles remarked to Sol about the public, "I know what they should have, but they don't know what they should have. So we'll give them something that is—they can afford to buy that's really good."[45] It was a rephrasing of the Eames remark, "The best to the most for the least."[46] A 15-year flash was over, but the 30-year flash was not. As late as 1971, in the Two-Piece Secretarial Chair, the Eames Office was still exploring the implications of what new plastics would mean to the detail of the shockmount. Even more than that, Charles and Ray saw all the designs as a continuing and connected evolution.

Ray summed up what drew them to mass-production this way, "We were concerned about the use of time, people's labor, for the greatest result, so that one person could spend a long time making one chair and he would have made that nice chair and then other people would not have that result, they would have something much less. But if that effort went into production, the idea of production, it would be at a higher level."[47]

Above left: An installation of the Eames stadium seating. The mass production of the Eameses' molded-plastic side shells was the fruition of a 15-year journey. Above right: Charles, staff members, and Ray (standing) pulling La Chaise from its mold

119

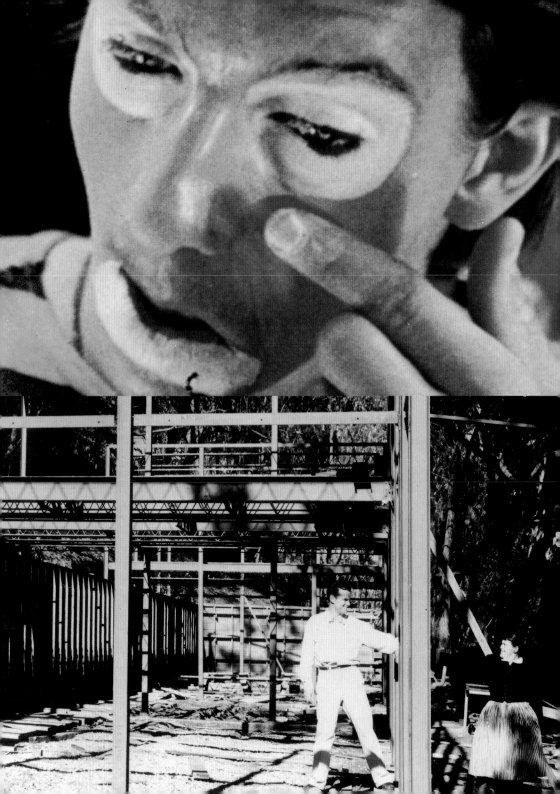

# Take Your Pleasure Seriously

In October 1965, the Eames Office's show *Nehru: His Life and His India* opened at the Smithsonian Institution in Washington, D.C. Ray's brother, Maurice, and his family, including his daughter Midge, then in her 20s, were among those invited by Charles and Ray to the event. Midge recalled that, "There were a host of Indian dignitaries and Washington *hoi polloi*. The reception was held in the new (then) Smithsonian building where the Foucault pendulum is." When the formalities had been taken care of, the party unfolded and Midge noticed that Charles and Maurice "appeared deep in conversation, then they walked off together. When they returned, all smiles, we learned of their trip. Charles had purchased a new ball, the superball, the small rubber ball with a tremendous bounce. Charles had discovered that, by bouncing it at just the right angle, it would bounce up the marble toilet stalls in the men's room, and he took [my father] off to demonstrate its . . . and his . . . prowess" with spectacular results.[1] Charles was, for a time, a real evangelist for the superball, giving them out quite often on his travels, and bringing some to his grandchildren in San Francisco. He was properly impressed when his grandson, Byron, managed to bounce the ball through his own third-story bedroom window on his first throw.[2]

Toys crop up all the time in the Eameses' work. As Charles pointed out, "Toys are not really as innocent as they look. Toys and games are the preludes to serious ideas."[3] In fact, around the time of the Nehru opening, Charles remarked "I visited a good toy store this morning—satiated? It was sick making. I longed for the desert . . . [but] among the great and elegant design exceptions is a toy produced this year that has swept the country. What is it? A small bouncing ball—[the] superball."[4] Charles and Ray were fascinated by toys. They collected them, used them in movies and showrooms, and sometimes simply wanted to have some around at the office. As Alex Funke recalled, the Eames Office "was given to great fits of enthusiasms" and so it was that someone discovered that you could drill a hole through a superball and put a pencil through the hole. Then you could bounce it with great force into the ceiling and watch the pencil shatter—an informal activity that continued until someone was almost blinded.[5]

Top: image from the Eames film *Clown Face* (1971), a training film made for the Ringling Brothers Clown College. Bottom: Charles and Ray playing in the framed structure of the Eames House (1949)

121

That such an idea would run its course at the Eames Office is a manifestation of the same spirit that pushes a chair material to the limit as well. Similarly, referring to a super-ball as "a great and elegant design exception" is an expression of the profound respect the Eameses had for anything that, through the hard work and discipline of the creator, led to an effortless and spontaneous experience for the user. They admired this same quality in the circus as well. They even made a training film for the Clown College of the Ringling Brothers Barnum and Bailey Circus, a simple, compelling record of some of the great clowns putting on their makeup: *Clown Face*. The creation of such a film was part of the fun. As Charles said, "We worked very hard at that—enjoying ourselves. We didn't let anything interfere with what we were doing—our hard work. That in itself was a great pleasure."[6] Agreed Ray in a different context, "Our personal lives and our working lives were combined everyday. There really wasn't any separate personal life."[7] In the film *Design Q&A*, Charles is asked, "Can design be used to create objects reserved solely for pleasure?" His answer: "Who would say that pleasure is not useful?"[8]

Charles and Ray had an expression they used around the office that encapsulated this: "Take your pleasure seriously." It was also an ideal that they truly lived, one that mani-fested itself in a million ways in their lives and work. And, indeed, when they later did the *Franklin and Jefferson* exhibition, for example, it was a quality they admired in the two men: Franklin and Jefferson took their pleasures seriously. Parke Meek commented about the con-nection between work and play for Charles, "You know, it was the fact that he just keeps hammering away. . . . He very seldom did anything for entertainment. Other than play. He made the work, sort of, a play thing."[9]

Former staff member and Cranbrook student Jill Mitchell recalled what might be consid-ered an unexpected permutation of taking pleasure seriously. "The wastebaskets [at the office] were lined with colored tissue paper. And so that whenever the wastebaskets were changed the colored tissue paper lying in the wastebaskets [was also] changed." When she returned to Cranbrook, her friends were skeptical. "'Oh, jeepers, that's preposterous'—but I could see that it was not preposterous; that it was absolutely the best way to deal with the wastebas-ket situation. And a solution to: how do you keep wastebaskets from being nasty inside?"[10]

The Eameses' friend Julian Blaustein commented on how things got done between Charles and Ray, "I don't think there was a definition to the way they worked: there wasn't a formal arrangement; they were there together. And they breathed the work. They breathed the work. And Ray did an awful lot to smooth the whole atmosphere. She too seemed in dis-array, but wasn't. . . . You [would] walk into Charles's office and on the drafting board, which was like a desk, you couldn't find anything. Couldn't find anything. You don't know how he ever got his job done. But that nice, neat package that he was as a man, with those little bow ties, the work came out just that way. It all came out effortlessly, it seemed."[11]

For many of Charles and Ray's friends not only was their partnership fascinating, but also their commitment to process. Billy Wilder remembered that "when you first met the Eameses, that's kind of interesting: they spoke a slightly different language. You thought they were, sort of, a little bit stammering and they'd never finish their sentences and you are a little bit bewildered at the beginning. They understood each other completely, but when they started off on the line, to get it perfect, they would sort of wipe out the first half up there and forget it and put it the other way, just to make it a little bit more comprehensive."[12]

Don Albinson remembered the Eameses as "very creative people, damned hard working people. They always worked, you know, at night—into the night. They worked till ten, eleven o'clock and then they'd go home for payoff time. Payoff time is when you tune in [to] the ends of all the movies on TV and watch the final scenes, a payoff in other words. And before going to bed you'd cut oranges into section and eat 'em this way. I went out there Christmas '45."[13] Albinson went on to describe one adventure that happened soon after he arrived: "We ran around the plant manager's house, I guess, with these sleigh bells so that the kids would think Santa Claus was out there, and I lived with Charles and Ray in their apartment, their Neutra apartment on Strathmore, for, oh God, I don't know, six, eight months. Long time. There was the three of us. . . . The furnishing in the apartment was— must have been a table and at least three chairs, and there were two papier-mâché horse heads, and I think some footprints, sort of, tacked up on the wall, and not much else. That was sort of the furnishings in this white, completely white, stark, clean Neutra apartment."[14]

Mara Bailey, the daughter of Dr. and Mrs. Bailey, who lived in the Neutra Case Study House next door to the Eames House, remembered that "Charles was the one that helped me learn my alphabet and how to write and how to print letters and numbers. And I distinctly remember him sitting on the patio outside the living room door, and he was sitting there in a chair, and I walked up. And he said, 'Well, gee, do you know how to write your letters yet?' 'Well, I don't know,' [I said]. So he worked with me all day, and then I got it! I got it. I got the A's and the B's and all that. Then a while later, Ray came—I was out playing again and Ray came and said, 'Well, let me see you do your letters.' And she showed me how to do really neat letters, not just your strip model, but with little dots at the N's and [at] the top of the A and how to have fun with a pencil and writing. . . . And they always had—Ray always had—chewing gum in the kitchen . . . in a particular drawer. And sometimes she was very generous and would open the drawer herself and hand us all gum all around."[15]

Drawers everywhere were like Harpo's pockets, filled with wonderful and surprising things. These were their collections of good stuff—not necessarily expensive or cheap, but, like the collections at the Eames House, good examples of things. These collections—eclec-

tic but not haphazard, some more systematic than others—might be paper samples, or handfuls of cut-out figures of office staff members for use in models, or crayons, or shells, or slippers, or pins, or a million other things. Charles and Ray considered this source material, a way of taking notes through collecting. Sometimes these artifacts would appear in their showrooms or photographs or movies, serving as a kind of repertory company of objects, with an almost talismanic function in the way the office connected to its own history.

One of Ray's lists from the mid-1950s

There were also the lists—Ray's lists. Ray was legendary for her outfits with deep pockets (Buddy Collette recalled "she always had that great dress, always great skirt on"[16]), which would be filled with lists and notes that she would constantly jot down, often on the back of the silvery inside linings of cigarette boxes. After carefully removing the linings from the cigarette packs (both Ray and Charles eventually gave up smoking), she flattened them out to use as her preferred note paper. She would produce these lists periodically to consult or add a new note, and then would download them later with certain members of the office staff.

Charles took notes too, especially in the form of photographs—visual notes of internal goings-on at the office: a Saul Steinberg improvisation might be recorded or a cover for the Committee for the First Amendment. But his pictures were often a way to note the world outside. Mike Sullivan recalled working late one night with Charles at the IBM exhibition space at 57th Street and Madison Avenue in Manhattan, when "we heard a lot of sirens—police sirens and [it] sounded like fire engines. And it was happening down near Park Avenue. And Charles says, 'Wow!' And you—we looked down, you could see all the lights flashing and there must have been some catastrophe of some sort, we thought. And he got—had the camera, and he used to wear his hat, this crushable Irish hat in the wintertime, and we go running. 'Come on!' he said. We ran down 57th Street. Evidently what happened was, there was some robbery, and the robbers were trapped in the building and all the police were surrounding 'em. And Charles was out in the middle of the street, shooting all of these different views of the police and the building and the lights going on. . . . He just had an inordinate interest in human affairs, you know? . . . When we were running down the street, and I was kidding him, I said, 'You look like Scoop Jackson in one of those B movies,' with the hat turned up, and shooting the pictures in the street, you know?"[17]

Sullivan, IBM's prime liaison to the Eames Office for over 20 years, became a close friend of the Eameses. He was with Ray when she was pulled over for speeding: "She showed me her driver's license, and she had erased 'date of birth.' 'That's none of their business,' she would tell me. 'It's none of their damn business.'"[18] Ray was very private about her birth date. Midge Kaiser, among many others, remembered Ray saying, "My life is an open book but my birth date is mine and mine alone."[19] Sullivan laughed as he remembered that "her other wonderful expression was, 'That person, as well-meaning as he is, is a dim bulb.' Charles had a great expression one time about someone he met, who was rather overbearing and with his own self-importance, et cetera. And Charles would say, 'Poor so-and-so, with his poolroom demeanor.' Great stuff. . . . Charles [said of another person], 'You know, I like them. I don't necessarily agree with them, but I respect the people with a point of view. A point of view. When they can, you know, defend that point of view. But if they can't, then they're just role-playing.' And he could sense that kind of stuff immediately."[20]

Another Sullivan story conveys the connection between the Eameses' can-do spirit and good work as an essential element in the quality of life. Sullivan remembered confiding in Charles a dream of his own, "'I wanna go around and photograph the graves of all these great actors that influenced my life, as a tribute to them. And photograph their gravesites, and just put it out as a published book whereby people could go when they see their films and pay their respects, that's all. And I talked to him about it once or twice, and he—and the third time I talked to him about it, he said to me, 'Michael?' 'Yeah?' He said, 'Don't talk about it—do it. Do it.' He said, 'It's a good idea,' you know? 'Just go and do it.' But I never did. He said, 'If I can help you, I will.'"[21]

Over the course of the Eameses' lives and work, these beliefs, ideas, and experiences coalesced into a formalized concept that they called the "New Covetables." Charles talked about this idea at length in the Norton Lectures, describing a humanity that had sort of painted itself into a corner "where information and imagery—and I think it's largely through television—[the world] has gotten so completely homogenized so that, in many respects, everybody has been getting the same. [And] it has been one of the things that's given rise over these past 20 years to a rising expectancy—rising to the point that there is and exists today a universal expectancy in which every person feels he has the right to everything everybody else has."[22]

Charles felt this development created a number of problems. For starters, there were so many consumer goods out there that one no longer needed to go through the trouble of selectivity. In fact, on the level of effort, even the most expensive product was cheapened because no real effort (beyond paying for it) was asked of the would-be owner. But Charles and Ray also saw a practical (one might even call it environmental) problem: if our standard of success is owning, say, a Mercedes, then we have doomed most of the world's population to failure because it will be physically impossible to make enough of those cars with the Earth's limited resources.

The solution the Eameses proposed, the New Covetables, would have certain characteristics: "It can't be too easy to get them. You must be able to have them. You must not be able to have them without first wanting them. The price must really have a price. It must be a real price, but . . . the coin in which that price is listed must be available to everyone. Now, the question is, what kind of things would qualify?"[23] In other words, the "coin of the realm" is not money, but effort, hard work. There is another quality: "The point is that these things will not diminish as they're divided. They're endless."[24]

So what sorts of things qualify? Charles listed some examples: learning to read a map; learning to speak Chinese; learning to ride a unicycle; graphing mathematical functions; getting to know a city; or even a story like "King Lear, the model of the inevitable situation which you can apply." The point with all these things is that "the coin of the realm . . . is the ability to give of yourself to the extent that you can master it." Charles pointed out that he himself had never learned to speak French, but that he could have; he had the coin but "I chose to spend it in other ways. I don't really regret having spent it as I have. But I didn't spend it that way."[25] The other wonderful thing is that if you acquire a New Covetable, it does not diminish it for the next person; it might even slightly increase its value for both of you.

The New Covetable was as much an Eames product as was the fiberglass chair. (In fact, the idea of New Covetables is, in a way, itself a New Covetable.) Ultimately, Charles and Ray viewed the Eames Office as a holistic practice within which all of the work was deeply interrelated, which made separating out furniture or exhibitions or any other facet counterproductive. Though there were various areas in the office and different project leaders, there were not really formal divisions. The people who worked on the Aquarium, on the chairs, and on the films were fluidly interwoven, and that is what the Eameses offered to their clients—and what the clients came to value. Charles and Ray imparted and invited a seamless dialogue between work and play on every level: in their own work, in their own lives, and in the gauntlet of connection they routinely laid down for their clients.

Deborah Sussman, when asked if Charles and Ray continued to enjoy themselves as the office got busier and busier over the years, replied, "the enjoyment—yes, basically, definitely yes, but on the other hand, it was so demanding that it would be exhausting. . . . The strain of pulling all that together, of innovating not in order to innovate but developing these innovative ways of explaining difficult ideas and phenomena [was] exhausting."[26] And, after a while, there were 20 cars in the parking lot. How did Charles and Ray manage to take pleasure seriously and still meet the payroll? The short answer is that they worked hard at it, but it wasn't always easy. Throughout the life of the office, Charles and Ray knew they also had to keep a business running, recognizing this as a simple necessity. Not only because their explorations often required the labor-intensive process of iteration after iteration, but because the presence of clients in the mix kept them grounded in a helpful way. A client coming to them was essentially a message from the "real" world that a given problem

Setting up an arrangement, including the pills, to be photographed for the House of Cards toy. Inset left: the image of pills as it finally appears. Inset right: the arrangement of spools being prepared

was valuable enough for someone to take the money to try to solve it.

Charles spoke often to his daughter, Lucia, about the importance of reinvesting in and reexamining the work.[27] But that reevaluation could be subtle. It could be the way there was always someone working with Herman Miller on the current productions, not simply on the new designs. Alex Funke felt that Charles and Ray perceived the ability to explore what interested them as the ultimate richness in life and, therefore, the proper way to use their own resources.[28] The furniture work and its royalties supported the running expenses of the office, but some clients contributed directly to the overhead as well. The relationship with Herman Miller permitted the furniture maker to be billed for some development costs, and IBM paid a retainer to the Eameses. Specific projects, such as World's Fair presentations or *Mathematica* or *Copernicus*, were billed individually. Other clients—Westinghouse, Polaroid, or the U.S. government—were billed on a project-by-project basis. Both the independence of the royalty stream and the multiplicity of major clients allowed the office to have a certain measure of control and autonomy. As Sussman commented: "Control was very important to Charles, and, in her own way, to Ray as well."[29] But such control did not just happen, it had to be carefully monitored and nurtured. The longest tenure of anyone at the Eames Office besides Charles and Ray was that of bookkeeper Mariea Poole, who provided a still-remem-

Certain objects formed a kind of visual repertory company and appeared in numerous different setups. Here, the butterfly kite appears in (from left to right) the film *Sofa Compact*, *Mathematica*, and a furniture shoot.

bered kind of iconic continuity within the office from 1951 to 1975.

Although the overhead of such an office was huge and the pressure intense, Charles and Ray were given to making sure they did not price themselves out of a project they found interesting. Parke Meek remembered that "it wasn't, like, some profiteering sort of game. [Charles] was never concerned with profit. I mean, somebody wanted to bid a job and—I'd try to figure out about what it would cost and I'd give him a price and he'd probably give 'em a price of half that much and I'd [say]: 'God, no way! We're gonna lose our [shirts]!' But . . . we did; we lost our [shirts] on a lot of jobs because he wanted to do [them]. And he knew [the client] couldn't afford it. So to hell with it! We'll lose money on it."[30] But even projects that didn't break even right away had the potential to do so in the long run, because Charles and Ray made sure to control those rights as well. It also meant that, in a subtle but important way, the clients saw by example that it was the work, not the billing, that made the Eames Office tick, which in turn could make the client more adventurous in the future.

Julian Blaustein, who often discussed the economics of the office with Charles, said: "Monetary sense of honor, the fiscal sense of honor, was easy for him, he just said, 'Look, I agreed to do it for this price.' He was careful, he tried to submit a budget that was realistic. But if he got ideas along the way that were costly, he didn't think it proper to go back to . . . say, IBM, and say, 'This is gonna cost another eighty-five thousand dollars.' He didn't think that proper at all."[31] One of the toughest projects in this regard was the *Franklin and Jefferson* exhibition in the mid-1970s. Don Orr, the Eameses' accountant, recalled a meeting when he told Charles that from a business standpoint he'd be better off returning the client's money than finishing the work the way he had hoped.[32] This was deeply frustrating, but Charles and Ray applied their own calculus of the difference between cost and worth; in the end, both IBM and the Eames Office absorbed some of the overage and the office completed the show in the Eameses' way.

Oftentimes work with a key client would not be a formal project, but the chance for the client's employees to learn directly from the Eameses. This could happen in lectures, presentations, or seminars in or out of the office. Some of the inspirations would last a lifetime. After Ray's death, a colleague at Westinghouse shared a story related at one such roundtable. Taken by Charles's observation that the clowns were the moralists of the circus, a designer at Westinghouse asked Charles if he would consider the composer John Cage to be a clown. Charles responded, "Yes, I think John Cage, too, would be flattered if he thought you took the role of clown seriously." Then Charles talked about a performance of Cage's that he and Ray had seen in Cologne, Germany, probably around 1954 — "the German audiences are a special kind." Cage, known for his experimental music, was performing on a bill with more traditional composers, such as Schumann and Schubert. Cage came out "looking great in white tie and tails and said 'Hello' and sat down. I don't know if you are familiar with Cage's music, but there's a prepared piano in which he has stuck sheets of tin and papers and he does this 'blump, plump' and in about ten seconds, he does, 'cleek, shoonk.' And it is a kind of thing that is a bit more effective in a drawing room because of the long spaces of time. If you put it in a big room, the ambient noises intrude on the thing so it sounds a little less organized."

Charles continued: "At any rate, the German audiences are funny. They go along trying to dig it. But after a while they are not digging it, and the audience would start to make funny noises. Then a German intellectual stood up in front and said something in German meaning 'Quiet!' Everybody started to be quiet. And pretty soon Cage went, 'plinck, plonck, shoonk, choonk, ploonch.' And then he slammed down the top of the music rack and it went 'whamm.' And some joker in the crowd now said, 'Hurray, biffy' — he yells out at Cage. And Cage goes on 'clunck.' Then somebody else hollers and there would be some catcalls. And Cage beaming. Then he takes a whistle and blows the whistle. Then the papers go flying and he goes on 'clunking.' And then the guys began stamping their feet, and they started yelling. Pretty soon they took a chair and slammed the chair down, and then they started breaking the furniture, and the people were stamping and they were yelling and Cage was going on 'clunking.' I don't know if you know Liphold — he's in the sculptoring business. I turned around at the height of this confusion and Liphold was standing on his chair screaming 'Wunderbar, wunderbar.' There was a radio area and I raced backstage at this point, to see if they were taping it, which the idiots weren't. It was the greatest Cage performance. It was a complete shambles, the furniture broken all over the place. And you know, they called off the rest of the program. And Cage afterwards was out of his mind with pleasure. He said, 'You know, the fellow that broke that first chair over that jardiniere, it just couldn't have come at a better moment.' This was genuine participation of the highest order. Now, I don't know whether you would call this a clown or what, but it somehow fits into this thing. And it was a very significant performance, the way it built. I just die at the fact that it was not recorded."[33]

# CHAPTER 11

# Case Study #8

In 1967 the Sisters of Immaculate Heart College in Los Angeles, California, announced a competition for the design of a new campus. Published on Valentine's Day, the brief was written by Charles Eames and follows here in its entirety:

The Sisters of the Immaculate Heart occupy a peculiar place in the heart of the community in which they work.

The uniqueness of this place in our hearts becomes evident when we know that they will be torn from (what we on the outside have considered) their comfortable quarters.

The significance of the move and the potentials in the new relationship to the other colleges at Claremont, have all the dramatic expectancy and risk that we have come to expect from Immaculate Hearts.

However, a new college means buildings, and buildings means architecture, and architecture means architects, and it all makes us break out in a cold sweat.

If only they were moving into an evacuated army barrack or an abandoned monastery or some really great old warehouse—then we would have complete faith.

But architecture on order is a different thing and those architects who could subjugate themselves to the real and evolving needs of such a community maintaining a relentless concern for quality—would be very rare.

What we, who love Immaculate Heart, want for the college is easier to taste than it is to say—

We guard ourselves against wants that could be hazardous—such as expressions of form or structure or monumentality or even an over-emphasis on beauty—

We want a college that will shelter those within it on the sad days as well as the gay days—

A system of buildings that will not be embarrassed by complete changes of program;

A structure that can be scotch taped, nailed into, thumb-tacked, and still not lose its dignity;

Spaces that will welcome and enhance teaching machines as well as celebrations and pageants;

Materials that will not tend to become shoddy and will still show a response to care.

One would hope that the experience of the buildings would seem so natural that the question of

Top: the future site of the Eames House; the final design of the house was set into the hillside behind the row of eucalyptus trees. Bottom: a model of the first design of the Eames House, the so-called "Bridge House," by Charles Eames and Eero Saarinen in 1945. The Entenza House (Case Study #9) is to the right. The row of trees above is represented by the dowels.

131

their having been designed could never come up.

We want these buildings to demand something of those who enter them and to enrich and shelter those who remain within.

We know now why gurus choose caves.[1]

Starting in the 1950s, the Eameses worked closely with the Sisters at Immaculate Heart. It was the Sisters who did the painstaking calligraphy on an exploded view of the lounge chair. Probably the best-known member of the order was Sister Mary Corita Kent, whose own exquisite and exalting serigraphy includes some classic images from the 1960s and 1970s. Sister Mary's teaching philosophy resonated with the Eameses' approach. (One of her Six Rules was "WORK. If you work, it will lead to something."[2]) More than a few Eames Office staff members had been educated at Immaculate Heart, which wove the Eames films into its teaching. Sister Magdalene Mary would at times project the films (especially *Toccata for Toy Trains*) in such a way that only a quadrant of the screen was visible, heightening the sense of color and abstraction for her students.[3] Though Charles's abstract prospectus was an expression of Immaculate Heart's special meaning and value, once more in the Eames work a specific charge became a gateway to broader concerns. This was as concise a distillation as the Eameses ever made from a dialogue that concerned them all their lives, that between self-expression and architecture.

Two decades earlier, in the late 1940s, Charles and Ray took up a different architectural challenge—the Case Study House Program—which, for them, opened the dialogue in another way. The project ultimately led to their most spectacular contribution to architecture in the classical sense of buildings that were actually built. Throughout their work, Charles and Ray extended the definition and practice of architecture and design, and they did both in the broadest sense. While this expansive definition of architecture is critical to understanding who Charles and Ray were, it is equally important to recognize that when called upon to design a real and specific building, they delivered in a quite timeless way.

Located in Pacific Palisades, California, the residence the Eameses created in 1949 for the Case Study House Program became their home for the rest of their lives. Generally known simply as the Eames House, it began life as Case Study House #8. The journey of creating this house—and the finished product—resonate with many of the themes of their other work: the guest/host relationship, the honest use of materials, universalizing from the specific, and, above all, the learn-by-doing process. This last theme is particularly striking because the medium of architecture does not usually allow repeated physical iterations of an idea to hone away the idiosyncrasies. In other words, it is one thing to build a chair over and over to get it right, but it is another thing entirely to build a home more than once to get it right. And yet, in the case of the Eames House, that is almost exactly what Charles and Ray did.

The Case Study House Program itself had an unusually high respect for process over prescribed form, a valuation that reflected Charles's influence (as well as being a measure of his common ground with John Entenza). In 1945, when the program was announced, Charles was on the editorial board of *Arts and Architecture* magazine, and Ray was credited as an advisor (she had also designed 24 of its front covers in the previous three years). John Entenza had been the magazine's publisher since 1938, when he bought it as *California Arts and Architecture* and then revamped its title and contents. His title change was ironic yet proper: ironic because it ended up representing to many around the world the ultimate California lifestyle, yet proper because it now had a far more universal voice.

Designer Terence Conran remembered waiting for each month's issue like it was a life preserver as he began his career in postwar London.[4]

Charles started talking with Entenza not long after he and Ray arrived in Los Angeles in 1941. He wrote to Eliot Noyes in August of that year, describing Entenza "as one of the very few out here fighting for its cause."[5] Charles wrote an article that fall for the magazine and then joined its board. The friendship between the Eameses and Entenza developed quickly, and eventually Entenza became one of the Eameses' biggest champions, providing a critical bridge between the experiments in the apartment and the mass production of the splints.

As it became possible to imagine an end to World War II, some people in the United States began to contemplate what the postwar landscape might look like, both literally and intellectually. Though milestones like the Battle of the Bulge, Iwo Jima, and Hiroshima still lay in the future, some of the challenges of the postwar environment were becoming quite clear. In January of 1945, *Arts and Architecture* announced the Case Study House Program. It called for the design of eight houses by eight architects in an ambitious attempt to not so much prescribe a solution or even just set an agenda, but rather, through example, to provide source material and experience for society as a whole. As Esther McCoy put it in her introduction to *Modern California Houses*, republished as *Case Study Houses 1945–1962*, "In 1945, Entenza abandoned his passive role as editor to play a dynamic one in postwar architecture. He announced that the magazine itself had become a client. Eight offices were commissioned to design eight houses. They were J. R. Davidson, Richard Neutra, Spaulding and Rex, Wurster and Bernardi, Ralph Rapson, Whitney Smith, Thornton Abell, Charles Eames and Eero Saarinen."[6]

The architects' designs would be published over the next eight months and then ultimately built. As the program developed, Entenza added a Case Study House #9, which

CASE STUDY #8

133

would become his own house, and then ultimately over two dozen more over almost two decades. The ambition of this program remains striking even after more than 50 years: the key realization was that it was not enough to publish drawings of houses that could point a new direction; they had to be built. And in fact the best measure of the program's success, given that most Americans do not live in Case Study houses, is the very fact that 24 of the projects (of the 35 designed) were actually built. This means that the buildings have entered the real world, where they can at least contribute to the dialogue—unlike, say, Charles's model house in St. Louis. Without being built, a house's meaning is hard to place.

As America faced the challenge of postwar housing (how do you house three million returning GIs all at once?), there were many options but essentially two basic approaches. The first, the one-size-fits-all approach, is exemplified by suburbs like Levittown, New York, with nearly identical homes in a Cape Cod or other traditional style, which over time are altered to greater or lesser degrees by the homeowners. Though this approach has the potential pitfalls of any lowest-common denominator, it is a perfectly legitimate one and obviously has some-thing to recommend it. Indeed, most modern-day developments take this path.

The Case Study House Program took a completely different approach.[7] First of all, it embraced a belief that the modernist ideals could be part of the postwar home. Second, there was a sense that all the new technologies and materials of the war effort could be used to do something besides harm people. Third, and most important, was the name itself: each house would be a "case study" of the needs of a particular client. It would solve the problems of the client, but in as universal a way as possible. Each client would be under-stood to represent a different type of homeowner, so instead of fetishizing the client's needs, architects participating in the program would try to achieve the broadest possible solution. But a fourth point is important, too: none of the first three points were dogma. For example, some architects used traditional materials without breaching the values of the program. The Case Study House Program thus offered a strong, healthy push in a certain ideological direction, but without the baggage of pointless enforcement.

In 1945, John Entenza bought a three-acre parcel of property in Pacific Palisades from the Will Rogers estate. The property, in Santa Monica Canyon, had been part of Rogers's extensive holdings in the area (Will Rogers State Park is about two miles away), and he is said to have hoped to build a home on the property before his abrupt death in 1935. The site of the future Eames House was (and is) a stunning piece of land, but at the time it was located a bit too far out of town. Today the parcel is just another pixel in the matrix of the ever-spreading and fundamentally contiguous Los Angeles supercity. But in the 1940s it still felt far enough away from Hollywood, Beverly Hills, and Hancock Park (quite affluent areas of town) for residents of those areas to have weekend homes at these beaches. Photos of the area from that time show far fewer houses in the canyon itself. Today one would have to have a house an hour further up the coast to have a similar (but less complete) feeling of remove. The lots that Entenza bought were eventually the sites of four-and-a-half Case Study Houses: #8, #9, #18 (known as the West House, designed by Rodney Walker), and #21 (the Bailey House, designed by Richard Neutra). The half a house refers to another designed by Neutra but stripped of its number after he disavowed it.* All of the original Case Study Houses have been well taken care of or recently restored. The Entenza house, also carefully restored, has a major addition that blocks part of its original view. Nevertheless, the collective spirit of this little neighborhood remains remarkably intact today.

* After construction had begun, this house was traded in mid-construction to a new owner distinctly unsympathetic to the cause.

A gopher snake, photographed at the Eames House in the 1950s

Charles and Ray were the "hypothetical" clients of Case Study House #8: a working couple with no children living at home. (Lucia would soon be at college and there would be room for her in the second bedroom during visits.) They needed space for living and for working. The initial design solution, now referred to as the Bridge House, was by Charles Eames and Eero Saarinen. Never built, it was a cantilevered structure rooted on an east-facing hill that stuck out through a row of Eucalyptus trees. The cantilevered end was balanced dramatically on two pillars in the middle of a meadow. An unattached studio on the landward side of the main structure provided work space. Images of this model reveal the dramatic attraction it must have had for its designers. Compared to the Eames House as built, though, with its reserve and perfect siting, it seems what one might call "conventionally spectacular"—in other words, impressive but not as truly insightful.

The original designs of both Case Study Houses #8 and #9 were published together in December 1945. The two houses always made a pair: they had the same architects, the clients for both were friends, and both used similar structural components. But fittingly, the feeling of the two houses as published was strikingly different. After all, the needs of the client for House #8 were considerably different from those for the single client for House #9. The flexibility of the steel elements in adapting to the two (and ultimately three) designs was a clear success for the new materials dimension of the program.

If the Bridge House related to its site by rising above and snatching a spectacular ocean vista from the airspace of the meadow, then the Entenza house related to its oceanside site through a series of nested scales, kind of a "powers of 10," like a set of Russian dolls. At the center was what was called the "womb room," a sanctum with no windows or skylights and, indeed, even concealed a bit from the rest of the house. This was the private space without distractions that Entenza requested as a place where he could write. Next came the welcoming scale of the living room, perfect for a single man who did a lot of enter-

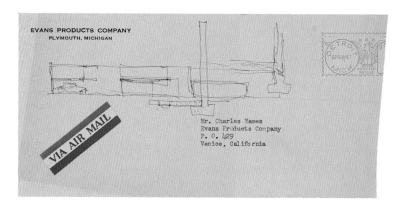

EVANS PRODUCTS COMPANY
PLYMOUTH, MICHIGAN

VIA AIR MAIL

Mr. Charles Eames
Evans Products Company
P. O. 429
Venice, California

Three of many
sketches from
the late 1940s
showing differ-
ent ways of uti-
lizing the origi-
nal ordered
material for the
house. The one
on the left is in
Charles's hand,
the middle in
Ray's hand, and
the right is in
both.

taining. Then, looking out the sliding glass windows (running the whole length of the ocean side of the house) one saw the scale of the meadow, and ultimately beyond that, the vast-ness of the Pacific Ocean itself.

Because both houses were made of steel, their construction was delayed by the postwar materials shortage. The Eames House had the advantage of being designed to be built completely of prefabricated parts. As Ray said, "It was the idea of using materials in a different way, materials that could be bought from a catalog. So that there was a continua-tion of the idea of mass production, so that people would not have to build stick by stick, but with material that comes ready-made—off-the-shelf in that sense."[8] But 1946 turned into 1947, and it was not until about 1948 that the material was actually delivered to the site. By that time much had happened to change Charles and Ray's understanding of the site. Nothing dramatic; in fact, very subtle. Charles and Ray had played. They had picnicked in the meadow. They had admired the row of trees along the bottom of the hill. Lucia Eames remembers many picnics on the site with Charles and Ray and often Entenza, who was an excellent cook. They had set up an archery target against the hill, flew kites, and in the end fell in love with the meadow.[9] When they looked at the delivered steel, Charles and Ray real-ized they had made the classic architectural error of choosing a beautiful site and then destroying it with a building. In a relatively short time, they redesigned the house to be built from the same pile of parts and, according to Esther McCoy, they needed to order only one extra beam to make the finished house.[*][10]

Many factors went into the transformation of the Bridge House into the Eames House. Above all, there was the desire to respect the meadow. Another was the recognition that the Bridge House design was fundamentally inefficient in its use of materials; much of the steel was used to support the main house. Charles viewed it "almost as a math prob-lem," to use Ray's words. "It was like a game to him."[11] How could one enclose the maxi-mum volume with the same steel? Another point may have been a 1947 exhibition at MoMA of Mies van der Rohe's work. Charles wrote about it for *Arts and Architecture*. In the exhibi-

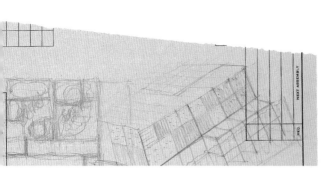

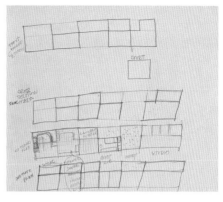

tion was a sketch—almost a doodle—of an idea for a house similar to the Bridge House. Fred Usher, who started working at the Eames Office around this time, recalled a feeling that this sketch had been a factor.[12] Though not a decisive issue, van der Rohe's doodle might have suggested a generic quality in the Bridge House—that it could have been anywhere. Similarly, the Bridge design required chopping down two substantial Eucalyptus trees in the row along the bottom of the hill. By itself, saving the two trees probably would not have been reason enough to change the design, but their imminent sacrifice must have resonated as a symbol of what was wrong with the original solution.

In redesigning the house, the Eameses played with many different configurations, some of which are published here for the first time. Each of these sketches uses the same essential vocabulary. Some of the sketches are in Ray's hand and some in Charles's and some in both. They were teasing out the issue—trying to follow their self-imposed rules and still make something better. In a sense, they were applying to this work of architecture their learn-by-doing process. Playing with the elements the first time around had given them some insights. But completing the drawings, living with the site, seeing the delivered materials, and spending time with the model—all these things together primed the pump for an intense couple of months of redesigning while under the gun. Not unlike Charles Darwin writing *On the Origin of Species* in a single year after 22 years of brooding on his data and ideas, the Eameses' earlier time was not wasted—it was what was necessary. The new plans were published in the May 1949 issue of *Arts and Architecture*.

The final design is very simple. Two buildings, simple boxes, are tucked into the hillside behind the row of trees. One houses the living space, the other the work space. A long, nearly 200-foot concrete retaining wall runs behind the structures so that the front of the buildings shows two stories to the world, but the back is set into the hill itself, insulating the buildings. The buildings are brothers but not twins. Each is two stories tall and can be measured in bays about 7-1/2 feet wide, but the module does not intrude. The house structure, closer to the ocean, is made up of eight bays (including an overhang of the patio), and

* Some have said that on a cursory glance, the structures are too different to use the exact same materials, but no detailed analysis has been done to settle the issue (which is a quibble because the key constraint in the redesign was the delivery of parts to the site). Any significant reordering of materials would have delayed building even longer.

* The precise cost is difficult to ascertain. The book *Eames Design* reports that Charles estimated the cost of building at $1.00 per square foot (versus $11.50 for wood-frame construction at the time), but that figure does not include the cost of the retaining wall or the Eames Office staff salaries.

the studio is made up of five bays. The patio between them is the width of four bays. Each structure has a two-story-high space on the end facing away from the other. The house is 1,500 square feet, and the studio, 1,000.

On the outside, the factory materials that make up the buildings are shown matter-of-factly, not with pride or shame. Factory windows and X-trusses provide the texture of the exterior. Color panels (orange, blue, gold, and others) are arranged on the grid. The effect is similar to that of paintings by Piet Mondrian. In later years, Ray would often get annoyed with people who suggested the house was inspired by the Dutch modernist painter. She obviously knew his work and had even met him in New York, but her point was that the effect was an inevitable result of the structure, rather than the structure having been arranged to achieve the effect—not unlike her reaction in 1940: "How could it have turned out other than it did?"[13]

Construction of the house took only a few months. The frame was raised in a day and a half.[14] The parts may have been "off-the-shelf," but Charles and Ray had found some very interesting shelves. Fred Usher remarked that not many design offices would have had a marine supply catalog among their references, but the Eames Office did and that is where a key element of the spiral staircase came from.[15] Once again Charles and Ray went to the heart of the true constraint in addressing the problem. In other words, just because this was going to be a prefabricated residence didn't mean that one could consider only prefabricated residential materials. The finishing work took much fine-tuning and fitting by folks from the office. In the end, the ultimate cost was basically in the low range for a standard house.* The retaining wall, in particular, was a significant added expense, but in keeping with the Eameses' philosophy, everything was used to the maximum advantage. Even the dirt dug out from the hill was relocated, forming a privacy berm between Case Study Houses #8 and #9. Charles and Ray Eames moved in on Christmas Eve 1949.

Having lived with this house intimately in different ways all my life, most especially working there for almost 10 years, I am able to share some further thoughts. Having driven

up the long driveway between the other Case Study house lots literally thousands of times, past Dr. Bailey's roses and a glimpse of the Entenza house, and having seen the orange panel of the studio revealed like the corner of an opened ream of paper as one comes around the corner past the bushes, I must report that some things about the house remain stunning every time. Above all, there is the house's comfort in the landscape. I could fairly describe it as a pair of steel boxes, and yet in spite—or more likely because—of that honest use of materials, it feels more comfortable in nature than many so-called organic shapes. Utter respect for the natural world finds no conflict with the geometrically aligned grid.

But there is more: the spectacularly unspectacular blend of indoor and outdoor, a kind of way-it-should-be-ness, an almost soap-bubblelike quality that inspired Ford Peatross to call the house "a vessel for the objects within."[16] Then there are the reflections; windows that reflect back abstract patterns of eucalyptus bark, superimposing them on the human textures within. Elsewhere you see the meadow through windows, through the house, through the interior plants, all at once. There is a detail over the back patio—a black-and-white photograph of these same trees screened onto a textile, then mounted on a panel and screwed into the building. Just before twilight, when shadows still fall on the image and the natural light turns the reflections of the leaves monochromatic, it becomes almost impossible to tell where the building ends and the reflections begin. One truly believes Ray when she remarked "after 13 years of living in it, the building for me ceased to exist a long time ago."[17]

Evenings it is like a little jewel, set behind the row of trees dropped to black by the end of the gloaming. Later still, when the traffic fades enough to reveal the sounds of the sea, you begin to hear the crash of waves and it startles you the first time each night. And every once in a while, in a certain season, the mist makes it so you can't see one end of the house from the other. The morning light awakens warm eucalyptus shadows in the sliding panels of fiberglass resin that provide a rigid veil for some of the windows. The chiaroscuro dance of the distinctive crescent shadows surprises at first, because then you realize that by

In the 1950s, the living room of the Eames House took many different forms. Here are just a few, from left to right: ribbons hanging from the cross-beam; wood wind instruments in the alcove; two Hans Hofmann paintings (*Castor* and *Pollux*); and paper balls

CASE STUDY #8

139

Above, from left to right: a photograph of the eucalyptus trees, which was screened into a panel that is a permanent part of the house; self-portrait of Charles on the ladder in the studio; the living room of the house; view toward the ocean

a quirk of the coastline, the Eames House actually faces slightly east. And on that kind of bright morning, there is to me no more special interior view in Los Angeles (or possibly anywhere) than that over the railing of the master bedroom into the living room below.

There are other details. The alcove whose seat foreshadows the sofa compact and whose ceiling Charles and Ray adorned with Tivoli lights after a trip to Copenhagen. Or the iron planter on wheels, built in the shop at the 901 space, which allows an arrangement of potted plants to be completely repositioned with ease. Or the sliding panels that give privacy to the upstairs bedrooms. The last two are examples of how Charles and Ray valued flexibility over reifying a particular self-expression, which made it theirs even more. And then there are Charles and Ray's collections, captured, in the fractal world of the Eames Office, in the Eames film *House: after five years of living*.

For a class I taught on imagery, there was an exercise each year in which I showed students (none of whom had been to the Eames House or even knew of it) all forms of documentation on the house—the Eames film, my own film, some books, slides, flipbooks, even the relevant *Arts and Architecture* issues—to the point where the students begged for mercy, saying, "We know what the Eames House looks like." So I replied, "Okay. Just write a paragraph describing the house and bring it in next week." Next week was a field trip to the house.

So, gathering there, the students discovered how critical experience is to understanding architecture and learned the limits of imagery. Half of them found the house to be smaller than they expected; the other half found it bigger. But in discussing it, what they really could not get from the images—and I am afraid the pictures in this book cannot capture adequately—is the house's comfort in the landscape, the exquisiteness of the siting, the peacefulness of the meadow (all of which make the Eameses' rejection of the Bridge House design so utterly right). Photos can't convey or offer the thrill of walking behind the house and finding you are at the level of the second floor, or the discovery that the Pacific Coast Highway is so close but somehow shut off because, instead of reaching predictably for the cliff, the house carefully husbands its own privacy against the hill.

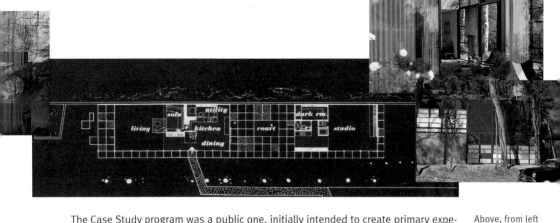

The Case Study program was a public one, initially intended to create primary experiences for visitors, readers, and architects. After the first three houses were built, more than 300,000 people visited them in the first six months alone[18] (tallies are not available for the later houses). Charles and Ray were always aware of this public dimension of the program and were generous throughout their lives to interested students and architects. But there were downsides to the high profile; namely, that while the house was still being built and the interiors done, young architects would wander up in the evening to see how work was progressing. A story was told in the architectural community that at one point "there was some very manifest problem with the casework in the kitchen . . . and, of course, every manifest problem you could see through the glass." Well, one evening when the house was still in this state, some young architects wandered up the driveway and peered through the kitchen window, where they saw a sign "stuck on the bookcase facing out through the glass, saying, 'Don't worry, guys. We'll figure it out.'"[19]

In another way, the process of making the Eames House reflects perfectly the way Charles and Ray had of keeping the hounds of final decisions at bay until finally things could drop into place. But they also knew when to stop. One of the original ideas had been to repaint the distinctive color panels every couple of years with a new color. But that idea, like superfluous idiosyncrasies on the lota, was simply shed with the passage of time. Because of the unique nature of the architects and the program, the brief to design Case Study House #8 offered apparent total freedom, but the architects were tough enough on themselves to impose their own meaningful discipline. Today, the exterior of the house looks pretty much like it did in 1950, while the interior looks very similar to the way it did in the very late 1950s and early 1960s. Embedded in that nuance of a decade is an important evolution in the office. But to get to that transition, one must ask other questions: if Case Study House #8 was such a success, why didn't the Eameses design more buildings, and why weren't they the ones designing that campus for Immaculate Heart?

Above, from left to right: floor plan of the Eames House and Studio; living room of the house seen from the patio; the studio just after construction was completed

# CHAPTER 12

# Films as Essays

The Eames House was very well received from the get go and was recognized as a landmark of modern architecture early in its life. So why didn't Charles and Ray do more architecture?

One answer is, of course, that they did. They designed the Herman Miller showroom on Beverly Boulevard in West Hollywood, California; a house for Max DePree of Herman Miller in Zeeland, Michigan; as well as two other buildings that were never built. But that's not a lot for three decades.

A better answer may be to say that they did do more architecture, but in different ways. Charles put it this way: "Furniture, and especially chairs, interest me because it is a piece of architecture on the human scale. . . . Architecture is frustrating. You work on an idea, but standing between you and the event itself are many traps: the finance committee, the contractor, the subcontractor, the engineer, even the politicians—all of them can really cause the concept to degenerate. Going into furniture, we have a more direct relationship with the end product—a better chance to keep the concept from degenerating. That's why architects design furniture—so you can design a piece of architecture you can hold in your hand."[1]

But it was more than just a matter of permits and the frustrations of architecture in general, because, after all, Charles, at least, already knew all this from his work in St. Louis. It was something deeper, a desire to address bigger problems in ways that could benefit more people. Traditional architecture solved the problems of a specific site. But any solution, no matter how wonderful, was necessarily limited to the building in question. It is significant that the traditional buildings the Eameses designed after completing their own home were either for friends or intended, like the Kwikset House, for mass production. The former honored friendships, the latter their idealistic vision for the future.

But there was another form of architecture the Eameses practiced that truly blossomed for them in the 1950s: film. Film was architecture on two levels: at times the Eames Office used film to literally model a proposed environment, but always the Eameses applied the structure and discipline of architecture to filmmaking. Filmmaking ideas had been perco-

A detail from the film *Tops* (1969)

143

Eight still frames from the Eames film, *Blacktop* (1952)

lating for some time (witness the conversations with Alexander Knox and Charles's first forays at Cranbrook). Even the studio of the Eames House was intended for film production, a function it served until 1958, when those efforts shifted to 901 Washington.

There is sometimes a misconception that the Eameses discovered film as a by-product of their furniture success, but the reality was much more holistic. Recall Charles's 1941 letter to Ray about writing and directing short subjects together. From the very beginning, Charles and Ray saw film as part of their world, and as they sought to create work of more universal value, communications became a logical place to devote some attention. Even in that 1941 letter, Charles seemed to sense that they would be making nonfiction films, in particular, ones in which they could express an idea overtly to the audience.

Ultimately the Eames Office produced more than 125 short films in 28 years. The shortest, *alpha*, runs just over a minute; the longest, *The World of Franklin and Jefferson*, clocks in at almost 29. Only a handful exceed 14 minutes. Together the films comprise a truly unique body of work of which Charles said, "They are not really films at all, just ways to get across an idea."[2] In a similar vein, when another writer pressed Charles to cooperate with an article about the films, Charles tried to talk him out of it saying, "They're simply tools."[3]

Though Charles had shot film at Cranbrook, that project had never been completed, and Charles and Ray realized they were far from proficient. So how could they learn more? By doing more. In developing their filmmaking, Charles and Ray restarted as they usually did, on their own, perhaps with some friends, getting the lay of the land. Given Charles and Ray's learn-by-doing approach, the Eames House and studio could not have been completed at a better time. The studio of the Eames House was created as the perfect incubation laboratory, not for furniture but for film. And that is exactly how they used it. In addition to shooting some footage of the house under construction, they made their first film, *Traveling Boy*, at the house in 1950. The film was never completed (it was occasionally shown with a record accompanying it), but it was an important next step.

*Blacktop* was their first completed film. Made in 1952, it is (as the subtitle says), *The Story of the Washing of a School Playground*. Charles happened to see the patterns

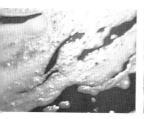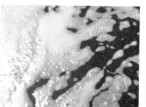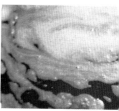

formed by the soap bubbles when the playground was washed at Westminister School, across Washington Boulevard from the Eames Office, and he and Ray decided to make a film of it. They shot most of it at the schoolyard with Don Albinson manning the hose, supplemented with shots done later in the driveway of the Eames House with the able assistance of the children of his neighbor, Dr. Bailey. In an interview, Ray explicitly compared the beginnings of the furniture to the beginnings of the films and then continued, "When we were working on the films, we worked on them at home at first because . . . we could have the freedom to make all the mistakes and trials."[4]

Blacktop was edited on a pair of rewinds in the studio at the Eames House—not on an editing machine, as would have been standard for the time. When cutting was finished and they wanted a print made, they learned that they had to cut the negative first. Charles called Sid Solow, the head of CFI (a film laboratory), and asked him to explain over the phone how to cut the negative into "A" and "B" rolls so that the film could be printed.[5] Negative cutting is an extremely precise and unforgiving process that is rarely, if ever, done by the creative filmmaker. But as he had with photography and furniture and architecture, Charles acquired the hands-on skills and technical understanding he would need to control the process to his satisfaction after other people got involved. The shifting shapes of the soap bubbles are accompanied by Wanda Landowska's recording of Bach's "Goldberg Variations." Blacktop is hypnotic in its visual poetry: "the uncommon beauty of common things"[6] was a phrase Charles often used.

Soon there were other films. Later in 1952, they made Parade: or Here They Come Down Our Street. Ray mused, "When we were making Parade, the movie, we just wanted to show close up these toys that we loved so, and we just hung them on the idea of a parade so you could see many things passing by. By looking at each one, you could see how they were constructed, whatever the material was. . . . And later on we read it was actually banned in one showing in Kansas for being a 'red,' or communist, film. Someone had later written: Indians with heads off going by banks and capitalism and the red balloon went up—all these things. We hadn't even noticed that there was a head missing on one of these little cast figures."[7] Needless to say, this was an unusual response to the film.

Eight still frames from the Eames film *Toccata for Toy Trains* (1957). These show part of the sequence in which a car is racing a train to a crossing.

Next came a 1953 film titled *A Communications Primer*. The film was an attempt to put information about the latest developments in communications theory into the hands of architects. This was an important film in many ways for the Eameses. Looking back on it half a century later, there is much that is extraordinary. First, there is the prescience that we were in fact entering an age of communications; second, the sheer ambition of choosing film to express an idea that others might tackle in writing; third, the explicit notion that the discipline of architecture might have a key role in the way communications systems would develop. Only in the Internet age did mainstream society recognize the decisive role of design in communications, not only in the way ideas were presented but also in the structure of information and the communications experience. Charles wrote to Ian McCallum of *Architectural Review*, "One of the reasons for our interest in the subject is our strong suspicion that the development and application of these related theories will be the greatest tool ever to have fallen into the hands of architects or planners."[8]

From the standpoint of the Eames story, *A Communications Primer* was the film that introduced Charles and Ray to IBM. As an artifact, it is important because it drew from a seminal multimedia experience called *Sample Lesson for a Hypothetical Course*. The work was also the first Eames film to be scored by Elmer Bernstein, an up-and-coming film composer recommended by the great Franz Waxman (whom they knew through Billy Wilder). The first meeting between Elmer and the Eameses was in the living room of the Eames House. Bernstein recalled sitting, the three of them, in the alcove: "Charles had a very special way of speaking. Charles always gave you the feeling he was thinking. He was very slow speaking, and my first impression—I don't know. I expected somebody who was going to be very glib and brilliant. Instant brilliance, you know. And Charles, of course, was not like that at all. Charles was a very quiet, thoughtful person. So, I was sort of . . . surprised by that. Whereas, later on—and it didn't take very long to realize that hidden in . . . what appeared to be slow and halting speech, was real genius."[9] They quickly settled on using a quartet, largely for financial reasons (constraints). Eventually, Elmer scored 30 Eames films.

One of the powerful things about the Eames films is that they are really Charles and Ray's essays. Though they expressed their ideas in many ways, very often the most concise

expression was through their films. One of the most important films in this regard is *Toccata for Toy Trains*. Made in 1957, it was all shot on a 4-by-8-foot tabletop in the studio of the Eames House. *Toccata* has a clear precursor in *Parade* and simply tells the story of a train that travels from one station to another. Like many of Charles and Ray's projects, it works on many levels at once. For kids, it is about 14 minutes of pure joy. To me, it is close to being a perfect film, a gem of cinematic experience with a beautiful Elmer Bernstein score. As you watch (at any age), you are pulled viscerally into the world of the toy trains. The trick to it visually is that it takes the objects at face value, accepting them as toys without trying to trick the viewer into thinking they are actual trains. This makes it more persuasive as a world. The film also demonstrates a spectacular understanding of scale: the toys are of many different sizes, but the illusion is that they are all of the same magnitude.

On another level, *Toccata* can be appreciated as a statement about design and even a comment on the shifts within modern society—not exactly nostalgia, but a matter-of-fact observation of a change in values. From a design standpoint, the message is made clear in a brief narration read by Charles:

> This is a film about toy trains.
>
> These are real toys, not scale models.
>
> That doesn't mean that toys are good and scale models are bad, but they are different. Most of the trains we have used are old, and some are quite old. The reason for this is per-haps that in the more recent years we seem to have lost the knack of making real toys.
>
> Most old ones have a direct and unembarrassed manner that give us a special kind of pleasure, a pleasure different from the admiration we may feel for the perfect little copy of the real thing.
>
> In a good old toy there's apt to be nothing self-conscious about the use of materials. What is wood is wood. What is tin is tin. What is cast is beautifully cast.
>
> It is possible that somewhere in all this is a clue to what sets the creative climate of any time, including our own.[10]

The narration lasts but a minute but invests the entire film with a powerful subtext.

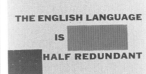
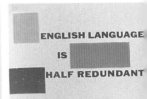

ENGLISH LANGUAGE     THE ENGLISH LANGUAGE     THE ENGLISH LANGUAGE     ENGLISH LANGUAGE

IS ABOUT     IS ABOUT     IS     IS

E-HALF REDUNDANT     HALF REDUNDANT     HALF REDUNDANT     HALF REDUNDANT

Eight frames from the Eames film *A Communications Primer* (1953), showing how even language uses redundancy to produce a high signal-to-noise ratio

A child may well ignore it, but the viewer who has listened is now seeing an essay about the honest use of materials. This is the poetry of ideas. And in this film, on the Eames House, and in the furniture, Charles and Ray explored the honest use of materials in three completely different mediums. This seamless connection between all their projects is really the key to understanding their design process. The Eameses created a fractal world of their own, and very often the films themselves were the mechanism of stitching such domains together.

*Toccata* took over a year to make, generally being shot in the evenings after work as the 901 office was completed. Often the day would begin with Charles and Ray planning the evening's shoot. Then Ray, Parke Meek, and at times Eames Office staff members such as Deborah Sussman, would spend the day preparing the film sets, while Charles worked on the furniture. Charles would then come back up and the shooting would begin. In a famous shot, the camera goes through a train, an effect achieved by animating a trip though a break-apart train, built car by car. Eventually they realized the rear window of one of the train cars had better have some sky behind it or the camera could never leave the train.[11] Other shots could be elaborate too: sometimes many hands were needed to wind or launch the toys and crank the rewinds. They used simple but clever geometry, so that one person could turn a crank and pull, say, four different trains at four different speeds: on a film rewind, each of four take-up reels of different diameters had a string attached to a different train. The narrowest reel would take up the string fastest, so that train would appear to move more quickly than the others. Simple but effective.[12] To create motion, sometimes the camera moved; other times it was the background that moved. The great Russian filmmaker Andrei Tarkovsky made the comment that "film is a mosaic made out of time."[13] The crafting of *Toccata for Toy Trains* is the perfect expression of that idea.

It is tempting to refer to the Eames films as educational films, which they are on many levels. But they are much more than that. In his 1975 article on the Eames films, director Paul Schrader closely connected the films to the work of Jorge Luis Borges.* He quotes a remark about Borges to the effect that until Borges we "had not imagined that there could be a poetry of ideas." Schrader suggests that until Eames, we had not imagined that there could be "a cinema of ideas."[14]

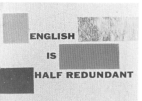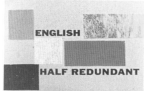

Charles once said that the films "come as a result of one of two situations: It's either a logical extension of some immediate problem we are working on, or it is something we have been wanting to do for a long time and can't put it off any longer."[15] One film that seems to be a bit of both is *House: after five years of living*, made, as the title implies, in 1955. The film is made up of about 300 slides shot over the first years they lived at the Eames House (including some images of the filmmaking being done in the studio). It is an experiment in conveying something about a piece of architecture entirely through stills presented in a film. Why would this be desirable?

Beyond being an interesting aesthetic exercise in its own right, *House* addressed one of the obvious constraints of filmmaking: the expense of the production itself. In the digital age we take for granted that nonprofessional moving pictures (home videos) can be distributed to a mass audience (via television or the Internet). But until the late 1980s, that was not really the case. Certainly in the 1950s, making a 35mm motion picture was a serious undertaking requiring a significant crew. But what if you were after something more subtle than simply recording a house (which, after all, you could probably do with a film crew in a week or two even at the most extravagant)? What if you wanted to capture those spontaneous moments of light that occur every morning for a while and then not at all for two months? You would need a tool that permitted you to do it on your own, on the spur of the moment, without the expense or the inconvenience of calling a crew together. That tool was the still camera.

When one looks at *House*, one is looking at the most beautiful light of the first five years of living at the Eames House. Afterward, a few sequences were photographed specially for the film to pull it together structurally, and then all of them were woven together with the *divertissement* written by Elmer Bernstein. Bernstein pointed out that writing for a collection of slides posed some challenges, but "that was more my problem than their problem because they'd lay all the slides out on a long table with light behind them, and then we'd go down the row looking at all the slides, and so that I could see what the images were going to be, but that was a very, very hard way to get feeling out of something. . . . Live action has a rhythm that you kind of pick up. Slides are static, obviously, except that the

* The article remains one of the best-pieces written about the Eames movie output. Schrader, who wrote *Taxi Driver* and directed *Cat People*, has been quoted as saying that the two biggest influences on him as a filmmaker were Charles Eames and Sam Peckinpah, a pair of filmmakers rarely spoken of in the same breath.

FILMS AS ESSAYS

149

Eight different stills from the Eames film *House: after five years of living* (1955)

way they used them it doesn't feel static."[16] One of the ways Bernstein and the Eameses communicated was through the use of bar charts, a kind of timeline of the film. There, with color pens and pencils, Charles and Ray would mark the visual arcs of the film. It was a uniquely visual way of scripting that Bernstein has never encountered in any of the more than 200 other scores he has collaborated on.[17]

Charles and Ray always wanted things done to the highest technical standards possible. They wanted the actual film to be made in Technicolor, a color-film process that used black-and-white film. Each Technicolor frame was literally shot three different times (once for each of the three components of color). The actual duplication of the slides onto film was done at the Eames Office by Parke Meek. Charles wanted a certain quality—a kind of confident leisure—to the dissolves (and if you look closely at the film, even on video, they have a different quality than most film dissolves). So Meek built a kind of Rube Goldberg optical printer in which a motor turned the camera one frame at a time, rotating a piece of plywood with nails sticking out, which then advanced a wheel with the appropriate color filters. At 24 frames per second, an image that appeared on the screen for 2 seconds required 48 frames of 35mm film to be shot 3 times each (one for each color filter for a total of 144 frames). This incredibly time-consuming process achieved stupendous results. People asked to learn the technique, but even though it was written up, no one else ever did it because it was too much work. Later, when Meek explained it to the Technicolor folks, they said it could not be done. As Parke said dryly, "I didn't know any better [so] I did it. . . . At times a lack of knowledge of the movie industry was a great advantage to us."[18]

Like the Newton Deck of Cards, the slide optical printer is a perfect example of the way Charles and Ray ensured that the tools of production were understood within the four walls of the Eames Office. A few years later, when the office created *Glimpses of the USA* (7 screens; 2,200 images; 12 minutes), Bob Staples and John Whitney figured out that if the office worked 24 hours a day, 7 days a week, using the traditional process, they would still not get the film done on time. But they were able to draw on their earlier technology and do it in-house. According to Staples, they "bought a metal lathe, stripped it down, hung it on the wall, put the camera on it. And now all of a sudden we had an animation camera. Well,

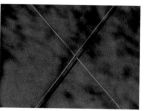

Charles wouldn't run out and spend twenty-five thousand dollars for an animation stand; he'd spend fifty thousand dollars having Parke make this out of a metal lathe.* To some degree he was not sure the technology was going to work, so he'd want to invent the wheel over and over and over again. But he did a great job, you know? I mean, this is how you learned things."[19] Stories like this recur throughout the annals of the Eames Office. At considerable expense of time, trouble, and money, the Eames Office was creating something many people take for granted in the age of desktop publishing: the ability to publish in-house commercial-quality work on quite noncommercial topics.

* This oft-quoted figure, which some feel was exaggerated, would have been primarily labor. Parke spoke of getting the lathe for the price of scrap.

Under the shadow of Hollywood, the Eames Office achieved a rare mix: they used the mainstream standards as a marker of technical excellence while hewing to their unique vision. Elmer Bernstein, today an Oscar-winning legend of cinema (*To Kill a Mockingbird* and *The Age of Innocence*), was uniquely positioned to see both sides:

I think that the execution of most of those films was on a very, very high level. In terms of expertise and the use of the medium, but . . . I felt no similarity between what we were doing and what was going on in the other world. First of all, Ray and Charles looked at the world in a totally different way anyway. I mean, they didn't perceive the world anything like what commercial films perceived the world like. . . . I think these films were an offering done with love. It's as simple as that. Certainly on the part of the Eameses, and certainly for sure on the part of Ray. For Charles I think they were investigations or looks at things that he wanted to look at for one reason or another.[20]

One way to experience the difference is to watch the Billy Wilder film, *The Spirit of St. Louis*, starring Jimmy Stewart. Charles directed the second-unit sequences of the plane being constructed. To the end of his life he remembered the thrill of opening a crate and discovering an original Wright Cyclone engine (like the kind in the actual plane), which was shot for the film. The Wilder and Eames sensibilities are quite different; the two Eames montages feel strikingly contemporary. In the film, it is like seeing the Eames film *Fiberglass Chairs* spliced into the middle of a 1950s classic like Wilder's *Stalag 17*.

An anecdote from the production of *Toccata for Toy Trains* suggests a connection of

Many different film sets: Charles filming Elmer Bernstein for the 1964 World's Fair presentation, *Think*; Ray on the set of *The Good Years*; Billy Wilder on the set of *The Spirit of St Louis*; Billy and Audrey Wilder

Charles to another famous (albeit fictional) Missourian, Tom Sawyer. One of D. J. DePree's sons came back to Michigan from the Eames Office. Some of the other folks at Herman Miller asked him how the trip was: It was fine. *What did you do?* Well, we spent a lot of time winding up toys and pulling trains along a track. *You're kidding.* Well, I had been doing it for a while, and I was feeling a little odd about it until I started talking to the guy next to me after a couple of hours. His name was Billy Wilder.[21]

Parke Meek recalled that the only breaks during the shooting of the same film were to watch their favorite television show, *Stars of Jazz*. One week the show featured Oscar Peterson improvising a jazz soundtrack over the Eames film, *Blacktop*. At the end of the show the announcer said that next week's show would include a new film by Charles Eames. As Parke Meek noted, "That's the first [we'd] heard of it." Rather than being alarmed or indignant, Charles and Ray saw it as a great excuse to make a film. So they took down the trains, shot some tops in black and white, cut them together, and sent in the roll of film. There was an interesting lesson in serendipity in it all. As Parke remembered it, during editing they tried all sorts of different musical tracks to see how they flowed—they all worked great. But when the person doing it on TV tried, it didn't work. It seemed to be because "there are just so many accidental places things would hit on anything else, but when you try you can't make anything hit."[22]

Throughout most of the 1950s, just about all the work with the Eameses and Bernstein was done at the Eames House. Bernstein remembers, "we'd all sit in there and . . . there was a curious . . . admixture of business and, kind of, social intercourse going on. So that the work never seemed, sort of, clinical, because it was always part of social interaction somehow."[23] But around 1958, the Eames Office had the opportunity to expand into the rest of the warehouse in Venice, and it did so. Bernstein remarked later that there were no more meetings at the house, and "what appeared to happen was that Ray and Charles moved virtually their entire lives into Venice, to the warehouse."[24] While that may be a bit of an overstatement, there is no question that the creative center of gravity shifted to 901.

If you look at photos of the Eames House living room where the meetings took place, throughout the 1950s the objects and configurations constantly changed. There was a

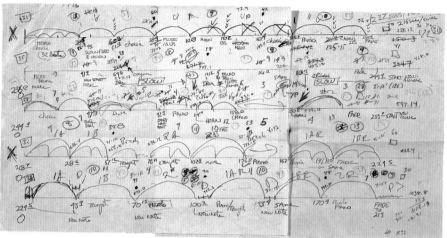

Above left to
right: on the set
of the interactive
videodisk
Merlin; filming
the tanks at the
office; filming
the beginning of
*Kaleidoscope
Jazz Chair*
(1960); the edit-
ing bench in the
studio of the
Eames House.
Left: a bar chart
for *Toccata for
Toy Trains*

definite trend toward more and more objects. But by the early 1960s, the room looked much
the way it does today. In forestry they would call this a "climax community": the way a pond
silts in to become a meadow, which gives way to an ecosystem of shrublike trees and then,
in turn, a deciduous forest, and finally a mature vibrant pine forest that stands indefinitely.
The interior of the Eames House achieved a visual climax community at the decade's turn —
the house remained vital and beloved and lived in, but it became primarily a home. In a
sense, it had nurtured the filmmaking dimension of Charles and Ray's work, but now they
were comfortable fully integrating it into the mainstream of the office's efforts at 901.

# CHAPTER 13

# The Guest/Host Relationship

One of the most powerful forces in the Eames work, a force that can be identified in virtually every major project the Eameses undertook, is the guest/host relationship. Charles felt that this was one of the most basic, even primal, human relationships. Every society in the world valued this relationship. It existed in a nomad's tent and a raja's court. Charles felt that it was also part of how one designed an exhibition or a chair or a building. He often suggested that one of the challenges of the modern city was that if we are all guests, then "who are the hosts?"[1]

I leave it to the reader to consider connections between the guest/host relationship and Charles and Ray's upbringings. Exposure to familial theater and dining establishments may well have been important, but such ideas drift toward the literal rather than the universal. And the guest/host relationship as Charles and Ray expressed it seemed to be an essential part of the human race itself. Though this thread can be seen in many specific Eames projects, one can argue that, in a sense, its most complete Eamesian expression was in the space at 901 itself, particularly after the office blossomed into the whole warehouse.

In 1943, 901 West Washington Boulevard in Venice, California, became the home of the Eames Office. Faded words "Bay Cities Garage" from its life as a garage lingered on outside walls throughout the tenure of the office there. For the first years, the Eames Office used just the front three offices. Manufacturing was done in the back, first by Evans, then by Herman Miller. Finally, in 1958, the Eames Office took over the whole building. As is often the case, this expansion was a confluence of opportunity and need. Herman Miller no longer needed such a small factory (they had several others) and the Eames Office needed the space. Eventually the office would need still more room, and a kind of addition, known as the "New Building," was built in the late 1960s with a formal filming area as well as room for the archives and various collections. Outside was a patio and picnic area—indeed the first picnic scene for *Rough Sketch* was shot there (but that is getting far ahead of the story).

The late 1950s were a turning point for the Eames Office in a number of ways. Deborah Sussman, who was away from the office from 1956 to 1958, recalled that she

Charles Eames showing his friend Buckminster Fuller around the office

* In the corner of
each right-hand page
of this book is a flip-
book tour through
901.

† The bathrooms
were back in this
area as well, with
excellent examples
of the Hang-it-All in
each one.

returned to a much busier and bigger office in the throes of the *Mathematica* project. She remembered a distinct feeling that the whole scale had changed.[2] And it truly had.

The physical context of working at 901 bears description. Almost everyone who entered remarked on the almost surreal quality of opening the door and leaving behind a somewhat shabby street in a not-so-fashionable area of Los Angeles. A break-in to Ray's car is immortalized in the Eames film *Goods*, and in the 1980s, someone was gunned down right in front of the office as Ray was leaving work one night. The feeling of the area was gritty. Julian Blaustein called the nondescript exterior "a fraud. . . . You go in that front door and the fairyland is before you!"[* 3]

Buddy Collette described it as "like walking into another world."[4] Others said it was like walking "through the looking glass."[5] Or Santa's workshop. And it really was. There was no clue on the outside: just the number 901. You rang a bell. The door opened, and you entered the front office, where folks like Hap Johnson, Pamela Hedley, Etsu Garfias, or Frances Bishop were answering the phones. By the 1970s you would have seen them through a textile hanging by the door, shaping a kind of hallway to a reception area. If you worked at the Eames Office, you might turn right and head down the hall toward the graphics room, one of the original three rooms. On the way, you would pass Charles's office on the right with frosted windows for privacy and glowing light, and on the left, Ray's office, door nearly always closed, making an extremely private place for Ray and her collections. Then you would enter the graphics room, which received the warmest, most beautiful afternoon light. John Neuhart might be working there with Ray or Nancy Zaslavsky. Big wooden letters and an array of porcelain signs hung on the walls, along with various sorts of tools and implements of graphology, photos from *Photography and the City*, a memento of *SX-70*, and an Eames House of Cards. One of the extraordinary things about the office was that in addition to being vibrant and full of an amazing energy, it was a self-curated museum of impeccable taste. Everything there was Eames-related, not only because Charles and Ray had selected it, but because very often it had been part of a project.

If you were a guest at the office, you were met by your host and usually taken into the heart of the building through a different narrow passage (with a vast bulletin board of activities and events),[†] which then opened up into the library area with its rolling ladder and marble-top table. The music of the musical tower might be playing (especially if one of the grandchildren was there). If it wasn't, you might be invited to play it by launching a marble to the top of a kind of gravity xylophone, where the marble would play a tune by cascading down prearranged keys (cardboard for the downbeats). Often an intern's first challenge was to come up with a new tune.

You probably wouldn't notice the door on the left behind the tower, which led to

Clockwise from top left: graphics room of the Eames Office at 901; note from Philip and Phylis Morrison written on eucalyptus leaves; 901 could be a set too: Etsu Garfias in *SX-70* (1972); the big number 2 in Charles's office; production of the *Moveable Feasts* exhibition; another view of graphics room

* Ironically, after Ray's death the space was remodeled, and the new design locked in choices, whereas the Eameses focused on the flexibility and utility of the space.

one of the full darkrooms, but you might look to the right at someone going through the entrance to the New Building. That was probably Alex Funke bustling in there to do some shooting, or Pat Naritomi headed to work on the slides, or Mike Ripps skipping up the little ramp through the vaultlike metal doorway that had been blasted through the brick. Maybe you will get to peek in there later, but for now you follow your host, still in the main building. Big, blown-up black-and-white images array themselves everywhere on the walls: clowns, shells, clouds, movie sets. A plexiglass shelf has a dense grid of shells from the *Aquarium* project; a magnifier is placed over some of the tinier whorls. You might follow on to the kitchen, where Emily or Maria would have some coffee ready, or sit on the World's Fair seating bolted to a wall.

The whole effect was profound in its impact. One of the most surreal aspects of the space, particularly for people who visited every once in a while, was its flexibility. Many of the walls were held in place only with clamps, so that in a matter of hours the rooms in the central area could be completely reconfigured. These configurations happened all the time. It was in this central area that models or mock-ups of timelines would be displayed. Sometimes whole proposed rooms of exhibitions (including the Time-Life Building's lobby) would be put together life-size. Other times a vast model—like that of *Mathematica* or *Franklin and Jefferson*—would be there to scrutinize.

On opposite sides of this central crucible were two smaller areas named after two key staffers: one was known as "Jehane's area" and one as "Jeannine's area" (even after Jeannine Oppewall had left). The areas weren't cubicles but the other sides of a variety of flexible walls; some more or less permanent, some not. In Jehane's general vicinity, math ideas were on one wall, Kepler on another, Tycho Brahe on yet another. A forgotten street sign sat on the floor. The latest toy lay on a counter. Further afield, a fun-house mirror flanked one side of the doorway to Jeannine's, reflecting a staff member as she twirls the phone cord while she talks, all the lines blinking.

A little further back, the space narrowed again to a corridor, right angling in front of a huge, hanging Indian flag. On the left, the door to the screening room. On the right, a bland door past which resided the animation room with both the down-shooting animation stand and the original lathe bed-slide camera from *Glimpses of the USA* being converted to Eames staff member Bill Tondreau's new motion-control system. A huge circuit board, with transistors like biscuit tins, hangs on the corridor wall—another one of the fascinating but unintrusive artifacts from efforts past, like the nose cone of the glider that hung over the kitchen. Ray tended to guide these selections from the living archive. If you blinked, you would miss an insanely huge archive of current publications running in a thin flat blade through the building—not just design and architecture but science and history, academic journals, and current stacks of the newsweeklies.

Deeper still was the production area. Furniture prototypes were tried out here. Dick Donges could be looking at the latest prototype for the Chaise Lounge. This was roughly where chairs were manufactured by the Eames Office, Evans Products, and finally Herman Miller. The feeling of its history was real but not dwelled upon—new history was being made. There was a real loading dock for shipments in and out, a paint-spraying booth sporting its aerosol pentimentos, and row after row of catalogs—the sort of catalogs Fred Usher meant when he talked about the way Charles and Ray reached beyond the obvious when considering prefabricated parts for their house. Though some furniture was being worked on at the time of Charles's death, the production area was used for getting shows ready for shipment, checking quality, and fine-tuning a million details on the walls. Shelves on the brick wall held early production models. Elsewhere sat some strange wicker chairs—a gift from Billy Wilder, they had been passenger seats on the first Ford Tri-motor passenger plane. And, incredibly, in this area were fish tanks. If you were with Charles, an octopus would come up to the tank's glass to greet you. Charles would drop in a hermit crab for the cephalopod's delectation. A shark's egg was backlit so the embryo would be visible. Sam Passalacqua would be setting up a shot so Charles could shoot an archerfish gunning down a fly in cold water. You would get caught up in the sea creatures, and in these moments staff member Randy Walker might be buttonholing Charles with a question.

So you would look up and around, and there—extending the full width of the building up to the ceiling and blocking even the classic sturdy wood beam rafters—was a massive bluish gray wall, like an unexpectedly direct slice of the building. It was striking in its bluntness and contrast to the rest of the space. Pushing open thick doors revealed the workshop, and you would realize the wall was for keeping the sawdust out. Tools, tools, and more tools. It seemed to have everything, including some things most workshops do not: a 4-by-5-foot portrait of Gandhi and another blowup of Irving Penn's photo of the Aubuchon child—the latter was part of *A Communications Primer*.

The workshop was at the far rear of the building, but the tour is incomplete. You come back through the loading dock and head out to the patio, where Ray might now be arranging food at a little table. Behind the patio stood a garage on the site of a shed (now gone) that belonged to a colorful local character known as the Captain. Here work began for the new *Powers of Ten*. Then, surprisingly, considering that all of 901 seemed to overflow with stuff, there was a grassy area fenced off from the sidewalk, lush and brightened by the smell of eucalyptus. Above sat a strange creature in the form of a ceramic waterspout.

The New Building also opened onto the grassy expanse, and in there Mike Ripps would sit down to finish the last details on *SX-70*. There were also a little camera supply

room, a shooting stage, and the most amazing number of slides. Annette del Zoppo would be looking at some selects with Jehane Burns. Up the stairs of the New Building you would find a vast, truly daunting array of toys and innumerable cans of motion-picture film in the archives.

In short, 901 contained precisely the blend of intellectual and physical tools one would expect for the Eames Office to do what it did over the 35 years it worked there. The space itself seemed to monitor and convey its own history and provided opportunities for serendipity and sunlight for those who worked there and those who visited. It created a bit of the feeling of "garage culture" meets "collage culture," the can-do tinkerer value system merging seamlessly with an aesthetic that valued good artistry and arrangement, but did not quite fetishize them. More than one Eames Office staffer commented that visitors didn't stand a chance—in the sense that the whole apparatus of hosting was so huge and complete that the visitor's experience was thought through from the beginning.

Charles observed that architecture was about anticipating the needs of the guest, and 901 took that insight to a whole new level of experience. Staff member Jeannine Oppewall made an interesting and revealing comparison:

> If you were the client, it was like going to gamble in Las Vegas, you know? It's a closed, self-involved environment, in many ways. And I don't mean that in a bad sense. You don't see the outside, there aren't any clocks, it's red-flock wallpaper or whatever it is, and twenty-four hours a day this [Las Vegas] machine is just chewing and absorbing and taking you. And, it's something metaphorically similar to the [Eames] office in a way. It was a closed, insular world, so when you came into it, you had to accept that psychologically. I mean, it's very subtle, you know? You didn't go out to lunch and discuss things; you were in that environment and you discussed it there. You were a captive audience, in a way.[6]

And even for those who worked there, Oppewall pointed out, it was "such an attractive and consuming world that there was really no reason to leave."[7] And that was true day and night.

The whole experience of a visit to the Eames Office was overpowering, and the visceral ambience was only the beginning. There were other things; some seen, some not. Almost every visitor—whether an old friend (such as Billy Wilder, Lee Krasner, Robert Motherwell, or Barney Reese), a client (the DePrees, Mike Sullivan of IBM, Pete Seay of Westinghouse), a colleague (Gregory Peck from the National Council on the Arts), a potential client (Robert Redford), a curious guest (Nobel laureate C. N. Yang), or any of the thousands of people who came through—was treated to a screening in the conference room, usually a few films or a couple of the three-screen slide shows. There was a feeling of some-

thing akin to a magician's lair in the conference room because many of the films were only available at 901 (or when Charles spoke), and the three-screen slide shows were extremely difficult to put on anywhere else. Significant parts of the Eames Office media output were experienced only in the office's performance space, which was the conference room. Why? Alex Funke got part of the answer when he asked if he could install a dimmer on the lights. Charles said no. Funke replied, "Come on, Boss. All theaters have dimmers." Charles replied, "No, no, I want you to just turn off the lights because . . . I don't want it to look like we're showing them a movie. I want them to know that they're looking at something that's a piece of work, it's not a feature. . . . This is not a theater—this is part of my work space."[8]

Behind the scenes, little cards were being kept to record which films or slide shows each guest had seen, so that next time they could be shown something new. It all seemed very effortless, which is part of being a good host—not to make people feel bad about the trouble you have gone through. Charles sometimes used a saying he had picked up on the film sets in his MGM days when a particularly difficult shot had been pulled off—"the blood will never show."[9] In the same way, keeping notes on cards (and not just relying on memory) was the best way to assure a rich experience for all.

When the office would hear that someone was visiting—say the Sarabhais were in from the NID—films for the guests would be chosen based on the cards. (Even so, Charles or Ray might change the selections at the last minute, which meant, in a sense, they even modeled their screenings). At that point, said Funke, "the machine would swing into motion and the films would all be pulled out and laid ready, and the slide shows would be racked up in the trays, and the lamps would be set up and running. . . . But the thing was that you wanted it to be perfect; you didn't want to let [Charles] down."[10] If it was the corporate brass from IBM or Herman Miller, then Charles and Ray "wanted to make sure that it didn't look the same as it did the last time the customer'd been there. . . . So everything had to be changed around, new pictures put up, and so forth. There was always the great orgy of going around and filling up the potholes in the floor." A part of all this orchestration was

Left: Charles showing Lord Snowdon the IBM Pavilion model at the 1964 New York World's Fair. He is pulling the "people wall" up into position. Right: One of many photographs Charles took to record Ray's beautiful settings and arrangements

good business, but as Funke pointed out, a lot of it was just "a pride thing; you liked to have the place look spruced up."[11]

Mealtime was always a presentation—a picnic, whether outside or in the kitchen, prepared by Maria or Emily. Charles and Ray often invited a guest (or two or three) and a staff member or two to join them. Some, like Jehane, ate with them regularly; others, from time to time. (Wags at the office called it the "Club of the Wealthiest Planters," after a line describing high society in colonial Virginia in the film *The Look of America, 1750–1800*.)[12] Having a full-time cook may sound extravagant, but it accomplished a number of practical things—it reduced the time spent traveling to and from restaurants, created the fullest possible experience for the guests, and subtly encouraged people to visit Charles and Ray on the Eameses' own terms—without necessarily even realizing it. Charles and Ray were not particularly enamored of parties. Parke Meek remembered being at a party where someone in the design community was complaining about how unfair it was that Charles was so successful. It was about ten o'clock in the evening. Finally, Parke said, "Do you know what he's doing right now? Working."[13]

Charles and Ray talked often of the circus. It was a potent metaphor in their world. (And perhaps more than a metaphor. Charles and Ray are said to have considered a clown act. Lucia Eames remembers filling out a college application and asking her father for his profession. His answer: "Clown.")[14] The circus resonates a lot with the structure and organization of 901. On the first level, both were built upon a deep structure. Charles observed that a floor plan of a Big Top tent was basically the same as the Acropolis.[15] And like the circus, the Eames Office looked like a lot of fun—and it was (or could be)—but it took a lot of work to get there. Finally, both achieved and required a certain kind of spontaneity. At the Eames Office, spontaneity did not mean winging it; it meant working hard enough and practicing enough to achieve a deeper spontaneity, a deeper ability to react to and contribute to the situation at hand. If two people untrained as clowns attempted to put on a clown act without any practice, the result would likely be pretty terrible and the interactions with the crowd painful to watch—and this would make them lousy hosts. On the other hand, if they worked at clowning, practiced for months, both the show and the spontaneous interaction with the crowd would be greatly improved. They would be starting at a higher level. And if they got really good, it would look like no effort at all. This was the approach of the Office of Charles and Ray Eames at 901.

One particular event says a lot about this higher level of spontaneity. In talking with people who were in the audience, the emotion of the experience still ranks as one of the purest joys in their lives. In 1967 Herman Miller decided to invite their foreign licensees (who at that time built the company's furniture overseas) to the United States for a tour to understand the parent company better, and also as a reward.

The licensees gathered in New York from all over the globe (Germany, Brazil, Japan, France, and England, to name a few) for the start of the two-week tour. They then traveled to Michigan, Chicago, and Santa Fe, and concluded in Los Angeles with a visit to Disneyland and a tour of the Eames Office. It was an incredible tour by all accounts, organized brilliantly by Con Boevy of Herman Miller. In New York, Herman Miller showroom tours and time with George Nelson were followed up with *Cabaret* on Broadway. In Michigan, they visited show-rooms and factories, each stop even better than the last. After a brief stay in Chicago, they stopped in Santa Fe, New Mexico, to meet Alexander Girard (head of textiles for Herman Miller) and view his spectacular folk art collection. The *pièce de résistance* was to be the last stop—Los Angeles: a visit to Disneyland, of course, a picnic lunch at the Eames House, and a tour of the Eames Office. The Herman Miller company valued its design history and for this group the name Eames was one to conjure with. By this point the caravan was about 75 people strong, including D.J. DePree, and Max and Hugh DePree.[16]

True to form, Charles intended to be an extremely good host. Unbeknownst to Boevy and most from Herman Miller, Charles had persuaded some people to surreptitiously photograph the entire trip. The night before the group's visit to the office, staffers rushed the slides to an all-night color lab. Lunch at the Eames House went as planned, and every-one came next to 901. After the tour and a sampling of films and slide shows, Charles casu-ally announced that there was one more slide show. Suddenly, the Sousa march "Stars and Stripes Forever" blasted through a pair of movie-theater-sized Altec Lansing speakers, and a three-screen slide show of the licensees' trip burst onto the screen before them: beautiful images capturing the entire journey—even Disneyland from the day before. The surprise of the moment, the recognition of the effort that went into its creation, the music, the personal nature of it—all of this coalesced into pure emotion. People in the crowd were so moved they cried. Others were literally unable to speak for a time.[17]

The moment felt exactly right, and the slide show itself was a series of spontaneous choices—undoubtedly remembering remarks and comments overheard to maximize its res-onance—by everyone working on it in the intense final stretch to make it the best it could be. But the level of that spontaneity and improvisation was much higher and achieved a far more powerful result than if the office had simply decided that morning to do a slide show for their visitors. It would have been too late for real depth. This was being a good host.

The gesture is reminiscent of an effort a few years later, when Charles delivered six Norton Lectures at Harvard. Given every few weeks over the 1970-71 school year, the lec-tures were so popular they were moved to a bigger hall after the first two. The new venue was the Harvard Square Movie Theater. Four times that winter and spring the Eames Office

staff descended on the theater just after the regular movie ended at 10:30 P.M. and essentially refurbished it to their specifications. Film projectors had to be realigned, the six synchronized slide projectors (two per screen for dissolves) installed and housed in a sound-damping room built of furniture pads, the set dressed, the podiums and extra speakers installed. The crew worked straight through the night and the next day, finishing the testing and the sound checks just as the doors opened for the first guests at 7:00 P.M. The lobby and the whole theater were filled with flowers—a stunning and still remembered welcome for the crowd staggering in from Cambridge's winter cold. The Eames Office crew ran the shows (involving hitting dozens of cues as Charles gave his talk), grabbed a catnap, then had to tear down the whole thing, getting every trace removed from the theater just in time for the 10 A.M. matinee the next day. The flowers were taken home by the audience. It was a 36-hour charette each time to re-create in this theater, at least for the night, the level of presentation they had in 901.[18]

The Eameses and colleagues crafted another memorable audience experience when they developed their multimedia landmark *Sample Lesson for a Hypothetical Course*, wafting the odors of bread into the ducts of the space where they were screening the film *Bread*. As Charles and Ray knew, preparation permits a higher level of improvisation. Some people consider this approach to life too serious; others call it the reality of making wonderful things happen.

The Eameses' approach was not just dramatic and in public. In the oral history archives of the Eames Office, Jehane Burns Kuhn tells this story:

> I remember when someone, a young man, came to interview for a job, and he came into the office over the weekend. And I think Ray was away somewhere so that no one was about except the housekeeper and me and Charles to, sort of, look after this young man. And it somehow came about that Maria put on one of her extra specially good lunches, picnic lunches at the office. Charles charmed the young man with anecdotes over lunch, and the young man was given room and opportunity to do his stuff. And I think that we dropped him off at his motel and weren't quite sure that he'd been dropped off in the right place and went to some trouble to check up that he was okay, that he'd gotten [in]. . . . And then I remember after that, an exchange with Charles . . . an odd thing . . . for either of us to have remarked upon, 'Boy! Sometimes we go to a lot of trouble.' And I think it was Charles who said, 'We,'—and he meant we the office—'can't stand the idea of not being loved.' And I said, 'Uh-huh, [I] guess that's right.' He said, 'But it would be hard to wish to be any other way than that, wouldn't it?'[19]

Collage of images from the Norton Lectures, clockwise from top left: Charles preparing in the hotel room; setting up the faders on the lighting console; guests enjoying the flowers; Charles at the podium; guests picking flowers; the temporary projection booth; lights; soundtrack for the slide show *Sets* being cued up; the lobby in the quiet before the storm

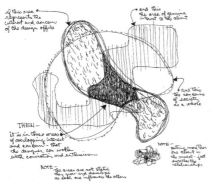

if this area
represents the
interest and concern
of the design office

and this
the area of genuine
interest to the client

and this
the concerns
of society
as a whole

THEN—

it is in these areas
of overlapping interest
and concern - that
the designer can work
with conviction and enthusiasm

NOTE these areas are not static
they grow and develop
as each one influences the others

NOTE putting more than
one client in
the model - just
amplifies the
relationships

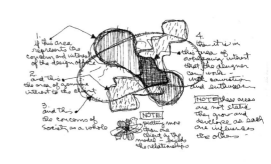

1.
if this area
represents the
concern and interest
of the design office

2.
and this
the area of genuine
interest to the client

3.
and this
the concerns of
society as a whole

4.
then it is in
this area of
overlapping interest
that the designer
can work
with conviction
and enthusiasm

NOTE these areas
are not static.
they grow and
develop as each
one influences
the others -

NOTE putting more
than one
client in the
model of
builds the
relationships

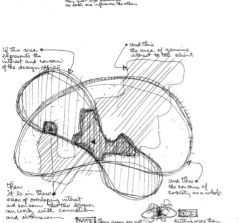

If this area
represents the
interest and concern
of the design office

and this
the area of genuine
interest to the client

then
it is in these
areas of overlapping interest
and concern - the designer
can work with conviction
and enthusiasm

and this
the concerns of
society as a whole

NOTE these areas are not
static - they grow
and develop - as
each one influences
the others

NOTE putting more than
one client in the model
builds the relationships -

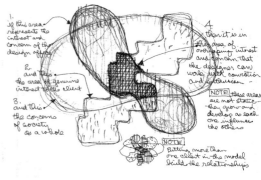

1.
if this area
represents the
interest and
concern of the
design office

2.
and this
the area of genuine
interest to the client

3.
and this
the concerns
of society
as a whole

4.
then it is in
this area of
overlapping interest
and concern that
the designer can
work with conviction
and enthusiasm

NOTE these areas
are not static.
they grow and
develop as each
one influences
the others

NOTE putting more than
one client in the model
build the relationships

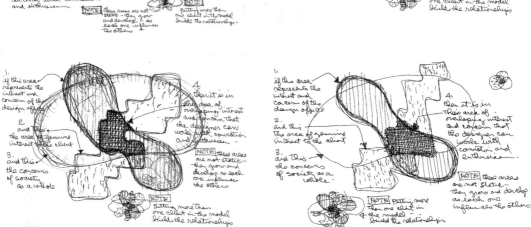

1.
if this area
represents the
interest and
concern of the
design office

2.
and this
the area of genuine
interest to the client

3.
and this
the concerns
of society
as a whole

4.
then it is in
this area of
overlapping interest
and concern that
the designer can
work with conviction
and enthusiasm

NOTE these areas
are not static -
they grow and
develop as each
one influences
the others

NOTE putting more than
one client in the model
build the relationships

1.
if this area
represents the
interest and
concern of the
design office

2.
and this
the area of genuine
interest to the client

3.
and this
the concerns
of society as a
whole.

4.
then it is in
this area of
overlapping interest
and concern that
the designer can
work with
conviction and
enthusiasm -

NOTE putting more
than one client in
the model
build the relationships

NOTE these areas
are not static.
they grow and develop
as each one
influences the others

# CHAPTER 14

# Constraints

In 1959, Charles was asked to bring pictures of the 901 space to a talk at the Royal College of Art in London. On some level, he did not like the idea of the intrusion, but he eventually got into a situation where he felt he had agreed to do it. He solved his dilemma by having Parke Meek and Jeremy Lepard build a kaleidoscope that he could film through. The result: the film *Kaleidoscope Shop*, a three-minute tour of the Eames Office filmed through a kaleidoscopic filter. As noted in the book *Eames Design*, this was a "kind of 'Eames' joke. [Charles] had complied with the request from the Royal College, but [did] not violate his sense of privacy."[1]

This kind of indirection on the nuts and bolts of their process was typical of the Eameses. One part modesty, it was also being good hosts and showmen—the blood will never show. But it also seemed to contradict the rigor and detail with which Charles and Ray communicated the interior life and spirit of other disciplines in exhibitions and films, until you remember that their reticence was also a kind of rigor, a sense of doing what was appropriate and not taking the easy way out. Obviously, any pictures of the office would have a curiosity value to an audience so far from Los Angeles, but they could not convey the spirit of the office. The kaleidoscope images themselves do not necessarily convey the spirit either, but the act of choosing them and presenting them comes much closer.

Furthermore, by showing transformation—the accelerated evolution of form into form—the changing images of *Kaleidoscope Shop* capture a singular quality of the office. In the Eames Office, Charles and Ray created a mechanism for maximizing the number of iterations of a concept they were exploring. One project was often reflected in another. This happened with films, with furniture, as well as with ideas. The film *Design Q&A* (1972), possibly the best and most entertaining film on design ever made, was the product of such a journey.

All of the Eames films are about design, reflect design, teach design—but almost none of the over 100 films made explicitly discuss the design process. The "almost" alludes to *Design Q&A*. It is only a slight exaggeration to say that watching this film will take you halfway to understanding the Eames design philosophy. (Charles's design diagram will take

Sketches by Charles of different versions of the design diagram (1969). The final appears on page 179.

167

you most of the rest of the way.) *Design Q&A* is also funny, in a very dry, Eamesian way: At one point, Charles is asked, "How would you define yourself with respect to a decorator? An interior architect? A stylist?" His answer: "I wouldn't."[2] The film takes the form of a questionnaire about issues related to design. The questions were written by Madame L'Amic, the curator of the exhibition of which the questionnaire was a part. Charles's answers were spoken by him and illustrated with still images, but it was nonetheless visually fast-moving.

Still in distribution and running only five minutes, it is no hardship to find and watch the whole film. But at the risk of oversummarizing the already concise, *Design Q&A* stresses two essential points that this primer has not yet addressed in detail: the role of constraints and the idea of the need. Charles felt that constraints were the key to the design process. In the film, Madame L'Amic asks Charles:

A: "Design depends largely on constraints."

Q: "What constraints?"

A: "The sum of all constraints. Here is one of the few effective keys to the design problem—the ability of the designer to recognize as many of the constraints as possible—his willingness and enthusiasm for working within these constraints. Constraints of price, of size, of strength, of balance, of surface, of time, and so forth. Each problem has its own peculiar list."[3]

If constraints were the shaping force of the design process, then the guiding force was something called the *need*. Asked in the film what audience design addressed itself to, Charles did not take the bait. Instead he responded: "Design addresses itself to the need." Later, L'Amic asks: "What do you feel is the primary condition for the practice of design and for its propagation?" Charles's answer: "The recognition of need."[4]

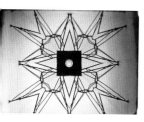  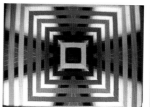 

Need is more primal than simply "I want" or "I would like." We all have our own definitions of things we need and, at any given moment, they are always a bit more serious than the things we want. Need in this sense does not necessarily mean market or audience—although that can be a part of it. In the Eames context, the need is the heart of the problem at hand—but quite possibly not as stated. Whether intangible or real, need tends to be an essential dimension of the problem that has inherent within it the possibility of design success (not simply box-office success), even if that success is ultimately subjective. (Q: "Can design be used for the creation of works reserved solely for pleasure?" A: "Who would say pleasure is not useful?"[5])

Charles was, of course, aware of market considerations, but was not driven by them. People sometimes say that Charles and Ray worked for Herman Miller, which isn't exactly true. They had a covenant with Herman Miller that was a relationship between two independent entities. Quite often someone from Herman Miller said, "Oh, I think there is a market for such and such a piece of furniture." And Charles would nod and say, "Sounds interesting"—and nothing would ever be heard about it again. On occasion the answer was "no" even after the job was taken. In the early 1950s, for example, Anheuser-Busch asked the Eames Office to redesign the Budweiser logo. The Eameses returned the project six months later, saying the logo was fine the way it was. (Many designers—just from a business standpoint—would have drooled at this opportunity.) Parke Meek mused that other designers put out a greater number of designs in a single season than the Eames Office put out in an entire decade.[6]

It was part of the DePree family's—D.J. and his sons Max and Hugh—wisdom to realize that it was in Herman Miller's long-term self-interest to be sure Charles and Ray worked in the way they felt comfortable.[7] Sometimes the company's suggestions made sense to the Eameses and offered the opportunity for realistic implementation. When Herman Miller pointed out the need for good, reliable, maintainable seating to handle the unique pressures of airport use, the Eames Office went into high gear. Dulles and O'Hare airports were the first clients of the Eames Tandem Sling Seating (sometimes called Eames Airport Seating). But even in that case, Charles and Ray had already made a film about

Left: four images from *Kaleidoscope Jazz Chair* show the real space of the front office morph into the prismatic space. Left, below: a text panel from *Design Q & A* (1972). This page: four images from *Kaleidoscope Jazz Chair*: two of Eiffel Tower bases, one of fiberglass chair colors, and the Solar Do-Nothing Machine

CONSTRAINTS

169

Dulles called *Expanding Airport*, and had clearly been thinking about the issues for some time. Time and again the Eameses' projects, even those on one level initiated by clients, turned out to have an antecedent in the Eames Office and in the Eameses' thinking. Each project Charles and Ray undertook had a fresh, meaningful dimension that connected to their own multidimensional world. Similarly, projects initiated by the Eames Office—though very often the dividing line is hard to find—usually had an internal history behind them. The Lounge Chair is a good example.

An evolution of "antlers" for the Aluminum Group

Most people who know the name Eames tend to associate it with furniture, and the chair most people think of is the Eames Lounge Chair and Ottoman, which first went into production in 1956. It has become a symbol of quality, comfort, luxury, and good design. For some architects, the Lounge is the chair they get for themselves when they land their first important commission: for other folks, it is simply their favorite chair ever. Like many of the other Eames pieces, the Lounge Chair is in the permanent collection of the Museum of Modern Art in New York.

In the case of the Lounge Chair, what was the need? Ray said Charles described it to her without words, by quietly interlocking his hands together: "Charles said [the concept] was this: one hand fit in the other," she recalled, putting her own hands together. "The simple shell and the padded upholstery that would just fit in it. We just thought the idea was interesting enough; to have, at that moment, a large, comfortable easy chair, was a good idea."[8] Don Albinson, who worked on the design, recalls Charles saying, "Why don't we make an updated version of the old English club chair?"[9] In other contexts, Charles said he wanted to give it "the warm receptive look of a well-used first baseman's mitt."[10] So one might say the need was a chair you can sink into. It may sound funny using the word need in this context; after all, it is often associated with raw desperation. But in the design sense, it does have, if not a desperate quality, a raw one. It is the most basic and essential challenge that underlies every design task. Though one might distill it to a single point like "a chair you can sink into," as the Eameses practiced it, the need was a constellation of ideas, concerns, and issues that embrace, reform, and engage the leading edge of the concept. The need in its fullest form exists for some time only in the mind of the designer (or designers) who constantly revisits, rephrases, reassesses, and resharpens that need as the process moves forward. For Charles and Ray, the process edged toward completion when the solution began to become a diagram of the problem. Ultimately, one can look at the finished Lounge Chair itself as the best way to understand the need as the Eameses defined it.

Constraints were also brought to bear on the Lounge Chair. Charles once said the problem with plastic is that you can do anything with it. If you have to design a chair out of a rock you are stuck with the rock—if you are going to be using the material in an honest way.[11] The constraints of the Lounge Chair are not immediately obvious. Unlike many of the other chairs, low cost was never an object during this design. According to Parke Meek, Charles feared Herman Miller might never make back the cost of the tooling.[12] The apparent lack of constraint in cost imposed an unusual burden, because no design choice could be justified as cutting down on expense. In one sense, an important constraint became a feeling of high quality—every material had to be excellent (indeed the chair still looks and feels best today in fine leather). The requirements of mass production—repeatability and reliability of the manufacturing processes—provided another group of constraints. It may be that this matter of figuring out the true constraints is why the Lounge Chair took almost two years to design. In a sense, though, the exploration had been going on for 15 years before the Lounge Chair started in earnest. Never forget, the L in LCW stands for Lounge.[*] And some other experimental lounge chairs done in 1945 and 1946 were also shown in the 1946 exhibition at MoMA. And as well, some of the Organic chairs from 1940 share a family resemblance to the finished Lounge Chair. So when Charles mentioned the English club chair in the context of creating a lounge chair, it meant that he saw that that one thread of the unfinished molded-plywood journey might very well come to its resolution in the padding and feel of the club chair (or the baseball mitt).

Usually the goal in the Eameses' design work was not an image but an ideal. Harlan Moore remembered a time working on the cushioning for the Lounge Chair. He and Don Albinson had made up five different chairs with different kinds of cushions. Moore said, "I was standing there beaming saying, 'Oh, he's gonna pick one of these.' And he looked at all of 'em, and he didn't say a word. He just looked. He sat in one. He looked at the others. And he walked away. And I turned to Don and I said, 'What does that mean?' And Don says, 'That means he doesn't really like any of them.'. . . I'm a production-minded guy, you know. 'We can't waste all this time building all these crazy things. . . . We've got to have a decision. Charlie, you tell us what you want and we'll build it.' So we did it again, and again, and again. And I don't know how many we built."[13] Because in the end they were working toward an ideal that existed only in Charles and Ray's minds.[†]

What initially seemed like inefficiency was again the hands-on process. It was seeing how many different versions of the lota one could make and learning from each one. It was putting an idea out there and then not viewing it from the standpoint of "Is this a replica of my statement" but, "does this bring me closer to an even better idea?" Moore's experience served in another way. Every interaction with key people at the office served to bring them into the fold of not just understanding Charles and Ray's process but something more

CONSTRAINTS

171

* The first one was given as a present to Billy Wilder, which may be the source of the erroneous story that the chair was designed for him. There were also some early prototypes, which he was given. The Chaise Lounge, however, was designed for Wilder.

basic: literally understanding them. Moore continued, "that's how you begin to understand Charlie's body language. Or he would say something like, 'It would . . . uh . . . It looks like an unmade bed.' Well, is that good or bad?"[14]

The design process for this chair was brutally long, but as always with a hidden side benefit of learning more about the mass-production challenges. Shortly after it started there was a long interlude, as Charles and Ray traveled to Germany where, among other things, Charles shot slides that became the film *Two Baroque Churches in Germany*. Herman Miller despaired that the Lounge Chair would never be completed, but when Charles and Ray returned, the process went into full swing.[15] Don Albinson remembers having to make 13 different versions of the arm for the final chair.[16] (On the Soft Pad sofa Sam Passalacqua would do dozens of different arm shapes.[17]) The five-legged base for the chair was prompted by Charles's feeling that with a four-legged base, there would be too much of a tendency for it to look like it was pointing in the "right" or "wrong" direction depending on whether it lined up with one of the legs. With a five-points-to-the-star base, there would be no points-of-the-compass effect.[18] Julian Blaustein remembers Charles asking him to come over and read some scripts while sitting in a test chair, probably the Lounge Chair. When Charles came to check on him, Blaustein was asleep—"that gave him his answer."[19]

Finally in 1956, the Lounge Chair was ready for manufacture—but that did not mean the process was over. Dick Donges remembers, speaking of furniture designs in general, "I think even when the piece of furniture was manufactured for the first time, Charles was never really finished with it. I mean, as far as the design goes. And I think he would always go back and look at it."[20] This was especially true of the Lounge Chair design. Parke Meek remembers fabricating the first ones for the Herman Miller showrooms.[21] The first 50 or so sold were basically put together by hand after the mechanical tooling made the forms. Some others, including the one at the Eames House, were covered in glove leather.* As the chair became successful, the design process continued to engage the constraints of mass production. Some adjustments Charles and Ray made at this stage included changing the way the cushions clipped on and the material for the buttons. As Charles said often, "The details are not the details. The details make the product."[22] As late as the mid-1970s, some

20 years later, Charles was discussing with Willi Fehlbaum of Vitra, one of the European licensees for the furniture, ways to improve the manufacture and design of the Eames Lounge Chair. As Donges observed, "a piece of furniture was really never done."[23] In fact, the office devoted a significant amount of effort to monitoring quality. Charles and Ray often visited showrooms and the factory floor to check on quality; they even banned the brown-leather version from the showrooms.

Two Eames Office projects bear the name Eames Lounge Chair: the iconic furniture and a film they made about it. Comparing them may give some insight into the roles of constraints and need. In 1956, Charles and Ray got word that Herman Miller had achieved a bit of a coup: the chair would be unveiled on national television on the highly rated *Home* show, hosted by Arlene Francis. In about a week. On the spur of the moment, Charles and Ray decided that what was needed was a little film about the chair and how it was made. They made a two-minute film of Dick Hoffman, who worked in the back of 901 for Herman Miller, assembling a Lounge Chair from scratch in sped-up motion to show how the chair was put together and packed. Then they asked their friend Elmer Bernstein to improvise a little score, which he did on the piano. Within a few days the film *Eames Lounge Chair* was completed and aired. Charles called this sort of thing "spontaneous production," and it perfectly illustrated his expression: "The best you can do between now and Tuesday is a kind of best you can do."[24]

From the standpoint of constraints, the counterpoint between the two Lounge Chair projects—one taking two years and the other five days—is wonderful. The office was supremely capable of moving in both ways—whichever way was appropriate. Because making a film was part of the fabric of the office, it was not a precious event. It was as much a part of the everyday rhythm as the nurturing of a long-term project such as the Lounge Chair itself.

And it was the nature of the office to subtly nurture and evolve projects. The film *Design Q&A* itself took a typically Eamesian journey of reiteration. Obviously, over years of work, a philosophy and process had developed, as well as a way of articulating that process. But an on-the-nose film on design was fraught with peril—it could easily be too

Eight stills from the Eames film Lounge Chair show the assembly of the chair. The film was made in just a few days.

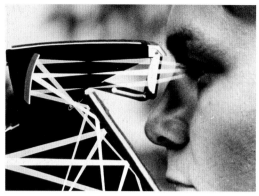

* The other three
designers were
Verner Panton
(Denmark), Joe
Colombo (Italy), and
Roger Tallon
(France).

† Land, founder of
Polaroid, was an
inventor, business-
man, and a real
showman whose
stockholders' meet-
ings were legendary
for their spectacle.

preachy, bland, pointless. In 1969, when the Eames Office was asked to participate in the show *What Is Design?* at the Louvre in Paris, a catalyst presented itself. Five designers were asked a group of questions by the show's curator, Madame L'Amic, and then invited to create a room that essentially answered those questions (the text answers themselves were included in the rooms as well). The Eames Office created a room called *Three Clients*, showing how the office had worked with Herman Miller, IBM, and the U.S. government. German designer Fritz Eichler created a room with virtually no text and simply huge industrial machines.*

In 1971, in preparation for the Norton Lectures, the Eameses used the questions and answers to create a multiscreen slide presentation. A young French woman, who was a friend of the Eames Office staff, was drafted to read the questions in Madame L'Amic's absence. This two-screen slide version was used in Lecture #5. Charles introduced it, acknowledging it as a work in progress, by using the future tense: "The pictures will be pictures from the office, pictures of work we're doing." (After it played, Charles deadpanned, "It is horrible having questionnaires read back to you."[25]) The next year, after more gentle iteration, it was honed a little further, including adding Laurindo Almeida's guitar, and then the film was completed. Though Charles was skeptical of questionnaires, he felt "presenting them straight in this way might give a little bit of insight."[26] In essence, it was the same "Q & A" that was in the exhibition. But each little step in the process had honed it more and more—the final print of any film tended to be a punctuation mark, though not always a period (as with the rough sketch *Powers of Ten*).

It is possible that the rarity within the oeuvre of such an overt design film may come across as false modesty. But examining Charles and Ray's film treatment of photography may give another insight into their caution. Many of the films are implicitly about photography because of the sheer beauty of the images, but there are only a few films explicitly on photography. Two films, in particular, stand out in this regard: *SX-70* and *Something about Photography*. They are very similar; both focus on the Polaroid SX-70 camera. Both

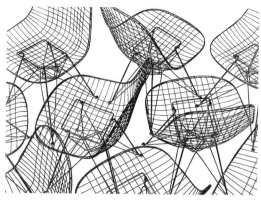

tell viewers something of how to take pictures.

Something about Photography is a good film; SX-70 is a great one. I think this is because the need in the Eamesian sense for SX-70 was a lot clearer. Named for a then-new Polaroid camera, SX-70 is a straightforward, visually lush explanation of how the camera works. It was made to introduce and explain the camera to Polaroid stockholders as part of a quintessential Edwin Land[†] stockholders' meeting. Charles and Ray were given one of the first five of the new cameras to play with, use, and ultimately film in order to show that the SX-70 could be used for more than mere snapshots. Something about Photography was suggested by Polaroid to be the first of an Eames film series to teach people what Charles knew about taking pictures. Though the film is good and fun and filled with sound advice, it lacks the transcendence present in SX-70. In that film, a crystal-clear technical explanation of the camera, accompanied by a luminous Elmer Bernstein score, becomes an ultimately moving meditation on the nature of photography before the viewer fully realizes it.

Charles's design diagram, also created for the What Is Design? show, helps under-score the difference. The ideas of the diagram resonate across many disciplines but focus on the design process. The diagram shows the overlap of concerns among three different entities: the area of interest to the designer, the area of interest to the client, and the area of interest to society as a whole. Charles and Ray's point was that, in the area where all three overlap, the designer can work with enthusiasm and conviction. In the case of Something about Photography, the need had not been as clearly defined, so the area of overlap was a bit murkier. It was there somewhere, but it was not as clear-cut as it was in SX-70.

It is important to note, in looking at the diagram, that the Eameses viewed the client not as an enemy but as a legitimate participant on the playing field. Oftentimes designers speak of the client as someone whom work is done in spite of. While Charles and Ray certainly spent time helping clients see the area of overlap, they always saw them as an essential and positive part of the equation. Recall Charles's letter to Ray in 1941 about

From left to right: a frame from SX-70; Llisa Demetrios in SX-70; Eames wire chairs; Charles and Ray working on aluminum group

possible films: "if it's given the right slant, it would have punch for the producer, public, and us."[27] All three were important from the beginning of their partnership. In a related vein, Charles once said that the most important thing an architect can do is teach clients how to spend their own money. Perhaps that is why "he got an enormous amount of respect from his clients,"[28] as Jeannine Oppewall said.

In addition to that, the office did something else. It nurtured ideas (sometimes quite a bit) on its own. The real benefit was related directly to the design diagram. By studying something on its own, the Eames Office could bring an idea to the point at which clients could see that an idea belonged in their area of the design diagram and, presumably, in the area of overlap as well. Exploration of new materials was an example of that. In addition to the molded-plywood and fiberglass chairs, the Eames Office worked extensively with two other materials: wire and aluminum.

The aluminum chairs are thought of by some as a kind of "second collection" after the various by-products of the 30-year flash. Aluminum is generally used as the support structure for a softer material that serves as the seat itself. Here again the office developed the understanding internally. Bob Staples learned to cast aluminum molds at 901 and carved the wooden "antlers"—the support—for the aluminum group chairs himself. As time went on, an idea was allowed to gel and then intersect again with the clients' needs. The Eames approach really encouraged universalizing from the specific. For example, the first Eames designs in aluminum were originally called the Indoor-Outdoor group (then later the Aluminum group). These were designed specifically for a house in Columbus, Indiana, that was being designed by Eero Saarinen and Alexander Girard for Irwin Miller. Girard and Saarinen were frustrated by "the lack of high-quality outdoor furniture on the market."[29] That was a genuine need that Charles and Ray could react to. Bob Staples echoed that. "I think his best product either came from his own head or from some legitimate client's request. Not just from Herman Miller, but when [the architects] wanted a new chair for the Chicago airport"[30] then it could be what Staples called "a love investigation"—a real passionate exploration of the idea. It is that feeling that the diagram captures.

The diagram is so simple that it defies too much interpretation. It is essential to the way Charles and Ray viewed their business and their interaction with clients. (Applied gently it resonates with their lives as well.) Consider the Airport Seating through this prism. In the area of interest to the designer, we will oversimplify and say that the Eames Office in 1962 was interested in airport seating and the *House of Science*. In the client area, Herman Miller was interested in the Action Office, which it was starting to develop, and in answering a request for airport seating. For the area concerning society as a whole, there was interest in *Lawrence of Arabia* and comfortable modern seating. Herman Miller had no connection to

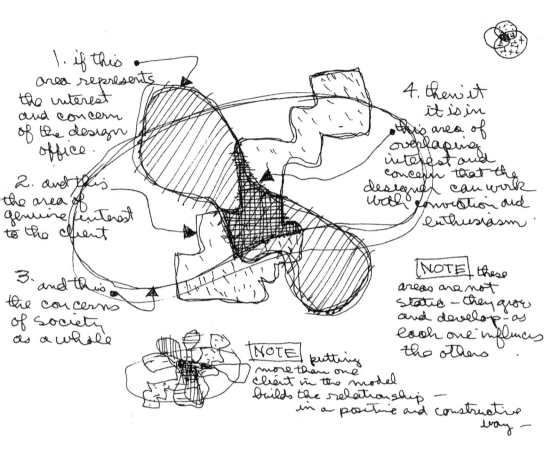

The final version of the 1969 design diagram showing the areas of overlapping interest and concern

*Lawrence of Arabia* (area 3) and only an oblique one to the *House of Science* (area 1). Action Office is successful, but with no direct interest to the Eames Office. The Airport Seating, however, is comfortable modern seating that addresses the challenges of the airport environment, designed so that seat pads can withstand tremendous and relentless use and be replaced easily and inexpensively. For this reason it remains a favorite of airport managers—the people on the frontlines—around the world.

The mutual self-interest of a furniture company and a design firm is fairly clear. The diagram's value becomes even greater when one finds the mathematics education of the general public within the right client's area of overlap.

# CHAPTER 15

# Mathematica

*Mathematica: A World of Numbers . . . and Beyond* is the direct ancestor of the modern museum exhibition. Undoubtedly, there had been other predecessors and precursors, but as an expression of the ability of an exhibition to be meaningful, fun, and interactive, *Mathematica* took exhibitions to a new level. It was also a spectacular statement of Charles and Ray's interest in science and its importance to them in almost the way of a New Covetable. In the history of the Eames Office, *Mathematica* was the first major endeavor to address primarily science as opposed to technology.

In late 1959 or early 1960, Tom Watson Jr. of IBM and the Eameses discussed the possible involvement of IBM with a new wing of the California Museum of Science and Industry. Charles and Ray proposed the idea of an exhibition that would convey some basic mathematical ideas with rich visual material and interactive exhibits. This idea ultimately became *Mathematica*; it was developed over the course of about a year and was installed at the museum in March 1961. *Mathematica* demonstrates beautifully the idea of natural overlap. If you analyze it through the design diagram, you see that mathematics was an area of genuine interest to the office—an evolving interest in education, but even more in the context of being as a contributor to the quality of life. Was it of genuine interest to the client? As Watson noted, IBM had a profound self-interest in an informed society, particularly in the area of mathematics.[1] Was it of interest to society? Well, there were two answers: in retrospect, the answer was clearly yes, given its success over the years; at the time, the answer was also yes, because society has always had a genuine interest in education.

Indeed, IBM's support of *Mathematica* was essentially the result of an ongoing conversation between Charles and Tom Watson about the importance of education and understanding. This was not simply a matter of "wouldn't it be nice for the company to support a good cause?" Charles tried to put it in a more hard-nosed context of genuine value for the company over the longer term—not just the notion that a well-educated public would in the long run be a healthier society and a better market for IBM's products, but also that a society with deeper understandings was a better one for IBM to operate within. As Charles said,

Image of infinity from the *Mathematica* exhibition

179

"I think I could even persuade them of the value of the toy films if I had to."[2]

While Charles and Ray had a high degree of respect for the government and its ability to solve some kinds of problems ("The proper public action can advance almost anything"[3]—notice the word proper), and indeed the government was an Eames client in many instances, they also felt strongly that corporations had a responsibility to think for the long term. This was not just a responsibility to society but also to themselves as businesses. Similarly, when it came to universities, education was too important to be left only to academia. Charles and Ray felt that education was not something business could slough off onto government but needed to help with. Charles had a lifelong wariness of attempts to compartmentalize so-called "good works." He and Ray wanted the qualities they valued to make their way into the fabric of everyday life, not to be thought of as a once-a-year visit to the opera. Business was part of everyday life, which is why the Eameses regarded business as a potentially important partner in this work.

In a way, it was like the difference between the model house program in St. Louis and the Case Study House Program: the latter had actual results, actual buildings. There was a practicality about the Eames approach that should not be lost under a gloss of aesthetic admiration. They did not view mass acceptance or economic success as the sole markers of success, but neither did they reject the informational value inherent in those kinds of success. Irving Berlin once said that "the mob is always right," meaning that the songs that became hits were the good ones. Charles and Ray did not agree, but neither were they so pleased with themselves that they thought the mob was always wrong. Appropriateness. With the Fiberglass Chair, commercial success was a measure of an effective solution to the design problem. For *Toccata for Toy Trains*, limited distribution (usually by the Eames Office and some business partners) and the ability to use it to effectively communicate during presentations inside and outside of the office were different but valid signs of success.

Similarly, *Mathematica* had its own set of high standards. In effect, the challenge the Eameses posed for themselves was to achieve the mass-communications goal of the Fiberglass Chair and the intimate level of ideas found in *Toccata for Toy Trains*—both in the same project. It "should be of interest to a bright student and not embarrass the most knowledgeable mathematician."[4] In particular, the Eameses were fascinated by an observation that they heard early on in their research: that although most people think of mathematics as being about numbers, the world of numbers actually represents only about 1 percent of the world of mathematics.[5] *Mathematica: A World of Numbers . . . and Beyond* made that idea extremely vivid to visitors.

As the first major exhibition of the new wing of the California Museum of Science and Industry, *Mathematica* had an ambitious target and the stakes were high. In science

Working on the mock-up of the *Mathematica* timeline. What started as a model of the content for internal purposes became a key feature of the exhibition. Inset: the same area of the final timeline

museums, the term permanent exhibition is usually more ironic than accurate in that such exhibitions usually turn over after several years. *Mathematica*'s initial run was open-ended, but no one really expected its 1961 opening to be so popular or its stay at the museum to last almost 37 years. In fact, *Mathematica* even outlasted the building itself, which was closed (and later demolished) in 1998. The exhibition has traveled since then, but it remains one of the longest-running, corporate-sponsored exhibitions in the United States. (Two copies of the exhibition, made by the Eames Office in the 1960s, have traveled as well.)

The education goals of *Mathematica*, though quite valuable, were not its only ends. Charles and Ray saw the ideas of it and other projects as the potential beginning of a new value system for society at large. Charles put the challenge of the exhibition this way: "One of the great secrets of science is the genuine fun and pleasure that scientists get out of it. One of the purposes of this exhibition is to let the cat out of the bag."[6] As happened often in Charles and Ray's work, the educational approach was not a matter of "a spoonful of sugar helping the medicine go down" but, instead, of finding the sugar within the medicine. If they could do that, they knew the rewards would be so much deeper for their guests, not to mention for themselves as hosts. If the pleasure came from the learning rather than the wrapper the designer put around it, then the possibility of real education existed. Putting the bar this

The case of
Mathematical
Models at the
beginning of the
original
*Mathematica*
installation in
Los Angeles

high meant, in the Eames process, that the design had to emerge from the science.

Speaking of their work in general, Charles once stated, "I think of our work as essentially that of tradesmen—the tools we use are often connected with the arts but we use them to solve problems which are assigned or we discern."[7] This understated observation is a profoundly accurate observation of their approach, and a walk through *Mathematica* will show why. Facing you at the entrance is a huge case, about 14 feet wide, 3 feet deep, 3 feet tall, which is raised up above the ground about 2 feet, with clear glass on all sides. It is labeled "Mathematical Models," but drawn in by the shapes inside, you may not notice that sign at all. Anticipating that possibility, there is a nice redundancy in the caption inside, above a series of beautiful forms, each expressing a mathematical concept. It says "Take a Good Look at These Models": the drunkards walk (an exhibit making a point about progressions in random behavior), a braid of rope, a beautiful brass piston that converts circular motion into linear motion, marvelous stone shapes and forms illustrating points in topology, and much more. Each item is visually compelling in its own way and connected as well to a field of mathematics.

After lingering there (and it is hard to say exactly why that first case is so compelling—beyond being good stuff—but it does; it isn't flashy, but it is quality), you may be drawn away by the sound of the nearby Probability Machine. Coming closer to it, you find yourself looking at a floor-to-ceiling, mostly transparent wall topped by a 200-peg grid about 6 feet by 5 feet. Through it, from the top center, in a slow but steady stream, drop 30,000 plastic balls toward a catchment at the bottom made of 17 vertical columns, each a few inches wide. The columns fill slowly after the balls randomly make their ping-pong way down through the grid. Some balls are bounced out to columns at the extreme ends. More end up in the center columns directly below the original opening. It takes about 15 minutes for the whole number to run through the cycle. Though the balls are poured in casually every time and ricochet into 30,000 different random paths, at the end, a bell curve always forms: most balls fill in the center columns and progressively fewer fall to the outside edges. The credibility of the experience for the visitor comes from the fact—as transparent as the plastic walls of the machine—that the result is so reliable (and so true) that the exhibition need count on nothing more than the laws of physics to get the same arrangement every time. It doesn't seem like a set-up. A quote from Sir Francis Galton, who discovered the bell curve, underscores the point: "The theory of probabilities is nothing more than good sense confirmed by calculation."

* One of the only criticisms of the show was the fact that this timeline had almost all men on it. In later years, Ray Eames resisted attempts to add women to the timeline, feeling that a patronizing tokenism was driving these requests. She felt, with the support of Ray Redheffer, that the standard of mathematical excellence for appearing in the timeline had been set without regard to gender.

There are other quotes hanging above you, hanging all over, and you notice one now: "A mathematician who is not also something of a poet is not likely to be a complete mathematician—Karl Weierstrauss."

Looking around, you can't miss the spectacular 40-foot-long, 8-foot-tall timeline of the Men of Modern Mathematics,* a textured swath running along the whole left-hand wall of the exhibition. As an object, it is immensely engaging—huge and elegant, with evident meaning, showing the history of mathematics from A.D. 1000 to the present. Arrayed with images and ideas, the timeline's conceptual heart is what looks like hundreds of rectangles containing portraits of the mathematicians, their achievements, and biographical background. Each rectangle is sized to reflect the length of the mathematician's life. The timeline rewards you at many levels. Standing back, you see clearly over time a genuine trend toward more and more meaningful work in mathematics, so much so that the information actually spills off toward the ceiling. Moving closer, you become transfixed by the stories, feeling like you could stand there reading forever.

The minimal-surfaces exhibit is in a box with four large, clear windows. Below these windows, you can push a button and a simple metal wire structure (a different shape on each side) is lowered into soapy water and pulled up. On the wire form, there is now a soap bubble covering it in the most efficient way possible. This is a kind of optimal geometry (for example, if the wire were in a ring, the soap would make a circular disk). One of the wire structures is a wire cube but, interestingly, the soap bubble does not simply fill in its sides.

Detail of the Minimal Surfaces exhibit; the Celestial Mechanics machine, teaching about the orbits of the planets; the original display area for the *Math Peep Shows* in 1961, viewed here by Lucia Eames and her children

Instead, the bubble coats the minimum amount of surface possible, so that each side looks pushed in, forming a miniature cube in the center. The panel explains a bit of the math of this unexpected result. You push the button again, and this time you admire the craftsmanship of the device itself—simple aluminum pulleys on line, which eventually trigger something to pop the bubble at its apex. If you know the Eames chairs, you see a possible relation to the form, but the bubble is popped and you follow the sounds of enthusiastic children over to an octagon-shaped piece with a Plexiglass dome on top of it. This is called the Celestial Mechanics exhibit. When you push a button here, a pinball is released into a white cone formed like a whirlpool immortalized in resin. The pinball circles slowly at first, but then faster and faster, relentlessly moving down into the vortex. Near the center of the cone, it circles almost insanely fast—very satisfying to people of all ages. The ball's transfixing and hypnotic motion mirrors the behavior of the planets: the sun's gravitational pull means that the outer planets orbit more slowly than those closer to the sun.

Behind this, opposite the timeline, another wall holds a raft of images and ideas: tornadoes, twin whelks, magic squares, R. Buckminster Fuller's domes, sand dollars, Koch snowflakes, chess moves, a Chinese geomancer's compass, and much more—some written, some photos, some graphics, some physical (there is even a real starfish mounted to the wall). There is the kid holding the mirror reflecting into infinity that you've seen in every geometry book. The exhibit is multidisciplinary without being cloying. Along with the images or objects on the wall, a cogent piece of text tells a story that pulls each item into the world of mathematics: the symmetry of the whelk, the math of the geodesic dome, the puzzle in every magic square.

Other exhibits call: a multiplication cube relates multiplying three numbers to the x-y-z axis. The first thing every visitor tries is 8 x 8 x 8, but then you realize the real rewards are in some of the smaller multiples. A Mobius strip has a moving train in the shape of an arrow that actually makes that one-sided journey. Fun-house mirrors teach a lesson about transposition. Projective Geometry creates an elaborate artifice whose details change depending on

which direction you look from (and, always, you notice the craftsmanship and details of the exhibit). Film loops showing five short films, each illustrating a specific mathematical idea, are called *IBM Math Peep Shows*.* Smiling as you read another set of sparkling graphics, you realize that you are enjoying a section on inside jokes for mathematicians.

It is impossible to summarize all of *Mathematica*. It is a truly interactive exhibition at all levels, and to go there with someone else is to lose that person for a while in the best possible way. Ray remarked that she and Charles saw no distinction between education and fun or play[8]—an attitude that is very clear in this show. Perhaps this is why this particular direction of their work became so important to them. They simply wanted to share this deep fun that they were capable of experiencing and producing. Elmer Bernstein commented tha he could feel, as time went on, their work becoming broader and broader in scope.

It is safe to say that there is not a museum science exhibition today that does not owe at least a little to *Mathematica*. What made the Eameses' exhibition different, better— perhaps stronger is the most appropriate word—than so many others? It always comes back to the process. The Eames Office in general, and Charles in particular, never delegated understanding. If something was in an exhibition, they had to understand it. The design flowed from the content.

The Eames Office ultimately would create over a dozen educational exhibitions on topics ranging from Copernicus and philosophical gardens to moveable feasts and Fibonacci, many of them focusing on classical physics. In the process, the office worked with many consultants over the years, brilliant people who contributed their insights to the education of the office and to the exhibitions and films themselves: I. Bernard Cohen (an expert on the science of Benjamin Franklin and Isaac Newton), Thomas Kuhn (who can be briefly seen in the Eames film *House of Science* reading his landmark work, *The Structure of Scientific Revolutions*), John Fessler, Owen Gingerich, and the Morrisons, among others.

Ray Redheffer, who was the chief consultant for *Mathematica*, commented that when he first started talking with Charles about the project, he (Redheffer) admitted that he

Left: detail of the image wall of *Mathematica*, teaching about the Fibonacci series. Right: Bob Staples and Jeannine Oppewall at work at the Eames Office, early 1970s

* The Eames Office considered doing the Banana Leaf parable as another peep show.

was not particularly known as a "popularizer" of mathematics. And Charles responded that that was not what they wanted. They wanted a good mathematician, more than a good lecturer.[9] It was the Eames Office's job to convey it, but to do that they needed content that was as unfiltered as possible. Without presuming they could replicate an entire lifetime of expertise, Charles and Ray needed to work as close to the content as possible to permit their instincts to engage as intensely as they could. They wanted people with that kind of wisdom helping them, but they needed to understand the material, too. Again, they stressed appropriateness. In the end, Redheffer felt that Charles could have made a real contribution to mathematics had he turned his attention that way. Redheffer cited, in particular, some thinking about topology and Venn diagrams.[10]

But there were times when even Redheffer questioned (at least at some level) the way the office worked. One day, with the deadline looming near, Redheffer came in to find 901 quiet and no one working on *Mathematica*. He started to get a bit irritated, and then finally he laughed it off when he saw that Charles had pressed everyone into making a flip-book birthday card for Eero Saarinen. (It showed an airplane towing a happy-birthday banner flying under the St. Louis Arch while under construction.[11])

However, Charles rejected the equation of "fun" with "easy" that permeates a certain kind of pop culture. In this sense, the Eameses were tough. In his lectures, Charles sometimes recalled seeing an educational Disney cartoon in which Donald Duck saw plants in the ground in the shape of cubes and said, "Ah, square roots." Though Donald always got a laugh, Charles's point was that the joke had nothing to do with the idea—and therefore the audience was far more likely to come away remembering the joke and not having any idea of what a square root was.[12]

In an interview together, friends and colleagues Philip and Phylis Morrison discussed the process of working on content with Charles. Philip commented that Charles "first had to grasp [an idea] himself to a degree, and then he could go ahead and make something of it. He worried at it, he teased at it, he struggled at it, he—." Here Phylis interjected, "He played with it." And Phil echoed that, continuing, "He played with it, he made jokes, he challenged it—all those things, until he was finally. . . . And then, it's a little thing which happened. And you [could see clearly that he got it]. You had made some point, and that would be it, and that would show up in the final thing in a good, helpful way. And not before that. And that's what almost nobody in that kind of business does." Morrison then went on to say that having been a consultant on many other projects in many kinds of offices, some of which had equally daunting artifacts around them, it was only at the Eames Office that the boss knew what they all meant.[13] Charles and Ray never delegated that understanding.

But part of grasping something was communicating it. Charles and Ray didn't lose

Clockwise from top left: detail of *Mathematica*; Charles explaining the multiplication cube to a young visitor; detail of the Multiplication cube; detail of the probability machine grid; early model of *Mathematica*; mock-up of probability machine at 901

Three short films
about math
and science:
*Newton's
Method* and
*Alpha,* two of the
films made with
Ray Redheffer;
image from
*Kepler's Laws*

track of that, either. Jehane Burns remembered a debate over the wording of some text for the René Descartes section of an exhibition. Burns translated the classic quote "Cogito ergo sum" as "I am thinking, therefore I exist," believing it was a more accurate verbiage, but Charles felt it was too mannered. He preferred "I think, therefore I am," which was the way most people recognized the idea. Burns said she "hated that, but I saw his point, and we did it his way."[14] Neither translation was entirely right or wrong, but the Eameses were following the balance they sought: "Innovate as a last resort."

Owen Gingerich, a consultant on a number of Eames Office projects, remembered returning to the office after a trip to Poland to start work on a process that would become

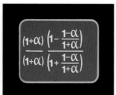

the *Copernicus* show. Obviously, one of its challenges was to convey the difference between the Copernican (sun-centered) system and the Ptolemaic (earth-centered) system. On the flight back from Europe, Charles worked out in his mind the mechanical gearing for a rugged device that would simultaneously show how both systems explained the orbits of the planets. When they landed, Charles had a sketch. This seemed strikingly brilliant to Gingerich at the time. He was curious, however, about whether or not it was in fact difficult, so he periodically assigned this task to his top graduate students in astrophysics at Harvard for extra credit. In 20 years, no student ever succeeded.[15]

*Mathematica's* five *IBM Math Peep Shows* became the seed of an idea for the Eameses. As Charles put it in the Norton Lectures, "A mathematician doesn't hire an essayist to do a paper on mathematics. And if he's going to do a film that is on the same subject, he himself essentially has to be the filmmaker."[16] Taking this concept to its logical conclusion, a few years later the Eames Office staff taught the rudiments of animation to Ray Redheffer. The results were three short films, each between one and four minutes long. These Eames–Redheffer films continue to be distributed today. Again, we see the Eames taking the learn-by-doing approach a little bit further: they not only let someone else learn by doing, but if they wanted to see what happened when they made the tools available, then they had to make them available.

Like so many of the Eameses' education-related projects, *Mathematica* offers the visitor direct experiences. The purpose is to give the visitor (or the viewer, in the case of the film) a credible, direct experience to add to their own internal library. Perhaps it was this quality that Philip Morrison was getting at when he referred to the beginning of Niels Bohr's first book on the philosophy of physics, "which says, 'Science has two goals. One is to order the world, and the second is to extend experience.' Understanding grows out of experience, experience and understanding have to go together." Morrison continued: "Now, all the people who write in the history of science and philosophy of science will say science's task is to order the world. That's not true! That's what philosophy's task is. And the difference is: science can extend experience, just as art can, but in a somewhat different way. And that extension is an essential part of the whole game. And if you forget that, you're in trouble. And in some way that's what Charles and Ray did: they were always extending experience by bringing things together, by looking at them closely and so on, in those ways. And they were not just trying to make abstract order out of things, nor were they trying to make just experience without exploration, without ordering. And, to some extent, they bridged the gap between science and art. And that's why, I think, their stuff is so splendid."[17]

Charles explored these ideas in his conclusions to the Norton Lectures: "I can never think that our pleasures, our rewards from the things around us, could ever possibly be diminished by additional knowledge about it. And the contrary is true. I heard Richard Feynman describe waves on the beach. He's a particle physicist and he was describing the waves in terms of insights that he felt and knew about the reactions of the particles within the wave, the relationship between the molecules of water, what happened as the light came into, the forces of gravity and the inertia [that] was taking place—and it was a description of a breaking wave because he had a tremendous appreciation of the exquisite beauty of what was going on, not only on the surface of the wave, but what was going on inside the surface of the wave and what had gone on beyond to make that wave possible. It was a delightful thing and no better pleasure or experience could I wish you all."[18]

The beauty of *Mathematica*, and indeed of all the Eames exhibitions, is the beauty of the molded-plywood sculpture they made on their early "Kazam! machine." When Charles and Ray made that sculpture, they saw no conflict between the goals of it being a beautiful sculpture and a technological test; similarly, with their exhibition, they saw no conflict between creating a beautiful spatial experience and a meaningful representation of the science. In fact, for the Eameses, both objectives had to be achieved in order for either to be. But how did they do that? A sculpture is one thing; a 3,000-square-foot exhibition is quite another. How did the design evolve to that point? In no small part it was because they created a way to maximize the number of iterations that each idea went through, polishing off the idiosyncrasies and getting to the heart of the matter. And one of the ways they did so was through another extraordinary development—the culture of 901 Washington Boulevard.

# CHAPTER 16

# 901 Culture

Who was the "we" of the Eames Office?

One answer is found along the top of every page in the *Eames Design* book, the massive catalogue raisonné that Ray was working on with the Neuharts at the time of her death. On each page there is a list of all the people who worked at the Eames Office at the time of the project. When you count the names you learn that there were 438 people who worked at the office from 1943 to 1979.[1] Then there are all the consultants and colleagues who worked on projects in the office—not staff members, but passionate participants nonetheless. And this probably misses some people who lasted only a few days.

They say that history is written by the victors, but it is often forgotten that oral history is delivered by the survivors. Every one of the people who worked at the Eames Office has his or her own history of it. Most have this history with them wherever they are; sadly, some have taken it to the grave. I have been fortunate enough to speak with many alums of the office as part of my Eames office oral histories. Some have shared their memories with other writers, have written their own stories, have talked to me on the phone or at the Eames House, or were recorded in a video guest book at a gathering after Ray's death.

Throughout this book I have used the terms "Charles Eames," "Ray Eames," "Office of Charles Eames," "Charles and Ray Eames," "Eames Office," and "Office of Charles and Ray Eames" more or less interchangeably. And there is a good reason for this. The many different projects and products of the Eames Office were all expressions of Charles and Ray's vision and a result of their design process. Without Charles and Ray's designs, vision, ideas, process, and intentions, these things rarely, if ever, would have existed and, undoubtedly (in the case of certain exhibits that might arguably have been commissioned from someone else), not in the form that they ultimately took. However, most of the time Charles and Ray did not do it alone. The work itself, the breadth of the work, and the ability to contribute to so many fields could not have occurred without the unique culture that Charles and Ray created at the Eames Office and the many talented people who worked there.

Phylis Morrison, who was at the office at the time of the Newton Cards and, later,

Eli Noyes, Ray and Charles, Deborah Sussman, Glenn Fleck, and Eliot Noyes posing against the wall of 901. Many photos were taken against this wall, including this one of some of the Eames Office staff members on July 4, 1965, in sunglasses designed by Deborah Sussman.

191

* One way of appreciating that continuity is that in 1943, when the office moved into 901, there were 24 people working there. Ten years later, 14 people worked there, but only 2 had been for 10 years: Charles and Ray. Of the 14 working in 1953, 4 (besides the two principals) were still among the 37 working in 1963. In 1973, of 34 people working, 2 had been there over 10 years, 2 over 20 (Mariea Poole and Parke Meek), and only 2 since the beginning. Also anchoring the office was this slowly changing core of key staffers, many of whom you have met in these pages.

after Charles's death, wrote the book *Powers of Ten* with her husband Philip and with Ray, offered this view: "I see many things in the work where there is something of Phil in it, where there is something of myself in it. But I see Jehane's phrase and I see Jeannine's idea and I see Dick Donges's hand and I see Alex's attention and that is what makes these things."[2]

How was that possible? How did these projects belong to both Charles and Ray as well as to the people they worked with? How was it that the Eameses' work spoke with one voice when so many different hands touched it?

One answer is inherent in the design process there: many different hands touched the work, but only two pairs touched all the work and decided where it began and when it ended.[*] Philip Morrison expressed it this way: "These are the pieces of the Office of Charles and Ray Eames. . . . It was a wonderful place. It's like the things you read about in Vasari's *The Lives of the Painters*. . . . In the midst of a very vigorous, thriving world, with all sorts of things going on, here's a group of people, a shifting group, but there's a center and a style and it all follows that. It isn't a very limiting one, but it does prevent individual departures that are very far from the main stem."[3]

But even this atelier analogy is only a partial answer, as it leaves out the framing of the problem, the guiding vision, and the exercise of a certain kind of control. It also implies something more static than the Eames Office, which was always feeling its way into new media and new areas. The common reference point at the office was the approach, centered on what was appropriate to the constraints and the need. Charles and Ray were not after a house style—Charles once said, "the extent to which you have a design style is the extent to which you have not solved the problem."[4] He often cited the example of the Hopi Kachina carver, for whom self-expression was the least important of goals. The best answer to how this common voice was achieved may lie in the culture of the office.

901 Washington Boulevard was where the work was done. Yet, more than a workshop, 901 was a kind of culture. If the office was trying in some senses to produce lotas, then 901 was the village. Jehane Burns said, "but it wasn't, in any recognizably ordinary sense of this century, a team effort either,"[5] suggesting it was far more guided and structured than it might have looked. Ralph Caplan remarked that when you walked in, everyone's brains were on the table.[6] It was also a culture in the sense that it had a history and artifacts that represented not solutions to be copied, but solutions that had worked.

Above all, the Eames Office was a place that had evolved to the point where Charles and Ray could maximize the number of iterations of an idea. Charles said, "If we have a slogan over the office it would be: Innovate as a last resort. More horrors are done in the name of innovation than any other."[7] Charles and Ray were adamant about this because they felt innovation for its own sake only severed the designer's connection to all of what works about the design in the status quo. (To choose an extreme example, you might say that cars always have four wheels, so you are going to be innovative and have 13.5 wheels. After all, no one has ever done that. Yes, you would have been innovative, but there is a common-sense history of why cars have four wheels that you are giving up for the sake of mere novelty.) The relentless iterations were what allowed the office to give innovations the test of time before they were even released.

Larry Bachmann, a writer friend of Charles's from the MGM days, said watching Charles at work was like watching one of those chess masters who can play a hundred chess matches at once, going around the office, a move here, a move there, and then returning eventually to play the next move of the first game without missing a beat.[8] Lucia Eames remembers her father telling her that he rested from one project by working on others.[9] Jeannine described it like this: "I mean, this is a man whose mind, when he sat down to concentrate on any one given thing, would always surprise you. Always."[10] Many former staffers talked about how intense that focus would be and then how it would be turned off as Charles moved on to the next project. Composer Buddy Collette put it this way: "It seems like he could handle many projects, or at least many thoughts. . . . I don't think I've ever worked with anybody that could stay with a project like that. . . . I don't even know whether he would take a phone call when we'd be talking like that."[11]

It was not always easy to work for Charles. Some people remembered him paying compliments to their work; others still feel they never got any. Perhaps Alex Funke was addressing that when he said, "You wanted it to be wonderful and you wanted him to say, 'Yes, that's nice: that's a good job.' He would always say, 'That's a good job; let's change this.' Because . . . one of the miraculous things about it is that just about anything you could do he could do better."[12] There may be exaggeration in it, but what it still really jibes with is Charles's deep understanding of so many different materials and techniques. He was able to make meaningful specific comments on the work being done. Once Charles and Ray understood the tools (for example, after their experiments with molded plywood), they then began expanding the universe of people involved with a clear sense of how to guide the process. Funke added, "and he was such a brilliant craftsman in addition to being a real, honest-to-God thinker. I think that was why he got the kind of dedication that he got from people."[13]

Understanding the importance of Ray's role was also part of working at the office, though it took some people a little longer to connect to Ray than to Charles. Jehane Burns remembered that it took her a full year or so to be able to communicate well with Ray.[14] Mike Ripps, who worked mostly as an editor at the office, remembered that Ray seemed a bit

standoffish at first and that he tended to go to Charles. But then, "Charles would remind me that Ray had the insight into these areas and that it was important to bring her into the process and not pass her by in any way. . . . I learned what an essential part Ray had [in] the rhythm and integrity of whatever the project was."[15] Ray inspired devotion as well, but in a different way. When Etsu Garfias finally chose to leave the Eames Office, she told her new employer that she would need two months before she could start. Her new employer was appalled that anyone would want that much time, but Etsu wanted the time to be sure that her replacement would take care of Ray properly. She cared that much.[16]

As in any new work environment, it takes a while to get to know the boss and the way he or she works. As Dick Donges said, "I think I, sort of, got the feel of Charles just by working [in the office]. When I first went to work there and started doing furniture, I certainly didn't have the feel for it that I had after seven or eight years. . . . And I think it's just body language, sort of feeling the way Charles would think about a piece of furniture."[17] Talking about taking pictures at the office, Parke Meek was a bit blunter: "You become a little Eames robot in a sense, I suppose, but it's fun."[18]

Staffer after staffer referred to getting a "feeling" or "sense" for what Charles and Ray wanted. It was a combination of the experience of working directly with Charles and Ray and of understanding the feeling of the office—one is tempted to say style, but it was more a process. With the office involved in so many different projects, as Don Albinson put it, "there wasn't any other way to do it,"[19] except by having a large staff. And Charles and Ray knew what they wanted from each staff member. Annette del Zoppo remembered Charles telling her not to trouble one gifted designer at the office with content. He felt that that was not the person's best contribution to the office.[20]

The dedication and devotion of the Eames Office staff was extraordinary. Working at the Eames Office was a form of exhaustion, exhilarating sometimes, but other times just plain tough. Jehane Burns observed wryly that there were times at two in the morning that one felt pleasure was being taken more seriously than one would have ever thought possi-

Two views of the
workshop space
at the back of
901

ble.[21] Harlan Moore, who worked on furniture in the early 1950s, said that "to be involved
with the Eameses wasn't a job, it was a commitment. And, when you [make] a commitment,
you're not only committing your [own] time but you're committing your spouse's time and
your family's time. And I can remember on a couple of occasions when Charlie was shooting
something and I'd be ready to go home from work at five o'clock at night and he'd say,
'Could you come back at seven? We'll want to do some filming.' I'd say, 'Sure.' And you
might be there till 11, you might be there till four in the morning because I don't believe
Charlie ever had a clock or a watch in those days."[22]

The work never ended. It took a certain kind of person to work there. An examination of the employment records revealed that there were a fair number of people (beyond
the 438) who started work at the Eames Office but didn't last more than a couple of days. It
just wasn't their kind of place. It was strange as well as tough. Ray recalled that people
would say, "I'll come work for you even if I just sweep the floors." And Charles would say,
"But do they really know how to sweep floors well? It's not easy."[23] They had a great nose
for people. Dick Donges said, with a good-natured laugh, that after 18 years "I never was
really hired. It was still a tryout at the end."[24] Fred Usher was hired for a never-ending three
weeks that lasted a few years.[25] This open-endedness was part of the way the office was
always inching forward and staying flexible.

But there was a kind of freedom at the office that was incredibly thrilling to the
right people. Jeannine Oppewall described it like this: "Charles could easily have been the
dictator and said, 'No, I want it this way.' But instead, his method was encouraging you to,
you know, 'Well, here's the rope. I hope you have enough of it to hang yourself with.' You
know. 'And by the way, come back and tell me if you think you're about to be hung.
Please.'"[26] The freedom to fail was key, because it meant real learning was possible in the
office. But like the circus, the constraints were there. There were some divisions and some
people tended to work in the woodshop or the camera department or any of a dozen or so
other areas. Other people were something akin to project managers for various productions.

And a given person might become responsible for the darkroom for a year or two and then move on to the animation area or a particular exhibit.

But the structure was oriented around Charles's sense of a person's gifts rather than formal positions. There was a phenomenon at the office that Alex Funke called "being close to the muzzle." It meant that you might happen to be walking by Charles's office when he was thinking about a project. Alex Funke was walking by the kitchen when "C. E. [Charles Eames] would say, 'Alex, we need you to do a timeline of technology [for] Franklin and Jefferson. Can you do that? We need it by tomorrow.' It was literally the case of being—Randy Walker, Mike Ripps—whoever happened to be in sight when the notion popped into his head."[27] But it also meant that staffers got to work on a number of different things at the office, which made the work exciting. Virtually everyone who worked there said they never had another job like it. It also kept alive the possibilities of unselfconscious design. Working on a technology timeline, Alex Funke was likely to focus on the content and keep the graphic choices within the overall voice.

It is amazing how often the people who worked there said their first task was something completely unrelated to their past experience. For Barbara Charles, it was an animation.[28] For Mike Ripps, it was laying out the artwork for a timeline in the *Franklin and Jefferson* proposal film.[29] For Deborah Sussman, it was making a mechanical drawing. She observed that "Charles was a genius at making you do that which you were least good at. He'd just know it. How did he know? I don't know how he knew."[30] It was, in some sense, a subtle test, to see the limits of people and a way of seeing if these were people who would fade in the stretch or really be able to come through in the flexible way the office required. It was also a small way to begin to internalize a bit of Charles and Ray's cross-disciplinary approach.

But maybe it was just a challenge, as Barbara Charles recalled: "You would be challenged to play darts with push pins. We would play killer Frisbee in the afternoon, everybody with a Frisbee, Charles and Ray too and throwing them at each other. Not only were you challenged to try to do your best work intellectually . . . but you also were challenged on any other score that he could think [of]."[31] Barbara Charles remembered a vivid moment early on: "He came by my desk. . . . I said, 'Charles, I'm really doing fine on all this art and history part of this show, but I really don't understand this scientific photography and I really think that you ought to get somebody else to work on the research for that part.' . . . And I remember Charles kind of leaned back and looked at me and said, 'Barbara, anybody in this day and age who can't read simple scientific literature is illiterate.' And I was totally taken aback. I had never been called illiterate in my life. And I just knuckled down and tried to keep working."[32]

Though Charles normally had an engaging, if intensely focused, approach, Jeannine Oppewall commented that, "those of us who were living there, in effect, saw that charm, but we saw a depth to it. It was a complicated, complex, interesting, deep personality. . . . He had a marvelous capacity for what he called 'St. Louis steelyard profanity.' I mean, it was poetic . . . in a way that was absolutely memorable." Charles could lose his temper—not often, but unforgettably, and "having witnessed that," Oppewall said, "I can honestly say no one else's temper tantrums will ever bother me."[33] Alex Funke witnessed such scenes and said that Charles's anger was "deep, controlled, and quick to pass. The worst thing was that you felt that you had let him down by letting him get so mad."[34] On the other hand, Fred Usher said, "I didn't know that aspect of Charles."[35] Jeannine continued: "I've also never met anyone who had the quality of righteous indignation that Charles was capable of having— and I think that's absolutely the right word. I mean, no one can ever intimidate me again in the way that Charles [was] capable of. In a good way, because he command[ed] respect. I mean, unless someone can . . . add a lot of charm into the mixture as well, why respect mere talent? You know, the man was not merely talented. He was also a complex and warm human being."[36]

The search for making things better could also be thrilling—or frustrating. As each project got close to its deadline, the pressure to complete it became intense. Percy Harris remembers this from the first years of the office: "That's why he took so long doing the photographs—because it had to be absolutely exactly what he wanted. . . . Everything had to be absolutely right according to their [Charles and Ray's] view. And so things took a long time. Ray would take a long time over things—I think that was part of the original relationship, that they both had that extraordinary desire for perfection and accuracy, and they would not ever hurry anything."[37] Julian Blaustein spoke of projects 30 years later in similar terms: "When I say that I'd get nervous, deep down I knew the job would be done because he said it would be. What was delaying the completion of the job was not a carelessness or an indifference, but a reaching out for that final idea, the cherry on the sundae that he knew was someplace out there."[38]

Twelve-hour days were routine at the Eames Office. Sooner or later, even the most dedicated and enthusiastic staff members would eventually leave for a variety of reasons. It could be family needs, time to start one's own office, a desire for more credit, a need to take a career in a different direction, or simply burnout. But all these reasons were simply another way of saying that an equation would have to exist inside a person's head to devote so much energy to the Eames Office, and at some point the balance of that equation was likely going to be affected by the fact that all of that person's effort was ultimately part of the Office of Charles and Ray Eames. The departures were often alarming to those left behind. Bob Staples observed that "the composition of the office would change when somebody like Don [Albinson] and Dale [Bauer] would leave. Or when Gordon [Ashby] left, or when I left, or when Glen [Fleck] left, or Deborah [Sussman] left, you thought, 'My God, it's gonna come absolutely to a screeching halt and tip over, and it's all gonna fall down.' Well, it never did. It never did. It just kept on going, you know. Maybe [it] changed direction a little bit, but it always moved, and that was because Charles was at the helm. Yeah, he'd lost his first mate, but, you know, we'll get through the storm. Seldom was it a convenient time for somebody to leave, because the work was never-ending."[39] Ray was also a critical element in this continuity.

Former staff member Anne Enkoji recalled working intensely on one area of the Copernicus exhibit for the longest time, and then being "completely blown away" by the completed exhibit. She had "no idea" how incredible it was going to be.[40] Barbara Charles spoke for herself and perhaps for others too when she said, "Each of us know[s] individually what we did. I know what I did and I'm sure Glen knows what he did and Bob knows what he did. When you are an employee, particularly in a place like that . . . the number of people is fluctuating from about 17 to 30 in the time I was there and it went much higher sometimes. You don't really know Charles's role, you don't know everything he is doing on the phone with people. . . . And it would be before presentations that we would see a lot of Charles because he would really be concerned about, finally, what are we going to show the client, finally, what is it looking like? But a lot of the intellectual germs of ideas were happening separate from us."[41] Charlie Kratka remembered how unfair he thought the credits were, so much so that it was part of why he left and set up his own shop. Then he began to understand some of what happened behind the scenes and "realized there is no other way to do it."[42]

Getting (and even understanding) credit is always a complicated issue in design. The people who worked at the Eames Office seem to recall very different feelings on this issue. Some would agree with Jeannine Oppewall's characteristically direct assessment: "I think most of the people who I respected who worked there had one quality in common, which was they were happy—I mean, this is going to sound a bit strange—happy to be exploited by a master, in the best sense of that word. I mean, everyone wants to give as much as he or she can and in return you get something as well. It was a trade-off. I certainly, speaking for myself, got an enormous amount out of it. I only hope that I was able to give to him something that he could use."[43]

Fred Usher took a somewhat different but related perspective: "A lot of us that worked there got a little bit upset because we didn't get any credit. It almost seemed like it was going to be a lifetime job and you were sort of anonymous. But on the other hand, because we worked there, we were famous among our peers. In other words, for no reason at all on the basis of merit. For years I was sort of a celebrity among my friends and everything because I worked at the Eames Office. So that is on one side, and on the other side you felt like your own creativity was getting submerged."[44]

Deborah Sussman also expressed ambivalence. Her time at the Eames Office was incredibly important to her (as were Charles and Ray personally), but she felt strongly that the issue of credit would be handled differently today. She wrote that when she showed Charles the credits for *Day of the Dead*, which she designed, he was a little stunned because he had never before included credits (besides his and Ray's) with the films.[45] Others felt a lot differently. Don Albinson, who had been a student of Charles's at Cranbrook, said he left after Charles wouldn't give him a co-credit he felt he should have for a piece of furniture.[46] Mercedes Matter, the wife of staff member Herbert Matter, told writer Joseph Giovannini that Charles took the idea from her of putting the skylight in the "womb room" of the Entenza House.[47]

On the one hand, one can argue point by point. For example, the womb room of the Entenza House has no skylight. So it is difficult to see precisely what credit Matter felt she was being denied. Additionally, Entenza had requested a room without distractions so he could concentrate in privacy (and, presumably, the architects listened to their client).[48] Or look at the common voice of the chairs before and after. Or one can look at the Eames films before *Day of the Dead* and see that most do have more than the two credits (such as "Washing by Don Albinson" in *Blacktop*). On a broader level, Elaine Jones, who saw many of Charles's lectures in her role as publicist for Herman Miller, said Charles never failed in his talks to acknowledge the work and role of the Eames Office staff and to credit Ray, especially when Ray was not there with him.[49]

Yet even when the details may be picked apart, the general frustration over insufficient credits may represent a more important emotional truth. At times it must have been frustrating, perhaps even overpowering, to be part of the Eames Office, particularly for people who had creative ambitions of their own—which many did. No matter how much work they did, they were still doing what Charles and Ray wanted. The essential problem may

\* Bertoia had been a teacher at Cranbrook. When the U.S. government began to consider interning East Coast Italian citizens in World War II, Eero asked Charles if he could find Bertoia work to keep him safe.[51]

† This ad appears in the *Eames Design* book, but with the line "Eames Process" inadvertently cropped out. The complete ad is on page 103.

have been less "the credits" than the fact that the ultimate credit would always have only two names in it. The *Mathematica* exhibition had a credit panel with the names of many people who worked on it. But the top credit was the office credit, which bore the Eames name—accurately, even if frustratingly to some. The staff members themselves were living that design diagram from 1969, working within the overlap of their own interests and those of Charles and Ray's. At some point, most of these people wanted to move into the other parts of their own region of the diagram. As Jeannine put it, "make my own mistakes" on her own projects.[50]

The most bitter departures occurred in or around 1946, when Harry Bertoia,[*] Herbert Matter, Gregory Ain, and Griswald Raetze all left at the same time. All had come to the office with careers already under way. They said later that they felt they were promised that the Eames Office (called the Plyformed Wood Company during part of that time) would be a collective endeavor.[52] If true, there were many aspects of the company that were "uncollective" before the four even started as employees. First, the work was based on the process developed in Charles and Ray's Neutra apartment. In fact, in 1944, an ad designed by Herbert Matter and published in *Arts and Architecture* promoted plywood molded with the "Eames Process."[†][53] This would suggest a hierarchy of some kind. In addition, Percy Harris (along with Ain and Raetze, one of the first employees) remembered, "Everyone worked, and [Charles] kept control of the whole thing . . . because even though Herbert Matter did a lot of the photography at the office, anything special Charles would do himself."[54] Frances Bishop had a similar impression: "How would they know it was done? Because Charlie knew just how he wanted it and when it reached that point, then it was done. . . . Everything had to be just right. If it wasn't, it had to be done over again. Both of 'em, they were perfectionists."[55]

Charles had another quality, which Parke Meek described as "a knack [for] making people think they thought of what he wanted them to think of. [A] very important thing if you want to get something done is [to] make the other person think they thought of doing it.

And it works."[56] This was the case not only with staffers but with clients as well. Jeannine remarked that she "was always amazed to see how he was able to get what he wanted and to persuade [the clients] at the same time that he was giving them exactly what they needed and they wanted."[57] Harlan Moore may have been speaking of a similar quality when he said that "Charlie always had a way of discussing something and we would get off the subject; we'd start wandering off, and he had a way of bringing us all back together again."[58] While these qualities seem to complicate the issues of perception, they were keys to how the office worked. Charles and Ray thereby achieved far more than if they had tried to do everything themselves, yet they were still able to exert much of the same control.

 Charles and Ray had a way of trying out their ideas by talking things over with people. Their friend, Amanda Dunne, said, "that's how [they] worked with everybody."[59] They were secure enough that they were not focused on being sure the other person knew that they already knew (think of the story of the fiberglass chair at John Wills's shop, for example). But this too could lead to misunderstanding. After Ray's death, Lucia Eames was contacted by at least four different people who believed Ray had told them what she wanted on her tombstone.[‡ 60] They thought Ray had confided in them but on reflection they realized that they could well have misunderstood a casual seeking of outside opinion. Charles and Ray felt that in order to get a genuine critique of an idea from someone, they had to avoid revealing too much of their own views. As Julian Blaustein said, "When [Charles] asked you for your opinion, he wanted it. And when he didn't ask, he didn't need it."[61] Alexander Knox had a related but (he felt) embarrassing experience while discussing color with Charles and Ray at the Eames House: "Both of them were talking about taupes and browns and grays. I forgot what it was for. I thought it would be nicer to bring greens inside and for a little while, I think they agreed. I think they tried it out with some watercolor on large sheets or something and it looked horrid because it didn't look real. That is, you couldn't, you really couldn't bring a green inside unless it was a real green—a real object like a plant."[62]

 The filmmaking process suggests another way to consider the design process at the

Vignettes at 901: Charles with consultant I. Bernard Cohen; Ray adjusting a projector; a shoot in the new building; Yu Yoshioka working on the school seating; Sam Passalacqua caring for the aquariums; Jeannine Oppewall as the mother of the future

‡ In the end, Lucia decided to follow the instructions in Ray's will.

Eames Office. In many cases, that process is a lot like film directing—for example, *Dr. Strangelove* is as pure an expression of Stanley Kubrick's vision as *The Seventh Samurai* is of Akira Kurosawa's, and yet neither director could have made the films without a talented cast and crew. All those people made incredible contributions and yet the work has a single voice. The Eames Office had a bit of that feeling as well. At times it was literally directorial. Deborah Sussman remembered arriving in Mexico City to work on the film that became *Day of the Dead*. When she arrived at the hotel, she found that Charles had left "a note there which said, 'Go to the sugar market . . . and shoot the sugar sculptures and the people buying and selling them with the light coming through the canvas behind the sellers,'" as well as another note about how to expose the film properly. The guiding vision of the completed film was both subtle and pervasive.[63]

The staff members mentioned in the text of this book, cited in the acknowledgments, and others—such as Glen Fleck, Dolores Cantata, Dale Bauer, Peter Pearce, and John Neuhart—gave their hearts and souls to the work, as well as some of their best years. Their efforts are in the work of the Eames Office: in the three versions of *Powers of Ten*; in the three times that Mike Ripps shot the timeline for the *Franklin and Jefferson* proposal; in the life-size papier-mâché skeleton Deborah brought from that same trip for filming; in the images of the fish tanks and the 2,200 stills in *Glimpses of the USA*; in the 22 screens at the New York World's Fair; in over 100 films, dozens of exhibitions, and hundreds of different furniture designs. Barbara Charles commented, "I have always thought of the Eames Office as better than my college education. I was at the Eames Office for four years and I was at Oberlin for four years and they clearly both challenged me. But the Eames Office was the best education you could get."[64] Parke Meek put it another way: "Every day it was something different. You never knew what you were going to do."[65]

In the film *Design Q&A*, Charles answers two questions that directly address these various issues:

Q: "Is design the creation of an individual?"

A: "No, because to be realistic one must always admit the influence of those who have gone before."

Q: "Is design the creation of a group?"

A: "Very often."[66]

This last comment is given with a still shot of Charles at the camera surrounded by a number of Eames Office staff members. In the space between these two subtly asymmetrical answers may lie a sense of Charles and Ray's feelings on the issue.

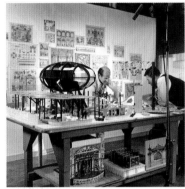

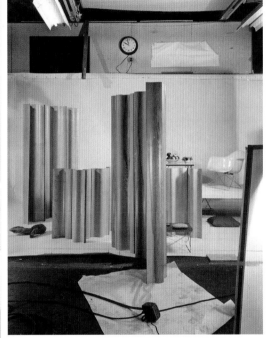

Clockwise from top left: Jehane Burns Kuhn by an exhibition mock-up; Richard Donges at work in the shop area; photographing screens at 901 (the writing on the bottom indicates how the picture should be cropped); work on the Aluminum Group; a model of the New York World's Fair

# CHAPTER 17

# Modeling

One of the keys to the Eameses' work was the use of physical and intellectual models as an integral part of the design and thinking processes. This was true at a number of levels. In a sense, one can make the case that the hands-on process—the endless iterations of an idea until the idiosyncrasies had been honed away—was nothing more or less than a series of models of the ultimate concept. The large and talented staff at the Eames Office was critical to the process of smoothing away the excess to get to the heart of things. What Charles said of Eero Saarinen's work could also be applied to his and Ray's: "There was a continuity that developed . . . where in a sense the architecture became the model of the problem."[1] The hands-on process thereby offered a way to be constantly modeling things to find out the essence of the idea within them.

It was also true in the more traditional sense of the word *model*. As the Eames Office began to make films, the lushness and richness of the models they created put them in a league by themselves. The office had already made beautiful models of the Case Study Houses, the *Good Design* exhibition, and other spaces. *Parade* and *Toccata for Toy Trains* were only the early phases of the wherewithal to shoot elaborate sets both in stills and films. In this sense, the Eameses modeled virtually every exhibition and physical project they explored. Charles and Ray took quite seriously the lessons learned from Eliel and Eero Saarinen of trying something out over and over. They also created models for multimedia presentations to try out the ideas and figure out the best presentation.

In the case of *Glimpses of the USA* (1959) at the American Pavilion in Moscow, building a miniature theater and trying different configurations of screens led Charles and Ray to the conclusion that five screens were not enough, while nine screens were too many. Seven screens gave viewers just enough information to process viscerally, without disorienting or alienating them. The Eames Office actually set up projectors for the miniature screens to try out the experience. Modeling was part of the whole learn-by-doing spirit of the office.

*The Sample Lesson for a Hypothetical Course* was a model for a whole idea of teaching, where a rich broth of images and ideas would become a shared experience for

Charles and Ray working with a model of *Mathematica* (circa 1960)

205

students and allow teachers and students to draw from the same incredibly rich page. Even the way projects were explored was a form of modeling. The massive mock-up of the timeline for *Mathematica* was a truly interactive model that allowed the staff to put ideas up or take them down. It actually started as a way to track the content, then became part of the show.[2] Charles could try an idea on for size. He could put up the name of an important mathematician—a candidate for the History Wall. It might only be a name and an image, but if it made sense it stood for the whole idea of the person; then the whole apparatus of further content creation would kick into gear and Ray Redheffer would craft one of his rich and nuanced biographies for that person. Or someone else at the office—Deborah Sussman, for instance—might be asked to weed out some of the excess from the timeline. Charles would then be able to peruse it at night and know exactly where the timeline stood at that moment, because he knew where the model stood at the moment—the model and the timeline were the same. Eventually, both grew in breadth and depth until it was time to make the actual timeline. The Eames Office never underestimated the value of a low-tech model.

In the Norton Lectures, Charles said, "the thing about models, about using them, is that a model doesn't have to be a total theory of a field. It doesn't have to be a golden thread that sort of leads you through a labyrinth. A model, a true model, in the experimental and feeling-your-way sense, can just be a kind of a tentative walk through the experience by which you can then retreat, consolidate yourself, re-group, and . . . take a try again."[3] In this sense, modeling became the intellectual equivalent of the many prototypes of the Eames chairs.

As this idea developed further, it took on a number of interesting qualities. First, it became important to teach this idea of modeling as an idea in and of itself. In other words, Charles and Ray sought to share with others the value they saw in this way of thinking, as they did in the IBM Pavilion *Think* presentation at the New York World's Fair (1964–65). The IBM Pavilion was another collaboration with Eero Saarinen, begun before his death. The former Saarinen Office, by then called Dinkeloo and Roche, was the architect; the Eames Office did the exhibitions. Of course, the Pavilion was itself modeled twice by the Eames Office in two short film presentations. Content and architecture were well integrated from the start. Ideas and panels from *Mathematica* were used for a scholar's walk. There was also a typewriter bar that allowed visitors to try out all of the new IBM typewriters. With all its parts taken together, the World's Fair was the Eames Office's largest project to date. Mechanical puppet shows discussed ideas about computers in a comical and very crowd-pleasing way, yet the takeaway ideas were meaningful; for example, the message of one was "a computer is simple (in a complex sort of way)."[4]

But the key message was contained in the *Think* presentation, shown on 14 big

screens and 8 small ones in the Ovoid Theater. It was the capstone to a completely immersive experience. Bleachers filled with people at the ground floor and then moved in their entirety into the theater (thus the name of the Eames film condensing the *Think* presentation, *View from the People Wall*). There an emcee made a presentation that indicated that the theater itself was an information machine, allowing visitors to look at many things from different perspectives. In it they tried to show that the process used by scientists or city planners to solve complicated problems was "essentially the same method we all use daily." One example shows a football coach using a chalkboard to explain a play to his team: "The diagram is as much a test model of a football play as the wind tunnel miniature is a test model of the X-15. . . .The flight characteristics [can be reduced to equations that] are mathematical models and they can be manipulated with even more flexibility than the miniature."[5] The ability to manipulate things more easily is obviously a valuable asset of any model.

Another example used in the multiscreen presentation was the planning of a dinner party. This dinner-party sequence worked on many different levels: as a useful idea, as a cinematic tour de force, and as comic entertainment. People who saw the presentation at the World's Fair remember it quite vividly, and Paul Goldberger of the *New Yorker* observed that it has held up quite well.[6]

STEP 1: STATING THE PROBLEM. The hostess decides to put on a dinner party for her husband's boss.

STEP 2: COLLECTING INFORMATION. The hostess considers whom she might invite to the party.

STEP 3: ABSTRACTING THE INFORMATION. She makes a list of who might come.

STEP 4: BUILDING THE MODEL. She sketches the table and tries out various seating arrangements.

STEP 5: MANIPULATING THE MODEL. She continues to try different positions around the table, zeroing in on her final result.[7]

Audrey Wilder appears as Cleo Fenwick, a vamp who is briefly considered as a guest—but "the wives won't like that." Ray used to joke that she and Charles gave John Houseman his first break as an actor (he appeared as the boss, Mr. Townsend, long before he won an Oscar for *The Paper Chase*). As the hostess muses on the alternative seating arrangements, the different potential positions are shown on the multiple screens in a kind

From left to right: Model of the 22-screen theater at the IBM pavilion; and two ideas presented on it during *Think*: arrows and the concept of "two-ness"

MODELING

207

of peremptory stop motion. On one screen, as Dr. Schlossberg is rejected, he is eliminated as if by a Scarsdale Blofeld. On another screen, a huge centerpiece is used to separate two feuding guests "after that incident last week." In the end, the dinner party is a success: and the steps the hostess uses are no different than the ones used in large-scale problem-solving.

In addition to being entertaining, the dinner-party sequence had a staggering coordination of imagery, suggesting another aspect of the idea under construction. A huge amount of footage was shot for this and the other parts of *Think*. Underlying it all was an essential sweetness and respect for the effort of being a good host. Surely Charles and Ray understood this both personally and professionally, as children observing their elders and as adults welcoming people into their world. They had a genuine respect for the effort and value of what was generally thought of as a "woman's role" at the time. If *Think* was a very explicit take on modeling, then the film *Aquarium* probably represents the best use of film both for presentation of a project and as the model.

One of the most important unexecuted projects at the Eames Office was a proposed National Fisheries Center and Aquarium for Washington, D.C. Even in the way the aquarium was unfinished and the office dealt with what was a significant disappointment, the project represented everything positive about the Eames design approach. As a case study, it showed that the Eames design process was not some rarified approach, but an intensely pragmatic one that allowed good answers to emerge. This project took the idea of modeling to a new level, in the sense that the finished film conveyed a powerful feeling of the intellectual and visceral experience of the proposed aquarium.

The *Aquarium* journey began when the Dinkeloo and Roche firm included Charles and Ray in the discussions of a national aquarium to be built in Washington, D.C. The respect between Kevin Roche and the Eameses allowed Charles and Ray to be involved, as exhibition designers, in conversations that would influence the actual building, though the Eames Office's formal charge was content design. The office's first step was typical. What was the best way to find out about how to take care of an aquarium? Set one up in the office. The Eames Office never delegated understanding; design had to reflect content. And though there were times when this seemed inefficient, it was not in the deepest sense, because that knowledge was then inside the office, part of the culture, not outside.

The aquarium project was the ultimate triumph of this approach. Long after the project had been closed, the Eameses maintained the aquariums at 901—take your pleasure seriously. The office aquariums contained mostly cold-water creatures from local waters, allowing for the easy supply of specimens. But these were not just a couple of fish tanks; they were 250- to 1,000-gallon aquariums with elaborate filtration systems. It was not a

matter of a few neon tetras; they were, in essence, a model of a large aquarium, allowing the office to stumble through all sorts of issues of feeding, collecting, replenishing, filtering, and a million other smaller pleasures on a modest scale. It also allowed Charles and the other staffers to photograph and film the creatures. From these experiences developed exhibit ideas like the *Push Again* machine. It would give you information on, say, anemones. One audio fact. Then, if you were intrigued, you would push again and there would be another fact that followed, and then another, and so on—an interesting kind of interactivity.

As the project developed, it became clear that an important phase would be the approval of funding by the U.S. Congress. This evolved quite naturally into a feeling that a film would be the best way of presenting the aquarium for several reasons. First, film could tell the story concisely in under 10 minutes—the length of a reel (a typical Eames constraint). Second, "Charles always maintained that when the lights went down and the film went on, the congressmen were not about to stand up and say, 'Oh, excuse me! I disagree with—' You had the whole floor. . . . You are willingly agreeing to submit yourself to that form. And you get less . . . argument in return," remembered Jeannine Oppewall, who worked on a number of film-models. "There's a psychology there that really works . . . [that] really understands the human animal, in a way."[8]

Another reason for the use of film (there was also an accompanying book) was a little more subtle. Charles and Ray believed the more complete the aquarium looked, the more likely Congress would be to approve funding for it. Therefore, the sense of the film was immediate, as if the aquarium existed, yet the film was couched in terms of a proposal—one that swept viewers away. I. Bernard Cohen, who consulted on other projects for the office, described some measure of the film's effectiveness: "Once when I was going with my wife out to Washington and we wanted to have something to do, so we said, 'Well, let's go see Charles's aquarium.' We tried and tried and tried—we couldn't find the damn thing. And then we both suddenly realized at about the same time that there had never been that aquarium. But it [had seemed] so real."[9]

A last reason was the most important. What made the aquarium unique was not the creatures but the way they would be perceived. As Charles said, "we made the central

Four vignettes of the production of the dinner party scene for the *Think* presentation: Charles directing Audrey Wilder; Ray fine-tuning the set; John Houseman as the boss; the successful party

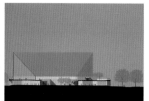

theme of the aquarium not a curiosity about the capriciousness of nature in building these fishes, but some insight as to what the laws were that made it happen that way."[10] Using film in the Eamesian way allowed the Eames Office to create a psychological environment from broad strokes of that idea, knowing full well that the actual aquarium would require a million little details (as *Mathematica* had) to achieve it.

*Aquarium*, narrated by Charles in an extremely understated manner, begins with an observation about a "fast-growing interest in the oceans."[11] The images follow in a way that amplify and anchor the narration. Early on there is an animation of the proposal and of the way it relates to Washington, D.C. Quick but visually persuasive, the film serves the important function of making the whole proposition specific. In fact, there is an almost free-association quality to the film in the sense that the constantly changing images remain anchored to the narrative. Stylistically, the nature of the imagery constantly changes as well: at the mention of a display of the Everglades, a camera moving along the model might cut directly to a shot of a snake moving in the water and then to a still photograph of the back of an alligator, artfully framed to accentuate the texture. There is no attempt to hide the artifice, which, in a way, makes it easier to accept the ideas. There is a great deal of inventiveness in the way archival material is presented, and stock shots punctuate nicely, offering production value and averting claustrophobia. At other times, flipping through old prints makes a point about a library.

Above all, the clarity of the images and the reason for their selection is never in doubt for the viewer. There are no words illustrated by obscure images, but often ideas are illustrated by abstract images. Abstraction without obscurity gives viewers the feeling that there really was an aquarium to film; otherwise, how could the film have been made? On another level the whole experience feels like a series of accelerated, simultaneous visual footnotes to an extremely exciting essay on a proposed aquarium. It feels profoundly thought out. There is a kind of persuasive stylization to the physical model, which was no accident. The project was the first one at the office for Barbara Charles, and she remembered learning "great lessons in the color gray. This sounds silly, but Charles was quite adamant when we made that model for the Aquarium that he didn't want us to pick any

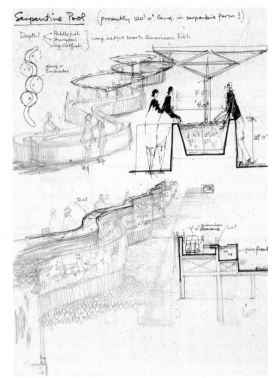

colors or any definite finishes . . . that he would have to live with in the long run. But yet we had to pick colors that would give the shape of the architecture, so at times we would do one wall a different gray than the other wall. . . . We were using color for shape and definition but not as color. It was really an interesting lesson . . . in that sense I got to know Ray initially, in that I would work with her on picking colors out of the fabulous paper drawers."[12]

In *Aquarium*, fascinating topics zip by as Charles weaves a narrative of an ideal but plausible facility. In a letter to Ray in early 1941, Charles wrote that it was important for them to talk practically about their future together: "We must see each other soon: this business of becoming 'dream people' in each other's minds is no good."[13] And in a sense that is exactly what happens when viewers watch *Aquarium* (and other Eames film models)—you want to see the area alluded to about locomotion (illustrating "the universal problem of how to get around").[14] In their own minds, viewer-visitors begin to make their own assumptions about the balance of living creatures, graphics, and media that will convey these ideas in the physical building, each one putting the pieces together in a slightly different way, making a "dream aquarium" instead. Evocative images are combined with evocative phrases: "the aquarium will show the microworld in a way that is meaningful."[15] The Eames films *Polyorchis Haplus* and *Decorator Crab* seem almost to be proposed clips for this area.

The proposed aquarium was an experiential cocktail of creatures, multimedia, and other content intended to reward the visitor by placing the flora and fauna in a richer context, whether evolutionarily, behaviorally, or even culturally. It is these contexts and the rich interchange between them that are largely missing from most public aquariums even to this day. *Aquarium* is a collective hallucination; as a viewer, you tend to like the one you put together in your own head because, after all, it is your own construction with your own per-

From left to right: six different images of the aquarium model in its broadest sense. Above: sketch of a proposed exhibition site

sonal connective tissue added to the kit-of-parts the film has given you. Paul Schrader commented that, unlike the worlds in Fellini films, which can only be fully inhabited by Fellini himself, Charles and Ray's aquarium is open to all.[16] That idea is related to a point Don Albinson made about Charles's wariness of sketching a chair out (as opposed to sketching with gestures and words): "You've eliminated a lot of possibilities by just making a couple of lines. He was shrewd enough to know that."[17] *Aquarium* is a kind of virtual reality for the viewer, a sort of image-making wherein the circuit is completed in the viewer's mind.

The aquarium project was ultimately approved by Congress, but the newly elected president, Richard Nixon, cut the funding. This was unquestionably disappointing. There was a real feeling around the office that it would have been a great project. But even in defeat, there was a feeling that the film served yet another purpose. Alex Funke recalled Charles saying it this way: "By doing this film we have tried to honestly present what *could* be. And, by doing that, we have set a standard that we hope whoever actually does the work will not fall below."[18] In other words, the film was a marker and model of a hypothetical aquarium. It created a feeling of "we took the idea this far, and when the baton is picked up again, the next designer can start from here."

In a sense, these models were the inverse of the typical honing process at the Eames Office. Where the design process was narrowing, narrowing, narrowing, the thought process the Eameses inspired in the viewer was spectacularly open. This aspect of modeling became increasingly important to the Eameses, and they developed the notion still further. Charles and Ray began to feel that, for citizens to be able to deal with the blizzard of information available today, they needed to develop models that addressed that information. A film like *Metropolitan Overview* can actually be seen as a model of a proposed system of how to present information.

The proposed aquarium would have given one set of tools for dealing with such information, particularly environmental issues: "each day brings news of new problems of things that need help and things too late to change."[19] The presentation *Think* provided a different set of tools. The common ground was the way the change in the quantity of information was becoming a quality of the information itself. Charles and Ray were among the early folks who identified and tried to grapple with the extraordinary rate of change and information that our society was just beginning to experience.

Charles put it this way in 1970: "We're working on an aquarium in the office, so naturally we have an aquarium. We have a lot of . . . marvelous little animals, mostly invertebrates and some fishes, that sort of cluster together, have high territoriality in the way they act and behave. And if those little animals feel too much of a stream, too much of a current flow, they're very uneasy. These animals are sort of geared to the status quo. . . . On the

A mock-up of the Revell Toy House (1959), designed by the Eames Office but never produced in quantity

other hand, there are the pelagic animals. And if that current stops, they're in trouble. They're dependent on change. Their whole idea of security is essentially when the current is flowing by them. That gives them the oxygen upon [which] they live, and that sort of frees them from other predators, it brings them closer to food. They're very secure in change. And I have a feeling in a way that we as a society and as a group are gradually becoming pelagic in our feeling. That if anyone is going to really feel secure, he must have not an insistence on the status quo, but he must feel secure . . . in change. I think that we've all now experienced this in a sense, where if you recognize a change and it's sort of like being in a place that you've never been before, and suddenly things become oriented, and a value appears that you'd never known before. And it seems to me that this is an aesthetic feeling."[20]

This quote encapsulates so much of the Eameses' approach, from the learn-by-doing process ("so naturally we have an aquarium") to the idea of being secure in change. The sheer flexibility of the Eames Office showed that these things were a part of its every fiber. But even deeper than that was the way the office embraced and pursued what Elmer Bernstein called Charles's "sort of unending agenda"[21] by applying a rigorous process. In the last decade of Charles and Ray's work, the need for these sorts of models was an explicit concern of the office.

# CHAPTER 18

# "If the Office Were an Island"

Charles and Ray Eames were a design team. The things created at the Eames Office were expressions of their joint vision and passion. In speaking of the work since the time they joined forces, just about invariably when I say "Charles," that includes Ray, and when I say "Ray," that includes Charles. Further, in the Eames work, everything does connect. If Ray is not behind the camera, does that mean her sensibility is absent as Charles takes the picture? If Charles is out of the room when Ray arranges the flowers he asked her to bring, is he somehow less involved? I would answer "no" to such questions. But how does that work? Who did what? Why do I say "just about invariably"?

The last question is the easiest to answer. I hedge because the very thought of speaking authoritatively about the workings of anyone else's—even a grandparent's—heart gives me pause and all the more so because Charles and Ray were so private. Alex Funke, who worked with them for seven years, called the Eameses "the most amazingly private people, [and] considering the fact that they were surrounded, eighteen, twenty hours a day by eighty other people, extraordinarily private. It may well be that [this wall of privacy] was something they'd created just so their energies didn't get spread so thinly, because of the tremendous, endless, interminable demands on them every minute of the day. Maybe . . . they had to turn inward in order to . . . counter that. I don't know."[1]

Funke again touched on this quality of privacy when asked what he thought would have happened if Ray rather than Charles had died first: "You know, [Charles] struggled on through all the . . . physical pain that he went through . . . and he never said anything about it—he just kept on going. I think he would have faced the loss of Ray [that same way], it would have been very hard, and then he would just have kept on working. But I can't say. It's very difficult because he was a very private man, and you really . . . knew very little about his real, deep down emotions. Occasionally, you'd see them glimmer through. But very rarely. . . . It was difficult to know, for example, a lot about his relationship with Ray. I mean, you saw them every day, but in terms of actually, you know, did they—when you didn't see them, when they were up to the house all by themselves, did they go at it like dogs

Charles and Ray Eames on the set of *Toccata for Toy Trains* (1957)

215

and cats? I don't know. Maybe. Hard to say. Difficult to know."[2]

It is a landscape, then, that suggests caution to anyone attempting to deconstruct into two neat piles "that indefinable, untouchable, unreachable something that was a part of the Eames magic,"[3] to use the words of their friend Elaine Jones. In considering the question of who did what, therefore, it might be best to begin with an answer, even if an unsatisfying one on some levels, because in some sense it is absolutely the right one: it doesn't matter. Charles and Ray were a partnership and a collaboration—two people who lived rich lives creating work together with lasting value and meaning. Each partner was implicit in the other. There are instances where you might give one or the other the edge, but in terms of the overall picture they worked together as a team. Furthermore, the work was beautiful and, thus, in itself a sufficient explanation of their connection. If the finished design was (to use Charles's phrase) "a model of the problem," then each finished project was yet another phrase in a description of the partnership's strength and strengths.

Not incidentally, Charles and Ray tended to answer such questions along these lines. Charles often said about Ray, "She is equally responsible with me for everything that goes on here."[4] A couple of years after Charles's death the *Detroit Free Press* reported that, "When asked the nature of their collaboration, Ray offers no explanation other than, 'We did everything together.'"[5] In a joint interview with the *St. Paul Pioneer Press* in 1975, Charles and Ray talked about this further: "the problem of who does what is an after-the-fact thing that people feel they have to ask. We never asked." The reporter continued, "It's always been a problem, agreed Ray, of people who say 'What did you do?' 'Whatever needed to be done at the moment.' Ray always answers."[6]

That practical answer, both disarming and disingenuous in some ways, probably captures a key fact: that it was a lot more important to other people than it was to the Eameses. Charles knew that Ray knew what their work and their working was about and Ray knew that Charles knew what it was about—and that was enough for them. Other people saw things that way too. Deborah Sussman used the term "current"[7] to describe Charles and Ray's connection: "they were always aware of each other and where they were and what was going on, liking it or not."[8] Alex Funke used a similar phrase: "Charles was always aware of her presence. He would always want her to be around. When we were shooting the tops, he would want to show her the tops. He would want to say, 'Look at this one.' She would be there but she very rarely said, 'Use the red one; don't use the blue one.' But I think what's happening here is that she didn't need to say, 'Use the red one; don't use the blue one.' It's like—it's almost like a kind of telepathy. It's like she strengthened Charles's view of what he was going to do."[9]

But they were not twins. Partnership does not mean two people repeating each other's tasks. What's the point? Elaine Jones, whose friendship with Charles and Ray began with her public relations work for Herman Miller, eventually left that firm to work closely with her husband, architect A. Quincy Jones, who had also been part of the Case Study Program. She observed, "I think people from the outside don't always know what's going on. When you're partners, you don't always go off together every place: one of you has to do one thing; one of you has to do another."[10] Ben Baldwin, the only person to really know both Charles and Ray before they met each other, put it this way: "The combination was an extraordinary one. I don't know of any other one like it . . . of two designers who really contributed enormously to each other's work, and they both had very strong gifts in different directions and yet somehow the same direction."[11] Thirty years later, another friend, Philip Morrison, said, "Ray makes a surround around Charles; Charles makes a direction for Ray."[12]

Charles saw everything through the prism of his architecture while Ray saw everything through the prism of her painting. For himself, Charles described "the whole bit as applying architecture to problems."[13] And of Ray he said, "Ray has a very good sense of what gives an idea or form its character, of how its relationships are formed. She can see when there is a wrong mix of ideas or materials, when the division between two ideas isn't clear. If this sounds like a structural or architectural idea—it is. But it has come to Ray through her painting."[14] Ray observed about their work together, "when we were working on the furniture and on the house and again in film, it never seemed [to be] leaving painting in any way because it was just another form."[15] Charles and Ray never felt that they were straying from their original fields. In essence, they applied the rigor and structure of their original disciplines to the work they did together.

In touching on their partnership, the temptation is always to figure out how to deconstruct it. Many people look at the Eames House and say that Charles must have done the hard, masculine modern edges and Ray must have done the soft feminine interiors. But not only is such a comment too tidy, it ignores the complexity inherent in most relationships generally and in Charles and Ray's specifically. Think of the drawings by both Charles and Ray as they worked on and pondered the final structure. And the corollary is that often after Charles returned from a trip, he would be followed by box after box of folk art and toys (such as the ones that populate the house) that he had shipped from the hotel. Lucia Eames recalled one time her father coming back from North Africa with a rug for the Eames House and pronouncing it just the one—and Ray agreeing with her wonderful laugh—they had been looking for.[16]

For a while, you imagine that, like a diamond cutter, you can strike just the right blow and see the two pieces of the gem, Charles and Ray in all their facets, the yield of a single explanation: husband and wife; painter and architect; man and woman; mother and

father; outgoing and quiet; artist and inventor; curves and straight edges; La Chaise and Eames Storage Unit; detail and overview. But such simplistic dichotomies usually collapse under their own weight. Ray is usually thought of as the one who loved little things. Yet think of all the wondrous close-ups that Charles shot in stills and movies. Think too of Ray's response when Arlene Francis asked her how she helps Charles "design those chairs." Ray responded, "By keeping track of the big idea."[17] Charles and Ray's 1956 appearance on Francis's *Home* show is a fascinating and engaging document of a time when a woman was unimaginable as anything but a helpmeet to her husband. Charles attempts to include Ray in the discussions, while Ray's natural shyness kicks in as the attention comes to her. Pat Kirkham wrote that Charles "squirmed" at the inability of Francis—an important pioneering woman broadcaster in her own right—to comprehend the Eameses' dynamic.[18]

Everyone who knew the Eameses or sees their work will bring his or her own feelings to it, but the extremes of observers' positions are astounding. Don Albinson, for example, seemed to feel that trying to give Ray equal credit was something done after the fact, a kind of political-correctness and that her involvement, even in the 1943 sculpture, was not dramatic.[19] This seems hard to reconcile with some of her beautiful biomorphic sketches. He felt that Ray's main focus was a more traditional one of caring for Charles. At the other extreme, Joseph Giovaninni has tried to suggest that primarily "Charles offered the technical achievement . . . (through the 1950s)."[20] This comment is also hard to reconcile with contemporary observations and, more emphatically, with, for example, even a glancing look at Charles's images and filmmaking of the 1940s and 1950s—not by any stretch the work of a technician.

When asked point-blank if Charles and Ray were equals, Jehane Burns Kuhn paused for a very long time and said, "If the office were an island, they would've been equals."[21] The delightful and essential paradox within that statement should be clear by now: in many ways the Eames Office was an island. The office had the incredible dimension of self-reliance and feeling of being another world, a world at a sufficiently intimate scale for those within it to learn the importance of listening to Charles and Ray's voices, with Ray's less overtly forceful but still important. The 901 culture itself allowed for the balance. In other ways, the office was not an island. Charles really seems to have set the larger course for the office, crafting its broad intellectual choices, though naturally in consultation with Ray. These were broad choices not merely in terms of theme, but also in terms of form, concept, getting an idea, and knowing how and where to push a design against the appropriate honing edge.

Jehane's comment also alludes to the fact that communication (in lectures as well as films and exhibitions) was an important dimension of the office. Charles gave the lectures. But the lectures he gave were not cold presentations of pre-agreed scripts, but one-man shows of his ideas. They were as scripted as the John Cage performance they saw in

Cologne, as spontaneous as the clowns in the circus he and Ray admired so much.

Almost everyone interviewed for the Eames Office oral histories had tried to puzzle out their own way of articulating what he or she saw in the partnership. Barbara Charles put it this way: "To me, Ray is the colors, the details, the quality . . . Charles is the intellectual ideas, the structures . . . that kind of Eamesian look in many ways that [you saw in the 901 film]—all those kinds of things around. While Charles loved them, Ray epitomized them."[22] Alex Funke offered this: "You have to realize that Ray's contribution was not very visible but it was extremely strong. 'Cause she really facilitated everything that happened. I mean, she didn't actually come out there and say, 'Move that light to the left or whatever,' but she was there, and she was talking to Charles, and she was discussing the work that was being done. . . . So her contribution is spread very thinly but because of that it's extremely strong. It's like a web that holds everything together."[23]

In reference to the photo shoots, Ray described Charles as "the best editor. I put things in and he takes them out."[24] Jehane remembered Charles saying much the same thing: "And that process was a tussle, very often. . . . Sometimes quite a sharp tussle. On the other hand, it meant that Charles knew that he could rely on Ray to put in things that he would want to take out, and that protected him, I think, from what might otherwise have been a sort of sparser, more austere, more sort of stereotyped modern movement effect, than he would in fact have wanted. He could rely on Ray to balance that."[25]

No discussion of Ray's contribution to the partnership would be complete without an acknowledgment of her gift for color and form. She had a legendary memory for color, keeping a vast collection of papers and colors at the office from which she could—and did—draw at will. Alex Funke: "And she would say, 'Well! Oh, I . . . I know just the color we want. It's the lining of an envelope that somebody sent me from Paris [30 years ago].' And she'd go and pull out the drawers in the graphics room and she would rummage through and she'd find by God this weighed-out flat envelope with this sky blue inside and say, 'There's the color!' And that would be—and it would be right; that would be the color that you wanted."[26] Dick Donges remembered a time on the *Franklin and Jefferson* project when a little sculpture was required: "She went up front, sat at her desk for a little while and . . . she had this piece of modeling clay and she sat there with a little, I don't know, it looked like a nail, a sharpened nail; and she made a little, tiny statue [of Jefferson] about that big that was terrific. I mean . . . it was enough there that you could tell what it was, but it wasn't so finished that [it] looked like she'd worked on it for months. And she was really terrific with that kind of thing, sort of visualizing. . . . And she was terrific at picking out flowers."[27] As Alex Funke said, "it's a million little things; it's not one big thing."[28]

Elmer Bernstein felt strongly that "Ray had the soul and temperament of an artist."[29]

Lou Danziger, a graphic designer and friend of the Eameses, seemed to agree: "If there was nothing but a drawer with pencils in it, the arrangement that Ray would make of those pencils would be art."[30] Film director and Eames friend Billy Wilder echoed both of them: "Ray is imbued with absolutely perfect taste. She is also I think a very good organizer—she's much less of a dreamer than Charles is. I think she sort of holds things together."[31] Kuhn, having heard similar comments made before, offered a significant caveat: "I think if that's true it's only true in a very buried sense. I think that Ray in terms of understanding was [a] realist, but not in terms of practice. I think that Ray was often quite unrealistic about what it takes to communicate to people and how one should treat people. And that Charles was the person

who had an absolutely fine-tuned sense of how to give people their due, which Ray did not have."[32] And yet Ray always had a certain graciousness about her. But what is striking is that all these comments are always a little protective of Ray, as if knowing that it is a given that she is junior partner.

But there was something else that Charles had. Ray put it very well when she said "a billion words could be talked about it [but] without knowing Charles there's no possible way to know this quality that he had of devotion and enjoyment and force."[33] Force. A part of any creation is an act of will, and in reading between the lines of many comments, perhaps one is seeing that the act of will was often Charles's in a different way than it was Ray's.

Jeannine Oppewall drew this distinction: "I think Charles had something Ray didn't quite have which was an ability, in public, on cue, to be logical, articulate, and terribly emotionally appealing. He had a charisma that people always responded to and was very good publicly. His speaking abilities and his warmth and his logic, in a way, I think, made him a more publicly accessible figure than Ray. Because Ray's method of thinking was not proceeding from point A through B through C to D to E. She hopped around. It was a different kind of mind. Equally as valid and equally as interesting, but not one in which I think naturally commanded the respect of whoever she happened to be coming in contact with."[34]

Although according to the conventional wisdom that Ray was not acknowledged or credited for her contributions in her lifetime, the reality is actually subtler and, in a way, more peculiar. Indeed, the 1946 show at MoMA was called *New Furniture by Charles Eames* and Charles was often referred to as the sole designer of the furniture. And yet, the Herman Miller timeline done in 1967 tracks the work of "Charles and Ray Eames." Charles himself always spoke of the endeavors in terms of "we." The vast majority of the films, starting in 1952, give credit to both Charles and Ray as filmmakers. And in 1961 Charles and Ray together won the first Arthur Drexler award for Industrial Design. The September 1966 issue (dedicated to the Eames work) of *Architectural Digest* edited by Peter and Alison Smithson is about Charles and Ray together—so clearly someone knew. The word was out there that this was a partnership.

Julian Blaustein felt that after a while, and in spite of Charles's clear statements about their partnership, "Charles began to realize that there was a little too much 'a Charles Eames this' and 'a Charles Eames that,' when he knew how much she contributed. And finally he insisted on the Ray and Charles Eames—or Charles and Ray Eames—credit line. My awareness of it was never that she asked for it. But he insisted on it."[35]

Ray did too, in her own way. Jeannine Oppewall, who was there in the 1970s, respected Ray's insistence on "a fair shake," even if it meant a little battle: "things like, you know, people in the office forgetting that it was called, actually, the 'Office of Charles and Ray Eames,' not 'Charles Eames Office.' I mean, that was a small and continuous little battle which I witnessed a lot. And she made me very aware that if you are a woman and you have serious contributions to give, that you must stand up for yourself and say, you know, 'You're on my toe, please get off it.' . . . I mean, I really think I learned a lot from her about how to say that. And in a nice way, not in a crazy way. Politely but deliberately."[36]

In the end it seems that both Charles and Ray realized that the things they loved most about their respective disciplines could best be achieved outside of them and this understanding may have been the true meaning of their partnership. Ray's paintings from the 1930s and 1940s are beautiful but not great in the way that her designs (meaning the partnership's designs) are great. Charles's buildings from the 1930s are marvelous, but not great in the way their Eames House is. A subtle but possibly important difference is that, on the whole, the path that Charles and Ray traveled after they met was more closely connected to his past than hers. Perhaps Jehane was getting at this when she discussed the way Ray talked about Charles and their work after his death: "She spoke as a full participant, but she made Charles the protagonist, I think. And she, sort of, both during his life and afterwards, sort of relied on his skills as a protagonist."[37]

I suspect the notion of the protagonist offers, at the very least, a useful model for consideration of the Eames partnership. When talking with those who knew Charles and Ray well, invariably with Ray the conversation will turn to her gift with form and color, and with Charles the conversation often turns to an attempt to define his specialness and convey the power of his mind. Elmer Bernstein commented: "It may have been that Ray would have been in his shadow. I dare say, I mean, one hates making this kind of qualitative judgments, but I dare say that it would be very hard to match Charles's brain, I think. I mean, he was a really superior mind. It was no reflection on anybody else who [was] around him, but I think

that Ray, per force, lived in the shadow of that mind. I think that most people perceived Ray as Charles's wife, not with disrespect. I don't mean any disrespect. I mean, I never had any problem with that because I worked with both of them all the time, and—except one or two rare occasions—my meetings were always with both of them."[38] Later, Bernstein went on, "I'll talk about my perception of him, because I've always felt, I felt at the time and I have felt since, that Charles, in particular as an individual, was the only real, authentic genius I've ever known personally, because that's the way Charles came across to me because of his grandeur of thought. I don't mean grandeur [as] in 'big,' but the ability of his mind to conceive things, or conceive and perceive things."[39]

Barbara Charles took a similar instinct one step further: "I can't imagine Ray without Charles, being great. Different, being an artist doing graphics and so on—I think she would have been very fine, but I don't think great in the sense the team was. I can imagine Charles being great without Ray, but quite different. You wouldn't have had a House of Cards. You wouldn't have had a lot of the things that have this very special pattern, texture, surface almost. It is almost the final touches, the final surfaces, I think of as very much the quality of Ray. And I think Charles would play off ideas on her, and I can't speak for the earlier chairs because I just wasn't there, but by the time I arrived and I worked primarily on the *Aquarium* and a lot of the IBM projects, they were very much intellectual projects [and] Ray tended to get involved in the presentation and the details but not in the content."[40]

Sol Fingerhut, who had worked on the fiberglass chairs, saw something related but different: "Charles was in charge. He was the one that was in charge. And Ray was like a . . . I would say, like second-in-command on the thing. But the decisions, the real decisions, were Charles's decisions. There were things that he'd delegate, or let her. . . . 'Delegate' is probably the wrong word, because of the relationship that existed, but there were decisions that he would let her make—or he would be influenced by her decisions on colors and other things. At least on our program; I don't know how it was on others. But I would say that there was no question that Charles was the one that made the decisions."[41]

Jeannine, who started at the office in 1970, speculated on how this affected Charles and Ray early on: "I think at some point it probably did provoke some tensions in the relationship, but I never felt that they were impossible to get 'round. Well, I mean, she married a difficult man, let's face it, you know? I mean, this is not an easy guy. This is not somebody who just says, 'Yes, dear, anything you want.' That's a different kind of relationship. If she'd wanted somebody like that, I'm sure she could have had it. But clearly she didn't . . . And whatever is the logical outcome of that, well okay, that's just the way it is, you know? And you either battle it and give it up and take up, you know, your life on your own in another way or you come to terms with it. . . . I think she was very gracious and very smart about it. I mean, she knew herself and figured out what she wanted and what she needed. And who among us is capable of doing anything more than that? I don't know."[42]

Elmer describes conversations about the music: "Ray contributed whenever she wanted. There wasn't any sense of protocol between the two of them, but Charles did most of the talking, and that was fine as far as Ray was concerned. But when Ray contributed, she would also get on a roll sometime and take over, and also carry on for quite a while on her own."[43] Ray's childhood friend, Barney Reese, who regularly saw Charles and Ray over the years, had this to say: "Well, I couldn't think of it as anything except theirs. It's theirs. Because being with them together, and the way they deferred to each other, [it seemed] no one wanted to be the leader of the band."[44]

But perhaps there is something even more nuanced going on. After all, in calling the House of Cards a "Ray" project, one cannot forget that Charles took those pictures. Or in considering the furniture, one cannot forget that Ray and Charles struggled together in the Neutra apartment. The nuance could be related to the example of the lota, particularly the idea of not needing to pursue self-expression for its own sake. In their designs, Charles and Ray saw or sensed that both of their essences were unavoidably in there. And perhaps there was a little of being a good host in the mystery, the idea that such ambiguity was the deepest way to acknowledge the incalculable chemistry that was going on.

Jehane put it this way: "And I saw the relationship between them as extremely close-textured, extremely close-textured, which had exasperation in it and great mutual reliance in it. I mean, there were very few things that Charles didn't check with Ray about at various stages." Jehane continued, laughing: "I remember Ray telling me that Charles had said, 'Ray, you should think before you speak.' And Ray said—Ray in telling me this—said, 'But that's not my way!' . . . It's hard to describe, but I would say they worked together in ways that were—absolutely couldn't have been otherwise for the nature of the office's successes in projects and [its] success as a form of life. And I think that the extent to which Charles just knew that certain aspects of things simply would be exactly the best they could possibly be because Ray would watch out for it was very, very, very strong."[45]

A lot of people who worked at the office invoked the family dynamic on the subject of Charles and Ray's relationship. Earlier in the same interview, Jehane recused herself, saying that asking her about Charles and Ray's relationship was like asking children about their parents' relationship—the same problems of perspective would come up.[46] And yet, as the interview went on, it was clear she had reflected a lot on this topic. Alex Funke invoked his parents too.[47] Deborah Sussman called Charles and Ray "like surrogate parents in a way."[48] Parke Meek said, "I realize I spent more time with Charles and Ray than I did with my own mother and father. In fact I sometimes—well, no, I don't feel I really knew them better. I feel

like I knew my mother and father very well. I like my mother and father too . . . [It's really that] I had two sets of parents. It was nice to turn thirty and have a new mom and daddy, you know. Very few people get that chance. It's a tough thing. . . . Boy, when you start measuring other people by [Charles and Ray], they don't measure up very well."[49]

"He was my intellectual parent . . . both Charles and Ray were," Jeanine Oppewall said, smiling as she continued, "I mean, I remember Charles once looking at a photograph of my father, and he pointed and said, 'Is this your biological parent?' And I said, 'Yes.' And we didn't need to say anything more after that. It was understood what the next comment was, you know? We both looked at each other and kind of smiled, you know? And I think I wasn't the only person that he had that kind of relationship with."[50] Indeed, for those who stayed on at the office for a long time, this familial dimension may account for some of the emotion associated with eventually moving on.

It is in the context of the Eameses' body of work that we should consider these subtle but important shadings in the partnership. Because if you think about all the dimensions of the hands-on process, the idea of the designer as director, and the special culture of 901, it becomes easier to see that only as a team could Charles and Ray have achieved their designs—in much the same way that a sandstone formation is sculpted by wind and water, both of which are ultimately expressions of a unified time.

But theirs was a life partnership as well as a design partnership. In my own memories, Charles and Ray are always together. And even if, in my mind's eye, I see Charles and me in the meadow of the house photographing spiderwebs, Ray is just off-stage arranging a (literally) picture-perfect breakfast in the kitchen of the Eames House: grapefruit halves and flawless toast. Or if Ray is picking me up at the airport as a kid, Charles is at 901 (working, I know, but waiting for me, as it seems when I am greeted). Or the two of them together as we have a picnic on the grass and flip olive pits onto the roof and Charles persuades me they are planning an orchard there sometime. They were always dignified in a kind of essential way. Two passages will have to stand for a million musings by friends and colleagues in our oral history archives. Michael Sullivan, who became a friend through the years of work at IBM, said simply: "Their relationship was one of love, truly. I mean, I would sit with them at meetings and things, and you observe. And Charles would lean over and hold her hand, or vice versa. Unconsciously. It wasn't . . . you know, it was just a natural kind of thing. They were very protective of each other, very much so."[51]

Sitting in the sunroom of their home, Philip and Phylis Morrison shared some of their observations of Charles and Ray's partnership. It was toward the very end of the interview when I usually ask if there is anything else I should have asked about. Philip offered first:

"I remember many occasions in the house and in the studio, where they would be working together on something, around some issue which was outside of 'em; they were both regarding it in the same way and trying to make—mold it, put it in place, put this brick in place somehow, in the still uncertain edifice that was being constructed. That's the image that I have all the time, that goes in all these places. I don't know if it's visual in any way, but it's [a] human relationship. . . . The shared task of making something which is both new and conforming, that's the thing. Like fitting—making a brick in a wall, that's the thing. Or, I guess, adding a piece of paint to a painting. It's the same thing: it has to be new. It wasn't there before. But it can't be foreign to what's there now. And that's a double thing, which is not easy to achieve. That's what it was all the time. But not just on paint, or not just on curve, but on everything: words, music, image, idea, need—everything. And that's the design element that they are talking about. Anything narrower is not right."

Phylis: "The damn thing is so ineffable. It was so rich, it had so many facets, it was so easy because by the time we actually got together there were so many thousands of pieces of subject matter which had been brought into the context—and so the context was glorious."

Philip: "They were sitting there in the studio—that was the wonderful part of it—in the office."

Phylis: "But they also were within us."

Philip: "I understand, but that was the great. . . . You could just tell by looking and walking into the [901] studio, you could tell it's a place that's very hard to duplicate. That's what the essence of it is. Anybody who duplicates that, in some way, will have a similar kind of control. But I don't know of anybody who does that. . . . The BBC has plenty of widgets on shelves, but nobody understands what they are, because the person who put them there, maybe he understood that one, but he didn't understand all the others. And there are plenty of people who understand wonderful things but they haven't got the pieces together and haven't made the imagery and tried to surround it and make them visual. But Ray and Charles did those things and that's a unique phenomenon, or pretty close to it."

Phylis: "On top of it all, of course, it made itself into a hard, but mighty good, way of living—and that is what Charles was really making—"

Philip: "That's right."

Phylis: "That is what Ray was really making—

Philip: "That's right."

Phylis: "And that is what they were making together."

Philip: "They were building a life together. Yes. Sure. Difficult."[52]

And then, after a few moments of being lost in warm reflection, the tape ran out, and the conversation with the Morrisons, though not exactly over, was complete.

# CHAPTER 19

# An Image Can Be an Idea

The final question of the film *Design Q & A* is: "What is the future of design?" There is no spoken answer, just Laurindo Almeida's guitar as we see images from the Eames House and its meadow. In some written transcripts of the film, the response is summarized as "No answer."[1] But this is, of course, wrong. The images are the answer and, in this case especially, suggest what Paul Schrader meant when he said, "Charles taught me that an image can also be an idea."[2]

Photography was critical to the Eameses' work and world. It was a form of investigating, celebrating, meditating, explaining, exploring, recording, communicating, teaching, sharing, playing, and much more. Even new staff members would be instructed to go and shoot a roll of film, which was then used in their evaluations. Charles often said that photography was a way of having your cake and eating it too: you had the pleasure of the moment as well as the pleasure of sharing it.[3] Many staff members took this love of photography with them long after they had moved on. With Ray's death, our family donated approximately 750,000 photographs to the Library of Congress, where they are now housed in the Prints and Photographs Division. They make up 5 percent of the entire collection, which is itself one of the largest in the world. Not all of those photographs were taken by Charles and Ray, but many were (Charles took by far the most by any individual photographer); the rest of the photographs were mostly taken by staff members during the course of productions.

Photography was not just done at the end of the day to sell furniture, it was actually part of the Eames Office design process. Dick Donges, who worked in the furniture shop, recalled that Charles and Ray "both had a very good eye. Charles had a terrific eye. He'd do a piece of furniture and not until he looked at that piece of furniture through a camera could he make really any criticism. But once he started photographing it, he knew exactly what was wrong with it."[4] When a prototype got to a stage of development at which "it looked fairly decent . . . he'd start photographing it with his Hasselblad or his 35mm . . . and as soon as he looked through that camera, he knew. . . . And we'd go back and rework it some more. [Maybe] the highlights weren't right, or the arms would be too fat, or the proportions

Detail of the Eames Tandem Sling Seating

227

or something would be out of whack. But he had a terrific eye through a camera."[5]

It was not just the details Charles was looking at, but the whole feeling of the chair. He was fascinated by unselfconscious choices and felt that one of the hardest things in the world was to get a fresh first look at something. Charles had a trick of being able to throw a pushpin into a wall. Sometimes a visitor would see him do it. Then Charles would suggest that the visitor try it. How? Just do it. And very often the visitor would get it the first time but would not be able to repeat it. Why? Charles felt it was because the person was too self-conscious to follow his or her instincts. Similarly, in the early 1950s Frank Newby interned at the office and recalled later how Charles would occasionally ask a staff member (they devel-

oped a code for this request that has been lost to memory) to hang the furniture pieces in development up in an unexpected way at the end of the day: upside down on the floor, sticking out of the wall, or turned on their side on the drafting table, whatever, wherever. The point was that Charles and Ray had no idea how they would display it, and in the morning, when coming in and seeing the piece unexpectedly, for that moment, they could have a fresh look at it.[6]

It is worth noting that the issue of appropriateness continues to weave itself into this story. After all, there was a tension between the tremendous iterations and their belief in first instincts. Charles and Ray were very practical: they wanted it both ways. So they used each approach where it was appropriate, recognizing that the more instincts they wove in, the better the iterations. And they weren't afraid to come back to the first answer if the iterations showed them it was still the best.

Photography was key to the warp and weft of Eames Office life. When a package arrived, especially one that was beautifully wrapped, it had to be photographed. Anything beautiful was celebrated. Etsu Garfias recalled, "Ray and gifts—I didn't know how she would do it, but it would look as though she never opened a gift. Because if she was really taken by the wrapping, the gift would stay there wrapped. . . . [But] then she would want to take a photo of the gift. And she would eventually open it."[7] Speaking from experience, I can report how frustrating this treatment of gifts was for a child at Charles's 70th birthday. But it was just part of life to see everything stop as Ray insisted on pictures being taken—and everyone there expected this and so had cameras at hand. At a lunch at the Eames Office a month or two before Ray died, she made certain there were photographs taken of Emily Mayeda's simple and lovely arrangement of food. It is significant, too, that the Eameses' most successful toy, the House of Cards, was a series of images on notched cards that could be built into structures. Intended originally for grandchildren (it came out the year my oldest sister was born) and family friends, the House of Cards was yet another fun way to weave into one's life images of what Charles and Ray called "good stuff from the animal, vegetable, and mineral kingdoms."[8]

Once, after a hurricane hit Mississippi, Charles's sister Adele called. She lived in Gulfport, which suffered severe damage. She said the storm was, in fact, devastating: houses floated down Main Street, trees were uprooted, power lines were down. She would not have access to a phone for a while and she was calling to tell Charles that she, her kids, and her husband were okay. Thus assured, Charles said, "Yes, but did you get pictures?" Jehane Burns Kuhn, for one, felt this story captured precisely the spirit of the Eames Office.[9]

Alex Funke remembered that one of the very first things he worked on at the office was a film called *Soft Pad*, which "grew out of the fact that we had a whole lot of Soft Pads sitting around. For some screwy reason the place was completely filled with these [Eames] Soft Pad Chairs. And Charles said, 'Hey, look at all these Soft Pads! Hey, why don't we take them out in the back and we'll shoot some pictures of 'em.' We took these out there and we photographed them in every kind of light and every kind of format known to man—because it was a

target of opportunity. Charles could never resist. If we had a lot of something sitting around, he couldn't resist taking pictures of it: it was just what you did." They even took some of the chairs up to the Eames House to shoot. Funke points out that "[Charles] was willing, without batting an eye, to commit the talents of three or four photographic people to going out day after day after day shooting these things. It was wonderful. So, of course, having generated all these pictures, the next thing is: why don't we make a slide show out of them?" Then, finally, this simple, concise slide show was turned into a film. "It was a little, bitty film that essentially he just kind of did. It's not a case of going to Herman Miller and selling it. Basically, he just went ahead and did it and then said, 'Here's a film for you.'"[10]

On a more somber, but profoundly similar vein, when Picasso died, Charles and Ray came to the office that Sunday and put together a slide show of photographs Charles had taken at an exhibition of Picasso's sculpture. Deborah Sussman and her new beau (and, later, husband), Paul Prezja, were there, as were Jehane Burns and a couple of others.[11] It was a very low-key event. The soundtrack was a recording of Gertrude Stein reading her own poem, "Portrait of Picasso," which starts, "If I told him would he like it." Jehane remembered, "It was all sculpture, and it made a lovely, lovely slide show. And it was just something that happened over the weekend, and it was occasionally shown to visitors, but it wasn't made for anything except the occasion."[12]

Taking pictures was an investigative technique for the Eameses as well. Owen Gingerich remembered a trip to Poland as being a key first step in the development of the Copernicus exhibition. When doing a film or project about a subject born 500 years earlier, "one of the constraints is what you have [that still survives]," Gingerich pointed out. "[Charles] said the problem with too many people is that in taking their pictures they try to do too many things at once with the same picture. . . . And I know that when we went photographing early that morning in Krakow, basically he was interested in textures."[13] Gingerich wasn't saying that Charles had the show previsualized, "because I don't suppose he was close enough to envisioning how it was going to be, but he knew whatever [it was, it] was going to show the tex-

ture. And very many of these detailed pictures"[14] ended up in the final exhibition.

Another time, Gingerich, a noted historian of science, arranged for Charles to photograph Nicholas Copernicus's own manuscript of *De revolutionibus*, the book Copernicus wrote that puts the sun at the center of the solar system. The keepers of the manuscript at Jagiellonian University in Krakow were extremely reluctant to permit it, but were eventually persuaded to allow a limited number of pages to be photographed. In fact, the book could only be opened 10 times (Gingerich could pick the pages) and that would be it. Charles shot about 20 rolls of film on those 10 openings, "and some of the greatest photographs of that manuscript are the pictures he took."[15]

Something else happened when returning from those trips. Alex Funke remembers: "One of the things that, of course, had always amazed people was that [Charles] could go off and shoot and be gone for a week or two and shoot 30 rolls, 40 rolls of Kodachrome, and come back and we'd send 'em into the lab and he could tell if there was one [slide] missing. We would lay all these rolls out and he'd say, 'Well, wait a minute, there's one missing. There's a shot missing here.' And [then somebody would say,] 'Oh my God, it's still in the box.' . . . For 600 frames there'd be one frame that somehow hadn't gotten laid out and he would remember that he'd shot it, which makes me think that he must've literally had a memory of every frame, which is probably why he was so good at editing stuff because . . . as he was shooting it, he had a picture of what the film was going to look like, and he was just . . . filling in the *scene missing* leader until it was done."[16]

The Eameses pioneered the use of multiple imagery in both time and space. Specifically, some of their innovations were temporal and had to do with quite fast cutting: images were layered upon one another and viewers were left considering the gestalt of what they had seen. Other innovations were spatial: the *Think* presentation had 22 screens, *Glimpses of the USA* had 7, *House of Science* had 6, and the slide shows generally had 3.

Opposite: a photograph of Copernicus's manuscript taken by Charles. This page: an image from *A Communications Primer* (1953)

*George Nelson always referred to this idea as "Art X."

Part of the thinking behind all this was being an extremely considerate host, a desire to give such a rich experience that there was no doubt that it had been worth the audience's time. But the need was always paramount. It was never about flashiness for its own sake.

We know from Alexander Knox that these ideas had been percolating for some time. The already abstract *Lecture 1* images (including a real flower pressed into a slide sleeve) in 1945 give proof of this, but *Sample Lesson for a Hypothetical Course*, initiated by Lamar Dodd at the University of Georgia in Athens was a critical milestone. Charles and Ray, along with Alexander Girard, were asked by Dodd and George Nelson to develop new ways of teaching the arts. After a mixed reception of their ideas from the university faculty, the team decided to put together a "sample lesson"* to give them a full hearing: "Instead of making a report, we made a film, or rather we put together an hour program made up of film and slides and words and clips of other films," said Ray. "It was intended as an example of how material could be used to give a base for student and teacher from which to develop and expand—not use up all the time, step by step." It was the learn-by-doing approach turned into teach-by-doing.[17]

The insight here was that students could apprehend the guts of most ideas, especially visual ones, in a moment. The result was that the panels on the walls and the films

being screened did not have to didactically make any special point. Instead, once one saw the *Bread* film (on breads from many different cultures) for example, the teacher could say: Now you remember such and such kind of bread, and then go on and make whatever larger point he or she wished. Irv Green of Zenith Plastics was at the presentation at UCLA and remembers two films from the presentation especially well. The first, a film about churches, "had a film [running] in the center screen. And to the right and to the left, [Charles] had slides projected. The film would keep going and they'd keep changing the slides. And they had all sorts of church designs—everything from Notre Dame to Chartres, and then all of a sudden, you got the smell of the incense which [had been] put into the air-conditioning system." Next came the film on bread; it "had everything from rye bread to tacos as I remember. [There was also] a Jewish challah and then he had pictures, slides of them cutting the stuff. Just kneading it as they were making it. And then all of a sudden, you got the smell of newly baked bread. Where [Charles] got it, how he did it, I don't know. And then the audience just gave out a big groan. Everybody was getting hungry. It was very, very unique."[18] Ray and Alexander Girard were there by the air-conditioning vents, first with the incense and then the fresh-baked bread. This was a true multimedia experience. As Alex Funke says, it was "the ultimate in guest-host relationing."[19] Many of the films the Eameses made offer (even without the olfactory effects) a kind of direct experience for the viewer. This makes them remarkable teaching tools in that they become a "base" of shared experience from which the student and teacher can draw.

There were other multiscreen experiences as well. The concept of the three screens was used widely at the office. Over a dozen three-screen slide shows were made at the Eames Office. The selection of the slides into three-screen passes was a constantly evolving process. Gordon Ashby underscored that "looking at a light and a white light table and having to focus on images again and again and again is one of the most fatiguing, energy-draining activities."[20] Charles and Ray would do it for hours. Jeannine Oppewall remembered helping with some of them: "I think that's one place where I learned an enormous amount about how to see. I think you come into the world with a certain predisposition . . . to see or not to see. But, I think, for me, that predisposition . . . was manufactured, or completed, I guess, in

the Eames Office. Because I spent so much time looking at the way Charles saw, and putting the three pieces together, and trying to understand why some things fit together better than others."[21] And, like many others, when Oppewall moved on, her experience at the Eames Office evolved further into her own sensibility and in her own work.

One of the biggest, most elaborate and ambitious multiscreen presentations was *Glimpses of the USA*. Made for the American exhibition in Moscow in 1959, *Glimpses* is a seven-screen presentation of extraordinarily rich image saturation. The American exhibition was part of a cultural-exchange program between the United States and the Soviet Union that took place in Sokolniki Park. Though the Buckminister Fuller dome, which housed the theater, was the most dramatic feature of the landscape, *Glimpses* was only one of a number of exhibits commissioned by the United States Information Agency to portray the American way of life. There was also a model kitchen and Steichen's *Family of Man* photography exhibit. The humanist cast of much of the American exhibition was due in part to the influence of George Nelson, who was asked to provide the overall design and organization for the show.

This exposition, intended as a small, tentative olive branch between two hostile superpowers, became most famous for the Nixon–Kruschev kitchen debate over the relative merits of capitalism versus communism. Charles and Ray witnessed the debate, which took place literally 50 feet from the theater that showed their film. In a joint interview with Ray, Charles remembered later that "Kruschev would pin Nixon down and Nixon would say about four times, 'Well, you've got to admit we have the best color television.'" Laughing, Ray chimed in, "Agony. Agony."[22]

The brief for *Glimpses* was to give the Soviet audience a feeling of what the United States was like. It seems clear that State Department was expecting a film with a lot of American flags and ideally some indication of military might. But, to use the language of the design diagram, Charles and Ray saw a natural overlap among what was good for themselves, for the U.S., and for the Soviet audience, and they instead offered a very human portrait of America which, in the end, was far more effective in communicating a positive message than the expected propaganda film would have been.

Relatively soon in the development of *Glimpses*, the Eameses settled on the multi-

Opposite: the concluding triptych from the 3-screen slide show G.E.M. (1970). This page: a triptych from *G.E.M.* showing images from the making of the film *Tops* (1969)

Model of the 7-
screen presenta-
tion *Glimpses of
the USA* (1959)

screen approach. As Charles said, "this was not a capricious method but rather a way of
establishing credibility and avoiding superlatives."[23] In other words, one freeway interchange shot fetishistically on a single screen could lead to the Soviet dismissal: "Well, we
have one in Kiev." But 70 shots of freeways in 20 seconds would tell the audience that, for
better or worse, freeways are part of the fabric of American life. As Charles said, "the audience recognizes an open set and this somehow raises the level of truthfulness."[24] The
Eameses used their understanding of the power of images to establish credibility with the
audience, but they were a little surprised at one aspect of the result. Parke Meek remembered Charles recognizing the irony of at least one cross-cultural connection being
expressed at a press conference after the film's screening, "All of 'em wondered how many
cars he had, and he says: 'I'm trying to tell 'em, that's not the way to go! We do not have.
. . . It's not the solution to the problem.' [Charles was saying:] 'Jesus! They want everything
we got. Well, look at us.'"[25]

       Charles was not hoping for a negative impression of *Glimpses* at all, but rather a
recognition that it was in many ways a description of an essentially good place, one that
could and should be examined. Given the political climate of the 1950s, it is incredible that
the first words of the film (spoken in English by Charles but translated into Russian at the

The actual installation. Note the graphic coherence of the 7 images actually used versus the ones in the model. Inset: a 7-screen pass from the final version

fair) were, "The same stars that shine down on Russia shine down on the United States. From the sky our cities would look much the same."[26] How did the Eameses get away with this? By flying below the radar. As Charles later told Owen Gingerich, "If you ask for criticism, you get it. If you don't, there is a chance everyone will be too busy to worry about it."[27] And this was exactly what happened—the negotiations and setups for the entire exhibition could have filled a book by themselves, keeping officialdom focused elsewhere. There was also the element of last minute-ness, which meant that by that point everyone was simply grateful that it existed. The Eames Office staff worked at full throttle for several months, modeling configurations, shooting images, editing, and writing. The final strands of film were shot in Vistavision (an 8-perforation film format similar to a 35mm slide that allowed a continuity of compositional style). Friends and family were pressed into service, too, including daughter Lucia shooting freeway exchanges and doorsteps in Boston. The music was the biggest orchestra Elmer Bernstein had yet recorded for an Eames score but, as always, it was a matter of appropriateness: the quartet that played for the Eames film *House* would not fill the vast theater the film was intended for. Charles and Ray and their team literally completed it the day the Eameses got on the SAS plane to Moscow with the prints.

When they arrived, it was time for the first showing on the actual screens of the

Buckminster Fuller theater. No one had seen it projected that way yet. Seven 35mm projectors came to life at the hands of an experienced Radio City Music Hall projectionist, transplanted to Moscow for the two-month duration. Americans and Russians who were setting up the American Pavilion gathered to watch, looking up at seven screens: four on top, three on the bottom. Each individual screen was 60 feet across, making the whole expanse almost as wide as a football field. Viewers had to stand back to take it all in. In just 12 minutes, 2,200 still images appeared on the screens. (There were also some brief sequences of motion pictures—ironworks and Marilyn Monroe—the latter courtesy of director Billy Wilder.) The cutting speed was about one pass (the seven images projected at one time) every two seconds, though the visual rhythm varied from time to time. The story told is simple, but the experience of viewing it is genuinely sensual and utterly immersive: It first sets the table with an overview of the land and then slides into a weekday in the life of Americans, touching on work, school, and home. Next there is a passage about Broadway, and then the weekend, filled with activity and "time for contemplation." Then, after an amazingly energetic and emotion-laden cluster of visuals accompanied by, but also embodying, jazz, *Glimpses* concludes with a simple sequence of people at home, people that could be anywhere. The very last image is of a simple bouquet of flowers.

When the film ended, silence filled the room. For a moment, the Eameses were not sure whether they had started an international incident, but in fact everyone—Americans and Russians alike—was overwhelmed by the power of the experience. In retrospect, it is clear that it was the dawn of a new day in recognizing the power of imagery. But there was something else in the air. As screening followed screening, there was always a whispering amongst the Russians in the audience at the end, and many were in tears. It finally emerged that by wonderful serendipity, the flowers that Ray had chosen for the finale (no flags, no missiles, no flyovers for Charles and Ray) were forget-me-nots—and the Russian word for that flower also means "forget-me-not" in Russian.[28] A gesture made in images carried the same meaning for both cultures, creating a kind of emotional rebus.

After 40 years, the descriptive power of *Glimpses* remains formidable; even reconstructed on seven television screens in a recent exhibition it was a compelling centerpiece. As projected in the dome, issues of credibility would have been dwarfed and obliterated by the viewers' sense that they had seen things for themselves. *The Christian Science Monitor* described the film as "by far the most exciting new use of the motion picture medium since the first Cinerama production."[29] Seen today, it satisfies as a work of visual power but also as a snapshot of America taken at one of the last cultural moments when one could be aware of the country's problems yet still feel deeply positive. Today, on the left and the right, that moment seems to have passed. Another reason it holds us is that the film is mul-

ticultural without being obvious about it. A glance at U.S. television programs, movies, or even mainstream publications from the 1950s and even 1960s would not reveal too many nonwhite faces, and yet the range of ethnicities in *Glimpses* is broad: African Americans are portrayed as part of the sweep of productive and familial life; Japanese Americans, 15 years after Executive Order 9066, illustrate all-American activities on the weekend; Native American ceremonies are woven into the section on faiths. It's unfortunate that this was an exception for the era, but it was. Though likely done consciously, this dimension appears unselfconsciously in the film—another kind of way-it-should-be-ness.

Charles said of this project that, "we were anxious to treat multimedia as a tool and not a show."[30] This applied to the other multiscreen presentations as well. He sometimes compared his use of multiple screens to giving a kid a hammer and that, "the chances are that everything he encounters will need hammering."[31] But a close examination reveals some fine-tuning of that hammer. As a photographer, Charles had a gift for close-ups and it is tempting to think of them as his "style." But *Glimpses* shows another side: though there are some beautiful passes in the film that consist of seven abstract details, the vast majority are wider shots where all seven have a structural and graphic quality in common (think of seven schools, seven bridges, seven desert vistas, seven people walking). This is because "design addresses itself to the need," and that was the need for this presentation. The multiple screens were a reflection of the Eameses' ability to look at different but similar examples in the same way. *House of Science*, presented at the Seattle World's Fair, was a little different, using six screens to tell one visual story. But for *Think*, shown at the New York World's Fair, the 22 multiple screens were a perfect expression of the idea of looking at the same thing in different ways, perhaps a reflection of the Eameses' method of circling around an idea to understand it.

Many of the films used only a single channel of imagery, but used it so quickly that it created a multiple-image effect. A project called *The Fabulous Fifties* encapsulates this approach and also was one of the few Eames films to reach a mass audience through television broadcast. The germ of the idea was pure Eames. In 1958, France was faced by the prospect of civil war as a result of the rebellion and insurrection in the Algerian colony. In

From left to right: three images from *Music of the Fifties* (1960); an image from the opening of *Fifties Dead Sequence* (1960). The Eameses also did a 3-screen slide show called *Cemeteries*.

237

the end, Charles de Gaulle was named premier and given huge powers, which culminated in the creation of a new French constitution that led to the Fifth Republic. The two-and-a-half-week interregnum before de Gaulle took power is referred to as "the de Gaulle crisis." As a simple test of an idea for quickly-made films that could be used to recap events, Charles asked John Neuhart, John Whitney, Parke Meek, and others to gather up newspaper images from the de Gaulle crisis. Charles shot them, treating them really like works of animation, and then set the sequence to the music of a French tune called "The Poor People of Paris."

They showed the film to producer Leland Hayward, and it was shown on CBS. Two years later, when Hayward was producing a television show called *The Fabulous Fifties*, he thought of Charles and Ray. Interspersed in this one-hour show (which included live segments with various actors) were five new short films created by the Eames Office, two of which were animated adaptations of popular books of the time.* The other three segments each applied a different constraint to the decade and shared with the audience what is revealed by considering the decade from that perspective. The first constraint looked at the 1950s from the standpoint of what happened in the "funny papers." In a few minutes, the Eameses' *Comics of the Fifties* sketched out the villains faced by Dick Tracy, Prince Valiant, and other characters in that action-packed ten-year period. The short also tipped a hat to new strips like *Peanuts*, *Beatle Bailey*, *Gordo*, *Steve Canyon*, and others.

The second constraint around which the Eameses built a film was deaths. Accompanied by a somber Elmer Bernstein dirge, *The Dead Sequence* shows images of famous people who had died in the 1950s. The audience may not necessarily have recognized all the faces and yet there were no captions. Elmer Bernstein asked Charles about that because the cutting "seemed so fast to me that you don't get a chance to absorb any of these images of the people that died in that decade, and Charles's reasoning was, once again, a highly visual concept—really highly visual concept. Yes, it was true that you would only [recognize] maybe one in 10, but even if you [only] recognized the really famous people, the general feeling . . . what happens to you is [that you] say, 'My goodness. I recognize this person. That means that all these other people that I'm looking at are really worthwhile, important people.' Just the magnitude is what's impressive, and of course then Charles was very, very much that way about visual stuff."[32]

All of the sequences show a mastery of the medium, but *Fifties Music Sequence* is a true landmark of media history. In nine and a half minutes, the Eameses recapitulated the music of the 1950s from many different genres—from classical to Broadway, Harry Belafonte to Perry Como, Alvin and the Chipmunks to Peggy Lee, the *Dragnet* theme to Van Cliburn. Virtually all films illustrating music (what we now call music videos) from that era were made as a single shot of a performer or performers playing a song. Even feature movies (whether musicals or not) that had nonperformance-based montages during music sequences basically used images that came from the narrative of the anchoring story. Charles and Ray blew that idea wide open with this film.

A musical overture, playing as a puppet theater curtain opens, begins a prescient smorgasbord of notes for virtually every idea in MTV's library: performance shots? Yes: in the Frank Sinatra sequence. Swooning fans? In the Elvis Presley sequence. Sexy teenyboppers? "Rock around the Clock." Literal illustrations of lyrics? Corks popping for "The Night They Invented Champagne." Lovers on a beach? Birds coasting on air as an oblique message of love? "Volare." Abstract images in time to the music? Russian Folk Music. Shots of the recording studio? Patsy Cline. Negativized images? The "River Kwai March." There are puppets, album covers, frogs, fruit, guns (for *Dragnet*), animation. It is really the first music video, which may seem like a dubious achievement in some ways, but as an effervescent explosion of pure cinema it is intoxicating. Because on top of all the visual play, *Fifties Music Sequence* has a kind of structure.

First, like a translucent membrane, an exquisite piece of music by Elmer Bernstein holds it all together. At first listen, it sounds like a simple series of music clips, but a second reveals that Bernstein created little interstitial pieces of score to stitch the whole film together. The recording of the music itself reveals yet another story: though the Eameses accepted constraints, they still pushed the limits of the technology as far as they could. Elmer recalled being in the CBS recording studio with four different two-inch tape machines[†] going as the engineers (with increasing frustration but ultimate success) tried to cue the huge machines to play precisely the right segment for editing into the clip. Some of the cuts in film and music last but a few seconds. Whereas digital technology allows this "sampling" to be done at home today, Elmer painstakingly crafted the piece required to make Charles and Ray's vision work.[33]

One of the most haunting sequences starts with an image of Judy Garland singing, and then, accompanied by Elmer's atmospheric refrain, a montage of stills of Garland. There is a progression, but you may not understand its meaning for a moment, and then you realize that Garland is getting younger and younger before your eyes but is always on stage, and then, in a flash, you realize something about her as a person before you are swept into the next montage. The entire segment concludes with a reprise of sound and image that is cut even faster, finally leading up to Ethel Merman singing "Everything's Coming Up Roses" from *Gypsy*.

The virtues of *The Fabulous Fifties* were not completely unsung, as Charles and Ray won a special Emmy award. But perhaps more meaningful kudos came the day after the airing, when Joseph Kennedy, the father of presidential candidate John F. Kennedy, called and said to Charles, "A film like that could help make my son president." Charles did not accept the offer and was the first to acknowledge that "without [it] his son got to be president, but [the request] was a marvelous tribute" to the use of the medium.[34]

† This was a physically large tape machine that recorded 24 tracks—the standard for the day, but almost obsolete today.

AN IMAGE CAN BE AN IDEA

239

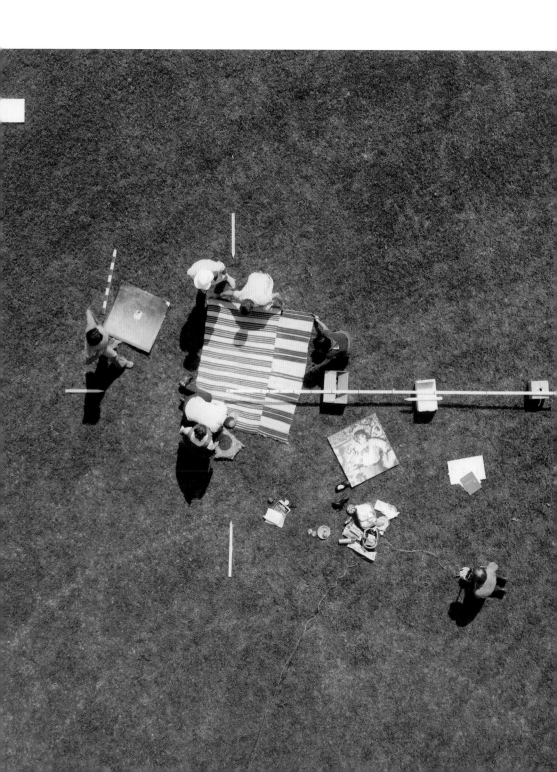

# CHAPTER 20

# Proposals, Sketches, and *Powers of Ten*

Elmer Bernstein saw Charles as having "a sort of unending agenda"[1] that expanded and expanded until the very end. The 1970s saw two projects in particular that embodied this expansive vision. Both of them, *The World of Franklin and Jefferson*, an exhibition, and *Powers of Ten*, a film, represent well the diverse intellectual scope of the Eames Office at the time.

The *Franklin and Jefferson* exhibition, the last huge (in terms of sheer manpower) project the Eames Office undertook during Charles and Ray's lifetime, is notable both for what it was and what it might have been. It was a visually rich and informationally exuberant experience of two key participants in America's revolutionary era, and one that resonated fascinatingly with Charles and Ray's own concerns. But though the client's original request was not nearly as rich as what the Eames Office eventually made, this bicentennial exhibition came close to being a full 25 years ahead of its time. The process and the potential make the exhibition a revealing close-to-closing project for the office.

In 1972, when a tribute to Thomas Jefferson was proposed for the country's upcoming bicentennial, Charles and Ray's initial suggestion was to put the Library of Congress online (or what we would now, 25 years later, call "online") on kiosks in the city halls of two dozen or so major U.S. cities. This echoed ideas the Eameses were exploring in a film called *Cable: The Immediate Future* (1972), which predicted in significant detail much of the functionality and potential of what we now know as the Internet.[*] The Library of Congress was selected not only because of its central position in the U.S. archival network, but also because it was an important example of what Charles called an "institution not committed to teaching."[2] These were institutions that, unlike universities, focused on the acquisition of information in its rawest form. They were free from the duties and to some extent the politics of universities (such as Charles had experienced at Washington University). The old Henry Ford Museum was another such institution—in three-dimensions. Henry Ford had asked his collectors to get one of everything—such as every variety of plow—rather than trying to pick the best or most handsome. In the Eameses' view, this meant the collection

Setting up the picnic scene for *Powers of Ten* (1977). Notice the blow-up of the 1968 version being used as a guide.

* The primary difference is that the hard-wiring of the network the Eameses presumed was cable and not telephone as it is today, but the film really explored the structure, rather than the technology, of the solution. Alex Funke, who was there at the time, felt that Charles was not crazy about the finished film but was fascinated by the ideas.

241

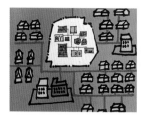

Images from four proposals, from left to right: *Cable: The Immediate Future*, an explanation of the technology; also from *Cable*, a proposed interactive presentation of public meetings; information center proposed in *Metropolitan Overview*; image regarding Newton's science in the *Franklin and Jefferson* proposal film

was more useful—after all, it is sometimes more important to see design failures than successes.[3] The Eameses felt that the Library of Congress on-line would make for a truly fitting Jeffersonian expression.

But the Bicentennial Commission wanted an exhibition on Thomas Jefferson, as did one of the venues, the Grand Palais in Paris, which had recently done a biographical exhibition on Lenin and had hoped that this would be the equivalent on Jefferson. The Eames Office later pursued some of the implications of the online kiosks in their interactive laserdisk projects, *Art Game* and *Merlin*, and in the *Metropolitan Overview* project. In responding to the commission, though, Charles and Ray used the making of the proposal film to suggest and model a major shift in the exhibition away from the "great man" mode into a dual focus on Franklin and Jefferson. This had the effect of turning the ostensible subjects into a prism through which to look at the times. A good deal of this thinking developed during the making of the *Franklin and Jefferson Proposal* film itself, suggesting yet another reward of the film-as-modeling technique.

The work and lives of Franklin and Jefferson resonated deeply with Charles and Ray and, in fact, suggest an alternative to the term "Renaissance man" (and woman) that has often been applied to the Eameses. In spirit, the Eameses were very much like Franklin or Jefferson, wilderness philosophers (in the Enlightenment sense) who were engaged with architecture, science, civic society, and anything else that interested them. As time went on, Charles and Ray found themselves more and more impressed by the Founding Fathers of the United States. Some dimensions in particular clearly resonated with them. In the Eameses' words, the Founding Fathers "were good learners, for example, in the sense of hands-on experience"[4] and tended to act "as if they owned the place, which made for a real continuity between their life and work."[5] Clearly, this was also a quality that the Eameses sought in the companies they worked with: in the case of all of their major clients, they made sure they could work directly with the person at the top.

The connections were so pronounced that Jehane Burns Kuhn, who worked on the Franklin and Jefferson content, "began to think . . . as the development of the show went on that what we were doing with both Jefferson and Franklin was to, sort of, do two portraits of different Charleses." She was certain that Charles would "have rather had dinner with Franklin than with Jefferson. I think he thought Franklin was better company. And Franklin being interested in such a wide range of practical matters, I think, appealed to him very much. And also Franklin's sort of slightly enigmatic quality. I mean, Franklin too was a person who was very comfortable with women, and one never quite knew what that amounted to."[6]

EL MUNDO DE

# FRANKLINY JEFFERSON

Museo Nacional de Antropología
del 16 de abril al 15 de junio, 1977

The completed exhibition, *The World of Franklin and Jefferson*, opened in Paris in January 1975, traveled to seven cities in five countries, finishing in Mexico City in June 1977. It opened in the United States in New York, continued to Chicago and Los Angeles, and was the main event for the office for around five years. The exhibition was well received in Europe. Charles commented that "half of Paris must have been photographed [near] the bison,"[7] referring to a huge stuffed bison that was part of the section of the exhibition on westward expansion.

Poster for *Franklin and Jefferson* exhibition at its last stop in Mexico City

However, when the show came to New York, Hilton Kramer of the *New York Times* seared it under the headline "What Is This Doing at the Metropolitan?" His essential argument was that without a lot of fine art in the show, it had no business being in the art museum.[8] Though the show's attendance was quite good throughout the United States, this criticism clearly stung. Ironically, of all the criticisms of the show, the question about whether it was appropriate for an art museum may seem strangest, because art museums routinely address civic and cultural issues today and not only with original fine artwork. Indeed, Charles and Ray were trying to move the audience beyond the objects to the ideas behind them. There were some 40,000 words of text in the exhibition—the intention was not that they all had to be read, but rather that the show had, at every point, the depth of content to reward the visitor. This was information overload, but instead of being in film, it was in space.

The show was also criticized for not attacking Jefferson's slaveholding more trenchantly. The show did address the issue of slavery, but it did not make that paradox the center of its treatment of Jefferson's character. Perhaps, on this question, one could ask: was Charles, as creator of an exhibition for the country's bicentennial, too polite a guest or too gracious a host? The Eameses felt, on balance, that Jefferson had done good things, and that it was dangerous to apply too blithely the standards of later generations. In fact, the Eameses actually seemed to be concerned with another, more structural, issue. Charles put it this way: "We hoped to clear away/short-circuit both 'indignation by hindsight' and 'hero-worship by hindsight,' so that people might be coaxed/provoked into thinking how these people met the demands of their circumstances, how they used their resources, and into

243

thinking about our demands and our resources. Jefferson said it himself: the way to honor them is not to cling religiously to their solutions, but to try to draw on something of their vigor and freshness of approach and apply it to our own different problems. It's not true that their problems were simpler. Everyone has problems as complex as his capacity to recognize a problem will allow."[9]

A last point: in his excellent book, *Fifteen Things Charles and Ray Teach Us*, Keith Yamashita cites "keep good company"[10] as one of the lessons. This was clearly another dimension of the world of Franklin and Jefferson that hit home for Charles and Ray. Charles and Ray themselves kept extremely good company. This was a matter of friendship, but also of keeping themselves honest. They often said, when approaching a problem, "We ask ourselves, what would Mies van der Rohe say? What would Bucky Fuller say?"[11] Then there were other compatriots in the world of design such as Eero Saarinen, Henry Dreyfuss, Isamu Kenmochi, and, of course, the friends-in-arms with Herman Miller, George Nelson, Isamu Noguchi, and Alexander Girard. Interestingly, Girard, with whom the Eameses collaborated, was someone whose work Ray had followed as a student (when she still went by Alessandro). In the 1940s, Charles was asked by Motorola to consider doing radio covers, but then he saw Girard's work and told Motorola they were in great shape.

In the realm of Hollywood, there were friends such as Billy Wilder and Philip Dunne (who wrote *How Green Was My Valley*), among others. Charlie Chaplin (and Noguchi) attended a Japanese tea ceremony at the Eames House once. Producer John Houseman was part of the Eameses' circle as well; they had consulted on Houseman's film *Executive Suite* (on the short list of films set in the furniture industry); the number on the wall of William Holden's office echoes the one that Sol Fingerhut saw in Charles's.

A short list of examples of "good company" would also have to include Philip and Phylis Morrison. He is an astrophysicist and member of the MIT faculty as well as having worked as a book editor at Scientific American for decades; she is a well-known teacher of teachers and innovator in education. The Morrisons were interviewed together for the Eames Office oral history project. She worked on staff at the Eames Office for a time, and Philip was a consultant for the office. Following her husband's comments about how the Eameses connected art and science, Phylis spoke slowly and precisely: "There is the word 'in-form.' And it says that the thing which brings the understanding comes from inside the structure of things. I think this is what Charles knew and brought out and into the light again and again."[12] The appropriate evolution of form from content was a hallmark of the Eames process. And the content and the form were never so completely in sync as they would be in *Powers of Ten*, fittingly though poignantly, the last major achievement of the Office of Charles and Ray Eames. The film was completed not too long before Charles's death.

After the somewhat anticlimactic response to the *Franklin and Jefferson* exhibition and its premature introduction of a new concept of in-formation into the Metropolitan, it is strangely triumphant that one of the last films Charles and Ray ever made would turn out to be one of their most important achievements of all. Tens of millions of people—students, teachers, poets, businessmen, gurus—all around the world, many of whom have never heard the name Eames, will remember these particular Eames images all their lives. It is a fitting capstone because it encapsulates so many dimensions of their vision and process. In 1998, the film was one of 25 added to the Library of Congress's National Historic Film Registry (in the same year that *The Last Picture Show* and *Bride of Frankenstein* were added). The registry includes 300 landmarks, from Chaplin's *Modern Times* to Welles's *Citizen Kane* and Lucas's *Star Wars*.

*Powers of Ten* is a recapitulation of the Eameses' work, process, and philosophy without being a repetition of it. The 1977 movie was really a punctuation mark on an extremely long journey of thinking about scale. One can trace the essential ideas back to some things Eliel Saarinen discussed at Cranbrook. Even before then, Charles's Christmas Card of 1931 captures a *Powers of Ten* view of St. Louis, and it is difficult to miss Ray's late 1930s' expressions of abstraction in the forms representing the proton.

In terms of description, *Powers of Ten* is extremely straightforward. Nine minutes long, it starts with the title and some brief credits over shots of a couple in Chicago having a picnic on a patch of grass not too far from Lake Michigan. After the meal, the man lays down for a nap while the woman props herself up against his leg and begins to read. From this point forward, the entire film is a single eight-minute-long shot. There are no cuts in the scenes I will here describe: The camera moves to a position directly above the picnickers. Around this time, the narrator (Philip Morrison) explains that we are looking at a square one meter by one meter, from exactly one meter away. From this point forward, the camera appears to pull away at such a rate that every 10 seconds we appear to be 10 times farther away from the picnic than we were 10 seconds before. As the narration says, "Our view will center on the picnickers long after they have been lost to sight." The camera starts to move away at a constant rate of acceleration. After 10 seconds, we are 10 seconds away and are $10^{+1}$ meters (or 10) meters away from the picnic. In a square 10 meters by 10 meters, we see the grassy area in which the couple is picnicking.

Thirty seconds into the journey, the camera appears to be a kilometer ($10^{+3}$ meters) away from the picnic, and we see a one-kilometer square centered on the picnickers and revealing just a piece of Lake Michigan. Seventy seconds after we started, we are 10,000 kilometers away ($10^{+7}$ meters), and we see a vista 10,000 kilometers (almost 7,000 miles) across—it is just about the diameter of the earth. Two minutes and 20 seconds (140 sec-

Four Images from *Rough Sketch*; the dashboard is shown clearly on the left of each frame

onds) later, we are $10^{+14}$ meters away; our view takes in the entire solar system. Our speed always increases at a constant rate until the camera slows and stops just beyond $10^{+24}$ meters or 100 million light years from the picnic, showing a view over 100 million light years square. "This emptiness is normal, the richness of our own neighborhood is the exception," says the narrator.

Then the camera zooms back in, traveling 10 times closer (a "power of ten") every two seconds. The feeling of scale is visceral. "Every two seconds we travel 90 percent of the distance to the picnic." Then we slow up at the picnicker's hand, now moving 10 times closer every 10 seconds. This time we explore the meaning of the negative powers of ten. After 20 seconds we are looking at square $10^{-2}$ meters across, that means it is a one-centimeter square of the man's skin that fills the frame. And still the camera looks closer: $10^{-5}$ meters (that's 0.00001 meters, or 10 microns) across is the scale of a white blood cell. Closer, into a chromosome in that cell, then into its DNA, then into the molecular structure of the DNA, then into the atoms that make up the molecule; $10^{-10}$ meters (an angstrom), the diameter of an atom, still moving in, past the electron shells, into the nucleus of the atom. Finally, the journey fades to black at $10^{-16}$, one-tenth the size of a proton. As the narrator says, "Our journey has taken us through 40 powers of ten. If now the field is one unit, then when we saw many clusters of galaxies together, it was ten to the fortieth, or one and 40 zeroes."[13]

The movie has many roots. Scale was a key concern for the Eameses from the beginning. Both Charles and Ray recalled Eliel Saarinen talking about always looking at things and problems from the next-smallest and the "next-largest frame of reference."[14] One can also look at the abstract photos that Charles took from 1945's *Lecture 1* onward as being about scale. The film *Toccata for Toy Trains* (1957) is, in some ways, the inverse of *Powers of Ten*: the latter makes scale apparent, whereas in the former the same acute understanding conceals it. Trains of many sizes were shot and woven into a seamless vision that all took place at one scale—the idealized scale of the world of the toys themselves. *A Communications Primer* (1953) shows a progression of copies, of copies, of copies into abstraction as well as a sequence on exponential growth. The film *2ⁿ* (1961) shows the exponential origins of the game of chess. And film after film used the scale of models brilliantly.

AN EAMES PRIMER

246

But philosophically for Charles and Ray, Eliel Saarinen's remarks are really the touchstone, and in this sense the film is truly a work of philosophy, a matter of literally stepping back to get a perspective. As Ray said, when they saw Kees Boeke's 1957 book, *Cosmic View*, "it suggested the possibility of making a film"[15] about these ideas. Boeke was an important Dutch educator and philosopher, and his book centers on a girl in a deck chair in Holland. It had been developed after World War II by him and his students as a solution both to the challenges of teaching scale and to the limited teaching resources then available.

From this suggestion, the path to the film shifts to the Eamesian learn-by-doing approach. The *Powers of Ten* made in 1977 was actually the third version of the film. In 1963, the Eameses shot a short demo about a minute or two long. Wanting to know how to make a film about exponential growth, Charles and Ray had done the most natural thing to them: they made a piece of film. They called it *Truck Test*. It was not a complete film at all. It was a test of whether they could make a continuous trucking (or moving) shot that would give the illusion of constantly accelerating motion. This film was very rarely shown and never to outsiders, because it was simply a silent technical test. The timing is slightly different—the rate of acceleration is actually a little slower. Charles and Ray asked Ray Redheffer (their consultant and friend from *Mathematica*) to work out the 240th root of 10, which was the number needed to determine the distance between each camera position.[16] Essentially, all three versions were animations, with the camera moving an ever-increasing amount (starting at the beginning of each power) until you get to the next power and it begins again. But the test is important because it shows once again that unselfconscious use of film as a tool, as a natural part of the process.

A few years later, when Philip Morrison and Ralph Caplan from the Commission on College Physics approached the Eameses about making some films as part of the commission's brief to develop films as teaching tools, naturally Charles and Ray suggested the *Powers of Ten* idea. In fact, some people with the commission thought Morrison and Caplan had suggested it to Charles and Ray—and no doubt they had as well; but as so often was the case with the Eameses, they brought clients into that area of natural overlap without the clients ever realizing it. The office made another film for the commission called *Lick Observatory*. One of the most exquisite of the slide films, it was intended to give students who might never visit a classic optical observatory a sense of that kind of place.

The Eameses' first completed film version of the idea was called *Rough Sketch for a Proposed Film Dealing with the Powers of Ten and the Relative Size of Things in the Universe*. First, notice the title. Like many Eames projects, it wore its "modelness" or "sketchness" on its sleeve. The Eameses felt that such an approach often let one focus more on the idea. In this case, not only is the film a model of the idea of scale, but it also acknowledges the arti-

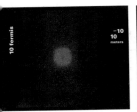

Eight powers of ten from the nucleus atom to the Milky Way from the 1977 film *Powers of Ten*

fice frequently—whether by adding an airplane to the golf course or by calling certain subatomic models out in the narration. It also does not zoom out (or in) quite as many powers as the 1977 version. *Rough Sketch* (as the 1968 version is generally known today; it was for a time referred to as *Powers of Ten* but that name is now reserved for the 1977 version) is basically black and white, and has a dashboard on the left side of the screen that shows the passage of time and compares it to earth time. What every viewer notices is the narration of Judith Bronowski, the Eames Office staffer who also took the lead on researching the film (Parke Meek was another key production person). Bronowski's voice is extremely cool and detached; that viewers often feel a bit lonelier at the edge of space in *Rough Sketch* than in *Powers of Ten* is in no small part due to the cool reserve of her narration.

Even today the relative merits of *Rough Sketch* and *Powers of Ten* is a meaningful topic for enthusiasts of the Eames films. The black-and-white version has the rough charm and integrity of a first effort, and yet the richness, precision, and sheer visual beauty of the color version is undeniable. One can easily admire both films, but *Powers of Ten* unquestionably hones off the idiosyncrasies of *Rough Sketch* in a way that makes the former more useful as a learning tool (which was, after all, the need) and a visceral experience from which the viewer can confidently extrapolate. In the color version, the Eameses chose not to acknowledge the models but instead to pursue a consistent realism. One measure of how effective they are comes at the end of *Powers of Ten*. When the journey stops at $10^{-16}$ meters, there is a frame filled with colorful, darting spots. The line spoken is: "Could these be some quarks in intense interaction?"[17] Twenty years later, the quark theory was proven and quarks were shown to be roughly $10^{-18}$ meters in size. At the Eames Office of today, we blew up the original $10^{-16}$ image 100 times for our CD-ROM, and the dots were exactly to the scale they should be to represent the quark. As so often happened, the Eames intuition was pitch perfect. The process of honing, of working with scientists like Philip Morrison and molecular biologist John Fessler, meant that throughout production everything was focused on understanding—not asking Philip Morrison to tell, but asking him to teach.

Alex Funke was, along with Michael Wiener, in charge of production on the 1977 film. He described the process of what to do with the number (the 240th root of 10): "You

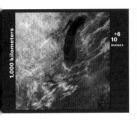   

start with [the camera] a small increment [of distance from the artwork] and then you multiply that distance by that magic number and then take that and multiply it again and again and again and again and again and again, so when you've done it 240 times [in other words, when you have shot all 240 film frames that make up 10 seconds], it's 10 times bigger. It's simple when you talk about it, but the mechanics of doing it are quite complicated. When you're up front [close to the artwork for a given power] you're moving—making movements that are so small you can't even see them. They're like little lines so close together. And at the far end you're making movements where the camera's moving at 6 or 8 inches per frame. And those are harmonically related. So that was solved: Parke and his gang solved it the first time and Mike Wiener and I solved it the second time. We reinvented the wheel completely" (in terms of the physical making of the dolly apparatus).[18]

Beyond the fact of making three versions of the project, which makes it, if not a 30-year flash, then a 15-year one, the process of making the last version of the film followed in other ways the practice of innovating as a last resort. The man at the picnic in *Rough Sketch* is Paul Bruhwiler, a Swiss designer who worked in the office at that time. By 1976, he had left the office but happened to be in town when they were planning to do the remake. Naturally he was pressed into service again. Etsu Garfias, the staff member who played the woman picnicker in *Powers of Ten*, remembered how carefully Ray duplicated the first picnic. After all, if they had Bruhwiler, then they could and, in fact, "had to re-create the first one. And find the exact blanket and the same bottle of wine. The same book. All of that had to be duplicated. And [Ray] was very careful and adamant about getting all of that straight. . . . She was sure that the [blanket] they put out was wrong. . . . And they finally found the right blanket. And she paid a great deal of attention to that. And those are things that are really important once you see the overall picture."[19] The real issue in re-creating the picnic so carefully was, again, a balance of priorities. They wanted to preserve what had worked and focus on what could be made better—after all, at the same time that they carefully recreated the setting, they were open to making the arguably far more dramatic change of adding a second person (Garfias) to the scene.

As a metaphor for the concerns of the office, the *Powers of Ten* film is certainly an

essay, not only in terms of the issue of perspective, but even more importantly because it teaches about constraints. *Powers of Ten* is so encompassing it is easy to forget that it is actually very narrow in focus. The whole journey is centered on one atom in one man's hand who happens to be in Chicago. And yet, simply by changing the perspective, that laser-focused journey ends up literally revealing the universe. This film is as pure an expression of the Eamesian idea of universalizing from the specific as is their Case Study House #8 or the design of the molded-plywood chair. They were always trying to satisfy the universal part of themselves. Once again one sees the liberating power of constraints.

Charles often spoke of a quality he called "way-it-should-be-ness." This quality was something to be desired in a design. It had to do with the idea of unselfconsciousness or unpretentiousness and, in a way, is the opposite of style for its own sake. What it meant was that when one looked at a design, one did not think "how clever" or "strange" or "new." Hopefully, one did not notice it all. Ideally, one thought it had been doing whatever it was doing forever. Another word for this is "timeless." A lot of Eames designs have that feeling. The furniture is of a time, but not trapped by it—like *Powers of Ten*. It unfolds so naturally and unselfconsciously that it seems easy; it even seems like filmmakers have always known how to do this shot. But they didn't before the Eames Office, despite other films that have tried to pursue this same idea. Some were "inspired" by *Powers of Ten* but at least one was made around the same time as *Rough Sketch*. Interestingly, though superficially similar, they all make different choices than *Powers of Ten*, with the effect that Owen Gingerich, who was a consultant on the film, recalled a meeting of members of his astrophysics department at Harvard. The question was whether to buy one of these other films for teaching purposes (for variety's sake) or a second copy of *Powers of Ten*. They voted for the second copy.[20] The movie truly offers that direct an experience of exponential growth.

*Powers of Ten* pulls together so many parts of the Eameses' approach that it is especially fitting that it centers on a picnic. For Charles and Ray, the picnic was an integral part of their lives. In the Norton Lectures Charles says, "We have a picnic every day at the office."[21] But, never forget: a picnic suggests both sides of the guest/host relationship. The sleeping man at the picnic has clearly been well hosted at the same time that we, the viewers, are guests at his picnic for our journey.

Opposite: production on *Rough Sketch* at 901, circa 1968. This page: attention to detail—Ray laying out the picnic, Charles checking the measurements. Notice Paul Bruhwiler (the man at the picnic) through the weeds at the bottom of the frame.

# CHAPTER 21

# Ten Years Apart

In August 1978, Charles headed to 901 Washington from the Eames House as he did every morning when he was living in Los Angeles. Driving down the long driveway past the other Case Study Houses to the city streets, he paused to talk with his neighbor and friend Stuart Bailey. Charles looked tired that morning, and Bailey was concerned enough to wonder to his own wife later if Charles would survive the year.[1] The *Franklin and Jefferson* exhibition had been exhausting, as had the *Powers of Ten* production. Ray commented later that she "wished it had not taken so much out of him."[2] Jehane Burns had a desk by the window: "I would see Charles drive up in the morning and I would see him sit in his car gathering himself before he stepped out of his car and walked in the back door. And [each day] I would see him sitting there for longer and longer. It took more of him to gather his resources and walk into the building. Because as soon as he walked into the building he was expending energy, getting things moving, keeping things moving, checking things."[3]

*Powers of Ten* was a triumph for Charles and Ray. Unlike most of their other films, educational distribution began almost right away through their recent relationship with Pyramid Films. But there were tribulations as well. The nature of the corporations they were dealing with started changing in the early 1970s. There were no longer people at the top "who acted as if they owned the place," but instead lots of middle managers who were as afraid of bold initiatives as the former leaders had once been open to them. Tom Watson Jr. had moved on from IBM; Edwin Land had been toppled from the head of Polaroid by the failure of the Polavision system. The process had changed at these and other companies. Alex Funke remembered one incident vividly: "It might have been *Something about Photography* or something. The people at Polaroid wanted to give [Charles] input on his work print!* They wanted to be able to comment on his work print! [For] God sakes! Here's a guy . . . who did the film for the American Exposition in Moscow when we were mortal enemies, presented the film in Moscow without anybody in the U.S. government even seeing one frame of it. He was annoyed. 'Who do those guys think they are? I know what I'm doing. . . .' They wanted to have—make sure their voice had been heard to justify their

Rose with molded-plywood airplane parts, mid 1940s

\* Essentially a final draft of a film

253

existence. And he knew that, but that's an example of how the joy had been slipping away."[4]

Herman Miller was a somewhat different situation. It was now publicly traded, but the DePree family still had an important hand in the helmsmanship of the firm. Though the Eames furniture was a smaller portion of the company's product mix, the Eames philosophy was still important to the values of the company. And those in charge recognized how critical the Eames furniture had been to the success of the firm. Nevertheless, corporations all across the United States were gaining a middle management that focused more and more on the short term, while Charles and Ray's messages were always geared to the long view. IBM's rejection of the Eameses' presentation of the interactive component of a personal computer was typically shortsighted. It was an idea that needed nurturing (and perhaps a new way of selling), and when IBM didn't do it, Apple beat them to the punch. In a very real sense, Charles and Ray had a greater commitment to the ideal of what IBM once saw itself to be than most of the new MBAs that they encountered at IBM.

The people who said "we need to be secure in change" were themselves thinking of changing their office in a radical way. Many people in the office sensed an inevitable transition. Jehane put it this way: "Charles was engaged in, at some level, a search for a person [to be a manager under himself and Ray]. Ray's take was 'It's terrible that the world can't produce a person to fill this slot.' I think that she never—as Charles never did explicitly—but I think that Ray not even implicitly really faced the idea that what the office was asking for was probably a contradiction in terms. That the chances of finding the sort of paragon who would have the strength and the experience to play that role and who would yet be willing to act the way staff members of the office had always been expected to act, as Charles and Ray's instruments—and I've said enough to make it clear that instruments is not a pejorative term—that [finding] such a person was sort of impossible."[5] Charles and Ray considered having Julian Blaustein work as a kind of producer in the office. Charles had long talks with Blaustein about it. Ray suggested Blaustein just show up and start in. But Blaustein said it could never work because if he and Charles disagreed, he (Blaustein) would assume that it was he, not Charles, who was wrong.[6]

Charles and Ray seriously considered closing the office down.[7] This would not have been the same as stopping work themselves, but it seemed like the only way Charles could keep the promise he had made to himself over 40 years earlier—to work only for the pleasure of the working. Elmer Bernstein, for one, saw the films like the prospective one on Monet (there had also been others on Daumier and Cézanne) as "late work," and this had concerned him.[8] But they were still in control of their choices and continued to attract and develop intriguing projects. Both the interactive laser disk and the *Metropolitan Overview* project had a kind of tantalizing potential. And, interestingly, it was for the film *Cézanne* that the Eames Office, particularly Bill Tondreau and Jane Spiller, developed one of the world's first motion-controlled movie cameras (such units are a staple of special effects production today). Controlled by a (literally) hand-wired computer, the Eames Office camera made sophisticated moves across a color slide to spare the real painting the damaging effects of movie lighting. But more than a mere conservation solution, the technique was, in a sense, the evolution of their slide films to a new level.[9]

But Charles was also getting older. In discussing the issue of whether Charles would have closed the office, many people imply that it was Charles's call alone, but, in fact, it was a dialogue between him and Ray. Charles once told a friend that Ray was concerned that they would lose the platform that had been so carefully built.[10] Charles also expressed a concern about what it would do to the staff (though at least one person told Charles that if that is what he had to do, she would not oppose it). If that was one facet, Jehane Burns softly suggests another: "He wasn't prepared for the idea that he would like a less-strenuous life."[11]

A day or two after talking to Dr. Bailey in the driveway, Charles once again traveled to the city of his birth. He was in St. Louis for two projects: photographing the exhibition of Monet paintings at the St. Louis Art Museum in Forest Park and working on exhibition ideas with the Missouri Botanical Gardens. The Botanical Gardens are on the site of Shaw's Gardens, about two blocks from where Charles was born. This trip closed another circle from his past, when he accepted an invitation from the new owners to visit his 1936 Meyer House. The next morning, August 21, 1978, Charles was scheduled to begin shooting at the Monet exhibition. For several hours he would have some of the most beautiful paintings in the world all to himself—this was much more than 10 openings of a book—and it was a self-generated target of opportunity. He was headed to the museum when suddenly he collapsed. He died almost instantly from a brain aneurysm. Charles Eames was 71 years old.

Any reflection about the impact of Charles's death on Ray personally would be close to meaningless. It was devastating, disorienting, tragic, sudden, horrible, immobilizing, sickening, angering, eviscerating, and beyond saddening to all of us who cared for or knew or loved him. To see her then was to know it was much worse for her.

Charles died on a weekend; most people at the office learned of his death early Monday morning. No matter how worn out some people worried he was getting, the essential thread running through the reactions to his death, even from those same people, was a feeling of his life being abruptly cut short. Daughter Lucia felt "the sun had dropped from the sky"[12] and all her fears for his health of the past years irreparably confirmed. Jeannine Oppewall, who had left the office a year or two before, was nonetheless angry with her intellectual parent for dying; "I wasn't through with him yet,"[13] she says. Selfishly, as a

grandson, I knew I would never be able to work at the office for a summer like my older sisters had. Parke Meek had a dream in which he found Charles in a hidden loft above the conference room saying, "Don't tell anyone I am back."[14] There was even a sense of being cheated of the chance to see how he would have closed the office. Jehane mused, "My instinctive feeling . . . is that he'd have gone off into the wilderness somewhere,"[15] like he had to Mexico before. Alex Funke, who had left the office a month or so before Charles died, remembers that his last project was something very, very small: filming a nineteenth-century German toy catalog. Nothing formally ever came of it. But Funke could see in discussing it with Charles how this might have been one of those germs of an idea that could have expanded for Charles and Ray into a whole world.[16]

Charles was cremated, and his ashes, held in a small wooden box made in the workshop by staff member Dick Donges, were buried not far from his father's grave in St. Louis. It was a simple ceremony attended by his wife, his daughter, his sister, and a handful of other people close to him.

Etsu Garfias remembers Ray's return. "Ray was wonderful when she came back. . . . I remember her having this meeting with us and us gathering out on the lawn [at the office], and her talking about her trip and what had to be done [next]."[17] But the office began to unravel. There were so many forces at work. Charles's leading role in the partnership left Ray unprepared to be a solo leader. But there were also the issues with the clients as well as natural tensions in the office—people torn between loyalty to Ray and a feeling that the magical years were over. It might have been impossible for Charles to keep the office together without Ray, but it certainly was for Ray without Charles.

Ray had a profound sense of loyalty to their clients. She even hired a kind of architectural office manager to fill the slot that she and Charles had been unable to fill so that those projects that had been started could be completed. But it didn't take. The clash of cultures was too strong. Besides, though the office had projects in the works, nothing of the stature of *Powers of Ten* or *Franklin and Jefferson* was in the offing. For Jehane, the moment it was over was an elusive one: "when the office ceased to be an office for me—and it's hard to say just when that was; it was sometime at the end of the year after Charles's death when I was still in touch with Ray and helping some—but when it was no longer a way of life for me, I really felt I didn't have a way of life. I mean, my world had gone, and it took me a long time to piece together another world. It had been very intense for me, very absorbing, very demanding. Obviously, also very rewarding."[18]

For James Hoekema, who worked on the laser disk project, the moment was very specific. It was during a 1979 meeting at IBM regarding the project, which had been revived somewhat after Charles's death. But the absence of Charles's driving force was felt acutely.

From the Eames Office there was Ray, Hoekema, Jehane, Howard Lathrop, and one other person and "I remember thinking, 'Well, that definitely is the end of it,' when one of these very senior guys at IBM asked very pointedly, 'Well, who can we call that could be our contact person that we can always count on to find out a definitive answer?'" Hoekema recalled, "Everybody said, 'Well, you can call me.'" Five different semi-autonomous Eames Office point people "was not the answer they were looking for. . . . [Afterward] we all knew that it wasn't going to go on much longer. And on the way back to the hotel after that meeting, this car full of . . . five of us all crammed into a rented car. We were driving down the highway in Connecticut somewhere looking for the restaurant someone told me about and we just didn't want to talk about the meeting and we didn't really have anything else to talk about. And somehow we started singing Lutheran hymns. It was the most bizarre sensation in the world. Somehow, we just—it was all we could do. And we had a very quiet dinner that night."[19]

Shortly thereafter, the transition accelerated and the office no longer sought new work. Ray entered a new phase of her life, which in many ways she blossomed into. For the rest of her life the Eames Office stayed open, in business and working out of 901. She became a kind of elder stateswoman of design. She wrapped up a few loose ends, films that had not been finished, and one piece of furniture: the teak and leather sofa. One film was especially important. Ray made a single-screen version of the three-screen slide show *Goods*. Charles's narration of the film was recorded during the Norton Lectures, and the film is an implicit tribute to him. He tells the story of a time Ray's car was broken into at 901: "everything in [her] car had been strewn all over the lot. There wasn't much missing. I think it was a beautifully wrapped broken alarm clock that was being sent to a grandchild for further dismantling, and I regretted this very much. But while going around and picking these things up, I came upon a bolt of cloth. And this was really distressing because . . . it was a bolt of wool, [that] when you take hold of it, why, you can feel the animal wax and oil in it somehow or other. . . . What was shocking about it was that the guy hadn't thought enough of it to take it."[20] The talk is, among other things, an expression of the way that goods in volume, still in their original packaging, can represent a connection between the end user and the person making the goods in the factory. It was a beginning to the idea of the New Covetables.

Ray became more of a public speaker in this time—driven by the need. And eventually she warmed to that role. Audiences loved her, were very supportive of her presentations, and felt privileged to meet and see her. Steve Cabella, an early collector of Eames furniture, also collected what he called Eames "moments"—places where he perceived or found a connection to Charles and Ray. Cabella remembered a talk at the Herbst Theater in San Francisco where Ray showed some multiscreen slide shows: "You could see the emo-

tion of the crowd, and people knew that Ray was there but they could also feel the absence of Charles—not that that lessened what was about to take place in front of them. It's just that they were sharing a certain sadness at seeing somebody gone, and seeing somebody there who you could tell was very much in love with that person. You could tell there was a little bit of a . . . half-moment there. You couldn't really tell that Charles was missing but you could see [that] Ray was trying to make up for you not having Charles there. And I thought that was just so sweet of her. It was very apparent in how she was trying to present the slide lectures. She wanted them to be exactly like it would have been if Charles was there or if you'd seen it 30 years ago or if you were going to see it 10 years in the future. She was very concerned that you left there having your visual moment to take home with you."

But the three-screen slide shows were notoriously hard to run outside the office. Cabella continued: "And, at one point during the presentation, the slide projectors had gone out of sequence and some were actually shutting off in their entirety, and Ray asked that everything be stopped so she could put it all back together the way it was supposed to be seen, so that she could make sure that you were having that moment [the way] they had worked to create it. If the moment had continued on with an absence of certain things, it just would not have been, I think, the same moment that she had wanted to present to everybody. And everybody . . . could see this, because the audience wanted her to stop . . . like she'd asked to stop so she could fix things. But the management of the series wanted her just to go on through with it [with a real attitude of] 'we'll fix it when we can.' And she was like, 'No, let's stop it now.' Save the moment, fix it, and continue on with the moment. The audience was in complete agreement with how Ray felt and it was very apparent; I've never seen an audience so . . . on the side of the performer, and we would have waited all night, whatever it took, because everybody realized we were being shown a rare visual and we wanted our own moments, I think—and I think everybody got them that night."[21]

Ray was retained as a consultant by both IBM and Herman Miller for the rest of her life. She worked on two books in this time. In both cases, her writing partners were married couples. The *Powers of Ten* book, written in collaboration with Philip and Phylis Morrison, uses visuals from the film on the right-hand page of the spread as the anchor of an experience of scale. Each power is elucidated through complementing text and images on the left-hand page. It was published in 1982, as the first volume of the Scientific American Library, a book series that popularized science but with the highest-possible integrity of content and contributor. The book is still in print.

Ray's other book began development in 1982. This was to be a book that portrayed the complete body of work of the Eameses. It was, of course, a completely logical and necessary book. In essence it was a kind of catalogue raisonné. The project became the classic

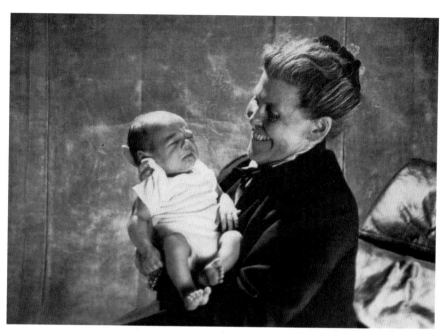

Ray with her
then
youngest
great-grand-
son Xander,
July 1988

*Eames Design*. Ray's vision of it was "a book without adjectives." After some time she asked John and Marilyn Neuhart to work with her on it. John had worked at the Eames Office, and Marilyn and John together had done a retrospective exhibition celebrating Charles and Ray's work in the mid-1970s. Though the end product has become a classic, the process was an extremely stressful one for all concerned. In the end, Ray felt that the publisher was supporting her coauthors more than her in the telling of her own life story (and, indeed, Abrams placed her name last on the author's list). From her coauthors' perspective, Ray could be an extremely difficult collaborator, a frustration that is clearly but reservedly expressed in their introduction to the book,[22] which was completed by them after Ray's death. Nevertheless, beautiful things sometimes take arduous journeys, and *Eames Design* is a fine example. At 440 pages with 3,500 illustrations, it wonderfully uses the rich self-documentation of the Eames Office to convey the breadth of the body of work.

   In the late 1980s, visitors to 901 were treated to a layout of the book on the walls of the Eames Office. It was a time of closure. Through this same time period Ray was cataloging the vast inventory of two-dimensional material intended for the Library of Congress. She had help from the library during the last five years, and most of the office staff was dedicated to this project. Her granddaughter, Lucia Atwood, also helped with the cataloging

TEN YEARS APART

259

effort. By this time Ray was living in the studio of the Eames House mostly for medical reasons—her back was giving her trouble. Nevertheless, she was always a gracious hostess to students, architects, and other visitors to the house. More than one group of budding designers was surprised when Ray greeted their class with a tray of long-stemmed strawberries dipped in chocolate—an Eames favorite; it was a memory to be treasured forever. In December 1987, Ray and Lucia went to the National Institute of Design in India to give the first Charles Eames Award to the ceramist Kamaladevi Chattopadhyay. This would be Ray's last trip to India.

By late July 1988, Ray had completed her text of the *Eames Design* book and identified all of the images in the archives (which only she could identify, though there were others that she hoped to review one last time). Around this time, Rolf Fehlbaum, her old friend and the head of Vitra International, the European manufacturer (which began making the furniture in the mid-1950s as a Herman Miller licensee), asked Ray to participate in a series of photoportraits the company was doing with important people in Vitra-manufactured furniture. Rolf wanted a picture of Ray sitting in the Chaise Lounge, and Ray asked if her new great-grandchild (her third) could be in the shot. Rolf said, "Of course." The picture is a marvelous one.

The child in question was my son Xander, and so I was shocked a few days later when I came to the Eames House. I was there to take Ray to a mutual friend's wedding. Ray was sitting in the kitchen with her forehead resting on the table. When she finally looked up to see me, she was completely gaunt and tired. I asked if we should skip the wedding, but she insisted we go. But this woman who always seemed to have boundless energy needed help up the stairs after the ceremony. Lucia came down from San Francisco to help, and a few days later Ray was in the hospital being treated for cancer.

Ray received some friends and family in the hospital, but we could all see that she was growing weaker. The cancer was viciously fast. A little over two weeks after she checked in, Ray was drifting in and out of consciousness, but she said at one point to a visitor, "I know what day tomorrow is." The next day, Ray Eames died on August 21, 1988—10 years to the day after Charles's death.

Ray had not wanted a funeral, but friends and family needed a gathering. Two days later at 901, many came to pay their respects informally with conversation and plates of long-stemmed strawberries dipped in chocolate. The feeling of sublime closure was both melancholy and celebratory. In a sense, this book started there, with a kind of video guestbook. We set up a camera in the slide area where people could share a few thoughts or stories. Many people shared stories and started conversations that continued as the "Oral History Archives" of the Eames Office.

Toward the end of that night, former staff members Annette del Zoppo and Parke Meek began talking and, as they did, they started pulling out boxes of slides from the shelves around them. First was a box of slides from Florence, Italy, where Charles had shot a three-screen slide show of the Baptistery. Then another box from another place, and another and another, each with its own memories. Annette's eyes fell on her own handwriting on a box of slides that she had labeled decades earlier. But now, in the box there was a note. Annette scrutinized it, saying to Parke, "See, this is Ray's handwriting and it says 'to identify.'" Annette knew how much time Ray had spent with slides like this, trying to capture as much detail as possible for future scholars. Annette had even helped a bit herself. She said to Parke, "Now that was the same as the one we just had in the [other] box, so you can identify that aloud. . . . This is Florence [Italy, too]. Maybe I should identify some of them—just write on them." Annette jotted down some notes and then they both started to laugh as they realized the poetic appropriateness of Ray's training still being with them even now that Ray was gone.[23]

Lucia asked Dick Donges, the same man who made the box for Charles's ashes, to make one for Ray's. A few days later, in a simple ceremony, Ray's ashes were laid to rest next to Charles's in the soil of St. Louis.

Chairs on the patio of the Eames House

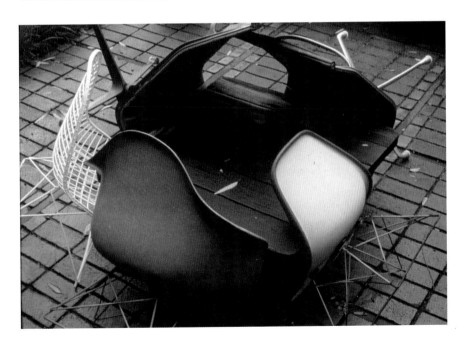

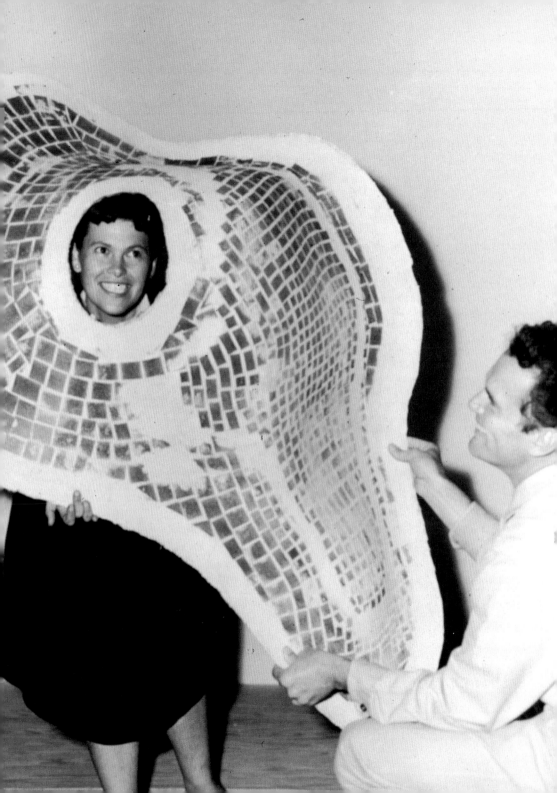

# CHAPTER 22

# Afterwords

It is the nature of biographies that they rarely have happy endings. And this primer has told enough of Charles and Ray's life stories to face that same issue. Even more important, Charles and Ray engaged so many dimensions of the modern world that to consider their work is to feel cheated that they are not still wrestling, improving, and nudging forward with compassion our society and its designs. But, because this is a primer and not a biography, the story will only be complete when you have finished the book and, perhaps, taken these thoughts into your own world.

Charles and Ray changed "how the 20th century sat down," the *Washington Post* once observed, but they also changed what we saw once we were off our feet. They changed what was in our rooms and what we saw on the various screens we sometimes have in those rooms. It is not just what they did but what they foresaw. Their work suggests a path where art and technology are not in conflict, where tradition can be a signpost for change, and where conveying ideas to a layperson need not be a reason for the well-versed to avert their eyes. Making an inexpensive chair was not an excuse for shoddiness but a legitimate design constraint born of necessity. As a new century begins, design has never been more in fashion, but it is not always a journey of integral understanding. For Charles and Ray, design was not an expression of style, but of "purpose." A sketch or a model was not an end, but the beginning of an engulfing process. The connection people feel consciously or unconsciously to the Eames work is a reflection of that vision, of working "in-form."

Many of Charles and Ray's contemporaries and colleagues are gone. Eero died young in 1961, Alexander Girard in 1993; George Nelson in 1986. Some of the people who helped tell this story have died as well, but many more are active and productive in a million realms. Charles and Ray touched many lives: some people began their careers at the Eames Office, some just intersected for a moment later in life. Even those who in the end felt wrung out by the intensity of the experience found it to be a keystone of their lives. Many of the staff members who contributed so much are listed in the acknowledgments.

The intention of this primer has been to pull together many of the intellectual pieces of the Eames puzzle and help the reader see the seamless connection between all the Eames work. But it is only a beginning. So, after your picnic, after your own models and your own rough drafts and iterations and your own did-you-get-pictures experiences, here are somewhat more specific ways to experience more of Charles and Ray's work.

Films. The over 125 Eames films are Charles and Ray's essays. About 54 are available in video form. Many libraries and independent video stores will have them. You must see *Design Q &A* (Volume 4, 1972). The following are also particularly important: Maija Grotell project (1941), *Blacktop* (1952), *Parade* (1952), *A Communications Primer* (1953), *House: after five years of living* (1955), *Day of the Dead* (1957), *Toccata for Toy Trains* (1957), *Glimpses of the USA* (1959), *Music of*

Charles and Ray playing with the form for La chaise, early 1950s

* People often ask about the irony of high prices for early Eames furniture, considering that one of their goals was low cost furniture. The answer may lie in an analogy: if you buy a copy of James Joyce's *Ulysses* in the bookstore, the reading experience—the exact words—will be identical to a first edition, but we have no problem understanding the increased value that a collector would pay more for the vintage book. Similarly, though the authorized contemporary manufacturings are not reproductions but the real thing, when it comes to the vintage examples, there is a special meaning to the thought that the designers themselves might have touched the chairs at the time.

the *Fifties* (1960), *Fifties Dead Sequence* (1960), *Comics of the Fifties* (1960), *IBM Math Peep Shows* (1961), *Truck Test* (1963), *View from the People Wall* (1965), *Aquarium* (1967), *Rough Sketch* (1968), *Tops* (1969), *Polyorchis Haplus* (1970), *Fiberglass Chairs* (1970), *Franklin and Jefferson Proposal* (1973), *Powers of Ten* (1977), and *Goods* (1982). This is the place to start. The flipbook in the lower right corner came from *901: after 45 years of working*, made by the author shortly after Ray's death.

Furniture. Most of the Eames designs are still being produced today. Herman Miller is the only authorized manufacturer of Eames furniture in the United States, the Americas, Asia, and all regions of the world outside Europe and the Middle East. Vitra International is the only authorized manufacturer in Europe and the Middle East. What does the term "authorized" mean? It means that the manufacturer has the permission of the Eames family to use the Eames name in association with the furniture. This comes with the proviso (which they willingly accept) that the Eames family has the right to set production standards both in terms of what is made and its quality. It was Charles and Ray's conscious decision that this authority remain with the family. Herman Miller and Vitra showrooms can be easily located in your city. Or try an airport. Or a restaurant. Or visit your local vintage furniture store, your local school, or maybe even a friend's house. You don't have to buy it to experience it.

The vintage market has accelerated in recent years with several pieces selling for over $100,000 (the record is for Charles and Ray's sculpture—$365,500). I feel uncomfortable citing these numbers because in themselves they should not be perceived as a mark of quality. Nevertheless they are part of the story. Though prices in the vintage market remains high for most early and/or rare examples, bargains still exist. And never buy for an investment what you wouldn't want to sit in or look at for its own sake.[*]

Books and writings. Five publications stand out: *Eames Design* (1989) by Ray Eames and John and Marilyn Neuhart; *Powers of Ten* (1982) by Ray Eames and Philip and Phylis Morrison; *Powers of Ten Interactive* (1999), a project of mine; *A Computer Perspective* (1973), a book the Eames Office made based on their own show; and *Fifteen Things Charles and Ray Teach Us* (2000) by Keith Yamashita.

House of Cards. The House of Cards Picture Deck is still in production (as is the Medium House of Cards) but not the Giant House of Cards, the Pattern Deck or the Computer Deck. The Newton Deck was never commercially available.

Multiscreen Presentations. These are the hardest to see, because the original scale was part of the experience. They were ephemera, like any good picnic. Only *Glimpses of the USA* (1959) has been reconstructed in any form—it was pieced together by the Eames Office of today and shown on 7 video screens for the *Legacy of Invention* show.[†]

The Eames House (Case Study #8). This is the Eames family homestead and the home of the Eames Office. Visitable by appointment only.

901 Washington Boulevard. When Ray died, the building was on the verge of being condemned for earthquake reasons. Lucia Eames was given six months to empty the building and begin seismic retrofitting. Yet Ray had felt it would be impossible to put everything back afterward (after all, she pointed out, it had taken them 45 years to do it the first time). She asked that 901 be sold to pay the taxes on the Eames House. After the seismic work, the interior was remodeled by architect Frank Israel and is still in use.

Three institutions have complete rooms from 901. Charles's office is on loan to Vitra International (at Weil-am-Rhein, Germany). The San Francisco Museum of Modern Art owns the projection room and conference room. The Los Angeles County Museum of Art owns the front office of 901. Some individual items were given to other museums, such as the Glider Nose Cone to MoMA in New York. In addition to the Eames family collection, two other institutions received major collections from 901:

Library of Congress. The largest single donation by far was, fittingly, to the Library of Congress in Washington, DC. The original commitment was made by Charles and Ray, and Lucia Eames donated 750,000 stills, slides, and drawings to the Prints and Photographs division where they are still being catalogued. The 160,000 items in the Manuscript Division are available to scholars. The intellectual property rights for these materials and all the Eames work are owned by the Eames family.

Vitra Design Museum. After Ray's death, the family felt very strongly that the collection of prototypes had to stay together because together they told a powerful story about process. A number of major American museums visited 901, but none were able to or were interested in taking this small but important collection intact. Fortunately, the Vitra Design Museum in Weil-am-Rhein, Germany—which also housed the collection of Charles and Ray's good friend Rolf Fehlbaum—was willing to keep them together.

Selected Architecture. The Entenza House was restored in the mid-1990's (and an addition added by the new owners). It is closed to the public. The Herman Miller showroom in West Hollywood has been gutted several times but the facade remains. Efforts to protect it continue. The Max DePree House is in very good condition and is privately owned.

NID. The National Institute of Design in India still thrives in Ahmedabad, India.

Websites. www.eamesoffice.com, www.powersof10.com, and www.loc.gov offer in-depth Eames-related content including bibliography, images, text, videos, and finding aids.

Charles and Ray's Early Work. At least five houses and a church still stand from Charles's time in St Louis. All, including the Meyer House, are privately owned and closed to the public. Check with local preservationists for details. St Mary's Church in Helena, Arkansas can be visited and is in excellent condition thanks to the commitment of the parish and community. *Changing Her Palette* contains a selection of images from Ray's early years.

Eames-Designed Exhibitions. *Mathematica* was installed in Los Angeles in 1961. The building that housed the exhibition is gone, but the exhibition itself travels. Another complete version is permanently installed at the Museum of Science in Boston. In Delhi, India, the *Nehru* exhibition has a permanent installation.

Other Displays. Several institutions reliably have exhibits dedicated to the Eameses. The Cranbrook Museum of Art in Bloomfield Hills, Michigan, and at MoMA in New York for starters. The Eames Office Gallery & Store in Santa Monica, California acts as a visitor center for the Eames House, and has rotating exhibitions. This list cannot include the many designs influenced by Charles and Ray, nor the many wonderful private collections, vintage furniture stores, and Maharam showrooms that offer still more ways that the work lives on.

The ending of this book became this list to underscore how much primary source material made by Charles and Ray Eames is already out there waiting to be explored. Experiencing any one Eames work enriches the next because you begin to see the connections and resonances more clearly. This is because, as I hope this book has suggested, Charles and Ray always made their ideas integral to their design and design process. And it is the universal part of all of us that Charles and Ray sought and found connection to.

For the Eameses, design was not a professional skill, but a life skill. The Eames House is a landmark, but it is and always was a home. Eames chairs are icons, but they were always comfortable. *Powers of Ten* is a philosophical statement, but it was always the best kind of thrill. And the people who knew and loved Charles and Ray probably miss most of all the chance to just talk to them again.

† Charles and Ray put the 22 screens of *Think* (1964) into the single-screen *View from the People Wall* (1965); they also made the 6 screens of *House of Science* (1962) into a single screen film in 1964. Images from *Sample Lesson for a Hypothetical Course* (for which *Bread* and *Calligraphy* were made) were included in *A Communications Primer*. The 3-screen slide shows have not been seen since Ray's death except for *Goods*, combined into one channel by Ray in 1982, and *Tanks* which was also reconstructed for the *Legacy of Invention* show.

# Acknowledgments

A book like this requires the help of many people over many years, but before thanking them, I want to underscore that the opinions in the book are mine and mine alone. I have sought to quote and paraphrase everyone involved fairly and accurately, but it does not necessarily mean that the individual in question agrees with the point that is being supported.

With that caveat, I begin by acknowledging my debt to Charles and Ray for a body of work that is so rewarding and engrossing to explore, consistently surprising and remarkable at every level. Next, I wish to thank my mother, Lucia Eames, for her commitment to maintaining the Eames legacy, for entrusting me with the directorship of the Eames Office for the past years, and for generously allowing me to include the Office's photographs and images (which are the vast majority of those in this book). Her recollections and insights particularly into Charles's years in St. Louis and at Cranbrook were invaluable.

I wish to thank the following Eames staff members, friends, and colleagues who have participated in the Eames Office Oral History Project: Don Albinson, Laurendo Almeida, Ron Arad, Gordon Ashby, Ben Baldwin, Bill and Roberta Ballantine, Saul and Elaine Bass, Annetta Beauchamp, Elmer Bernstein, John Berry, Frances Bishop, Julian Blaustein, Con Boevy, Ryland Breen, Barbara Charles, I. Bernard Cohen, Buddy Collette, Alan Colley, Dick Donges, Amanda Dunne, Lucia Eames, Sol Fingerhut, John Follis, Alex Funke, Etsu Garfias, Alice Gerdine, Owen Gingerich, Irv Green, Margaret Harris, Dorothy Jeakins, Johnny Johnson, Elaine Jones, the Kesl Family, Alexander Knox, Charles Kratka, Jehane Burns Kuhn, Sister Magdalene Mary, Parke Meek, Jill Mitchell, Harlan Moore, Philip and Phylis Morrison, Pep Nagelkirk, Molly Noyes, Jeannine Oppewall, Ford Peatross, Paul Rand, Ralph Rapson, Ray Redheffer, Barney Reese, Michael Ripps, Julius Shulman, Bob Staples, Jan Steward, Marianne Strangel, Mike Sullivan, Deborah Sussman, Fred Usher, Billy Wilder, and Tom Wolff. All of these people provided valuable background information and content for this book. The following people have not formally participated in the Oral History Project, but their experiences and thoughts shared in conversation contributed to my education as did all the attendees of the Eames Office reunions: Donald Albrecht, Tina Beebe, Randy Walker, Annette del Zoppo, John and Marilyn Neuhart, Virgil Mirano, Frank Romero, Hap Johnson, Pamela Hedley, Glenn Fleck, Frank Newby, Stuart Bailey, Adele Crispin, Tereza Jesus de Palma, Max Underwood, David Olney, Craig Hodgetts, Ming Fung, and Rolf Fehlbaum. (I wish to invite any other colleagues, friends, or acquaintances to send letters and recollections to the office should they desire.)

I also want to salute three people who had the vision to conduct Oral History interviews with Charles and Ray Eames in their lifetimes: Virginia Smith, Ruth Bowman, and Ralph Caplan. I know there were others, but these interviews were of particular use to me and are a reminder that an oral history on any topic is a gift to the future. Bob Viol of the Herman Miller archives was a generous resource, as were the folks at the Library of Congress, particularly in the Manuscript, Prints & Photographs, Interpretive Programs, and Photo Duplication Divisions, in particular, Irene Chambers, Ford Peatross, Meg MacAleer, Sam McCarthy, Marilyn Ibach, and Helena Zinkham. I also need to thank Alexander von Vegesack of the Vitra Design Museum, Christopher Mount and Pierre Adler for helping me find and explore some boxes in the library at the Museum of Modern Art in New York, Mark Coir of the Cranbrook Archives, and Gregory Wittkopp at Cranbrook Art

Museum, who were all generous with time and attention. Thanks to the Museum of Modern Art, New York, the Noyes family, the Saarinen family, Washington University, and Cranbrook Academy for letting us quote their materials. Midge Kaiser, James Kaiser, Celine Lawrence, Harry Loucks, Richard Wright, Laurent Torno, Stephen Leet, Rob Swanson, and (special thanks) Richard Olsen were real supporters of this project and offered considerable help.

The team at Rizzoli/Universe were a pleasure to work with: beginning with my editor, Alexandra Tart. Thanks also to Charles Miers, Ilaria Fusina, Gillian Scott, and Bonnie Eldon. Michael Hodgson at Ph.D, the designer of the book, did a heroic job. Also at Ph.D: Claudia Plasencia and Ann Enkoji. And a special thanks to Jim Rogers at Colortek. At the Eames Office: Bernadine Styburski, Michalene Seiler, Maureen Baine, Shelley Mills, and Kip Kotzen contributed particularly to the realization of this book; Russell Smith and Genevieve Fong have worked very hard on the Oral Histories over the years.

The following people also read a complete draft of this book and offered meaningful comments, insight, and good cheer: Byron Atwood, Lucia Atwood, John Berry, Gregg Buchbinder, Steve Cabella, Irene Chambers, Barbara Charles, Annette del Zoppo, Llisa Demetrios, Lucia Eames, Ann Enkoji, Rolf Fehlbaum, Alex Funke, Sam Gilbert, Carla Hartman, Michael Hodgson, John Hoke, Elaine Jones, Peter Loughrey, D. T. Max, Don Morehead, Philip and Phylis Morrison, Pat Mullane, Jeannine Oppewall, Bob Staples, and Deborah Sussman.

Lastly, I must thank my wife, Shelley, and our sons, Xander and Guthrie, for their infinite patience, flexibility, and support as I sought to find the time and energy to write this book.

## Abbreviations of Major Sources

CE, RE, & LE refer to Charles Eames, Ray Eames, & Lucia Eames. ES, EO, & StL refer to Eero Saarinen, Eames Office & St. Louis, MO. All interviews and conversations were conducted by the author in Los Angeles, California, unless indicated. All e-mails were to author.
\* Oral History participant

AF\* Alex Funke, interview, 1/1/92
AG\* Alice Gerdine, int., StL, 3/3/92
AK\* Alex Knox, int., Northumberland, England, 10/14/92
AN Alex Funke, conversation
AO Author's observation
AQ *Aquarium,* film, CE & RE, 1969
BA *Bulletin of American Academy of Arts & Sciences 27* (10/74)
BB\* Ben Baldwin, int., Sarasota, FL, 3/19/92
BC\* Barbara Charles, int., Washington, DC, 3/13/92
BD\* Buddy Collette, int., 8/22/93
BR\* Barney Reese, int., Sacramento, CA, 12/27/91
BW\* Billy Wilder, int., 10/88
CC CE, "City Hall," *Architectural Forum,* 5/43
CH Craig Hodgetts, conv., 1/20/01
CI CE, int. by Virginia Smith, 10/13/77
CL CE, letter to LE
CN CE, letter to Eliot Noyes
CP Eames Demetrios, *Changing Her Palette: Paintings by Ray Eames* (Santa Monica: Eames Office, 2000)
CQ CE, to Eliel Saarinen, ca. 1/24/38
CR CE, letters to RE, 1940–41
CW\* Celine Lawrence, int., StL, 12/90
DA\* Don Albinson, int., East Greenville, PA, 3/14/92
DD\* Dick Donges, int., 2/21/92
DH "A Designer's Home of His Own," *Life,* 9/11/52
DR\* Deborah Sussman, int., 2/5/92
DS\* Deborah Sussman, int., 1999
EB\* Elmer Bernstein, int., 1/13/92
ED John Neuhart, Marilyn Neuhart and Ray Eames, *Eames Design* (New York: Harry N. Abrams, 1989)
EG\* Etsu Garfias, int., 2/22/92
EJ\* Elaine Jones, int., 1/14/92
EM McCoy, Esther, *Case Study Houses 1945–62,* 2nd ed. (Los Angeles: Hennessey and Ingalls, 1977)
FB\* Frances Bishop, int., Grass Valley,

CA, 2/19/92
FR CE & RE, int. by Arlene Francis for *Home Show,* NBC, 1956
FU\* Fred Usher, int., Santa Barbara, CA, 2/10/92
HJ\* Huson Jackson, int., Lincoln, MA, ca. 11/95
HM\* Harlan Moore, int., 2/3/93
HR Herman Miller Archives
HS Haku Shah, e-mail, 3/23/01
IC\* I. B. Cohen, int., Belmont, MA, 3/17/92
IG\* Irv Green, int., 2/26/93
IN *Vogue,* 4/15/54
IR CE, RE, India Report, 1958
JB\* Julian Blaustein, int., 1/28/92
JK\* Jehane Burns Kuhn, int., Cambridge, MA, 3/16/92
JM\* Jill Mitchell, int., Boston, MA, 3/17/92
JO\* Jeannine Oppewall, int., 2/8/92
KE Jim Kaiser, e-mail, 4/20/01
KP "Kaiser Put in 16 Years," *Sacramento Bee,* 3/31/17
LB\* Larry Bachman, int., Oxford, England, 2/00
LC Courtesy Library of Congress Manuscript Division, Work of Charles and Ray Eames (numbers indicate box and folder location)
LG Donald Albrecht, ed., *The Work of Charles and Ray Eames: A Legacy of Invention* (New York: Harry N. Abrams, 1997)
LW Celine Lawrence Papers (collection of Eames Office)
LX Chronology by LE, 12/3/00
LZ Lucia Eames, conv., 3/00
MoMA Museum of Modern Art, NY
MM Midge Kaiser, e-mail, 4/28/01
MR\* Mike Ripps, int., 1/10/92
MS\* Mike Sullivan, int., White Plains, NY, 3/18/92
MU Mike Sullivan, e-mail, 6/24/01
NA CE, Norton Lecture #1, 10/26/70
NB CE, Norton Lecture #2, 11/2/70
NC CE, Norton Lecture #3 1/14/71
ND CE, Norton Lecture #4, 3/15/71
NE CE, Norton Lecture #5, 3/29/71
NF CE, Norton Lecture #6, 4/26/71
NR Eliot Noyes, letter to Alfred Barr, 8/2/41
NS Eliot Noyes, letter to ES
NT *The New York Times*
NY Eliot Noyes, letter to CE
NZ "Museum to Show Prize Furniture," *The New York Times.* 9/22/41

OG\* Owen Gingerich, int., Cambridge, MA, 3/92
OS Owen Gingerich, "A Conversation With Charles Eames," *The American Scholar,* summer 1977
PD *St. Louis Post-Dispatch*
PH\* Percy Harris, int., ca. 10/92
PJ Pupul Jayakar, *Designfolio 2,* NID, Ahmedabad, India 1/79
PM\* Parke Meek, int., 1/3/92
PN\* Phylis & Philip Morrison, int., Cambridge, MA, 3/16/92
PS Paul Schrader, "Poetry of Ideas," *Film Quarterly,* spring 1970
PT *The Powers of Ten,* film, CE & RE, 1977
QA *Design Q&A,* film, CE & RE, 1972
RG RE gathering video, 8/23/88
RM RE, letter to Edna Kaiser
RP\* Ralph Rapson, int., San Francisco, CA, 2/28/92
RS\* Bob Staples, int., Washington, DC, 3/13/92
RX RE int. by Ruth Bowman, 7/80–8/80
RZ RE int. by Ralph Caplan, 2/24/81
SD *Stockton Daily Evening Record,* 10/16/06
SE E. W. Seay, *The Ideas and Words of Charles Eames,* 11/1/81 (unpublished)
SG\* Sol Fingerhut, int., 2/27/92
SL Washington University, *Student Life*
TK Allan Temko, *Eero Saarinen,* (New York: George Braziller, Inc., 1962)
VU *View from the People Wall,* film, CE & RE, 1965

## Notes

CHAPTER 1: 1 . "A Review of the American National Exhibition in Moscow, 7/25–9/4/59, by Harold C. McClellan, General Manager" (report, 12/59). 2. Alison & Peter Smithson, *Architectural Design* 9/66: 16, 17. 3. HJ. 4. BR. 5. CH. 6. Rolf Fehlbaum, phone conv., ca. 1997. 7. AF. 8. DR.
CHAPTER 2: 1. MU. 2. AF. 3. ED: 405. 4. AO. 5. CR, 5/2/41. 6. MU. 7. AF. 8. *ibid.* 9. *ibid.* 10. JK. 11. AF. 12. Randy Walker, conv., 6/01. 13. MR. 14. DD. 15. DR. 16. AF. 17. Dr. Brian Josephson, e-mail, 11/7/00.
CHAPTER 3: 1. CI. 2. PJ. 3. *ibid.* 4. NF. 5. HS. 6. *ibid.* 7. RG. 8. PJ. 9. *ibid.* 10. SE. 11. RS. 12. FR. 13. IR. 14. *ibid.*
CHAPTER 4: 1. HR, DCM brochure

(Herman Miller, 2000). 2. AN, 1/92. 3. QA. 4. Richard Wright, *Eames Auction* (Chicago: Treadway/Toomey, 1999). 5. *Project in Home Furnishings*, MoMA, 6/24/40. 6. *ibid.* 7. Press release, MoMA 2/2/41. 8. *ibid.* 9. *Cranbrook Academy Newsletter*, 1941. 10. RX. 11. DA. 12. ED: 25. 13. NZ. 14. DA. 15. DA, JM. 16. DA. 17. *ibid.* 18. ES, to Eliot Noyes, 5/29/41. 19. Paul B. Posser, to ES, 7/24/41. 20. CN, 7/3/41. 21. RZ. 22. NR. 23. *ibid.* 24. F. T. Parrish, "Notes on Meeting with Eero Saarinen, Noyce & Saunders," 5/7/41. 25. CN, 9/2/41. 26. NZ. 27. CI. 28. *ibid.* 29. DH. 30. Eliot Noyes, to CE, 1/8/42. 31. RZ. 32. *ibid.* 33. AF. 34. Eliot Noyes, *Organic Design in Home Furnishings*, MoMA, 9/24/41–11/9/41. 35. LZ. 36. RZ. 37. W. Scott and CE, "A New Emergency Splint of Plyformed Wood," *U.S. Naval Bulletin*, 9/43: 1423-28. 38. CI. 39. ED: 33. 40. "The Best of the Century," *Time Magazine*, 12/31/99: 73–77. 41. RS. 42. LG, 74.

CHAPTER 5: 1. BA: 23. 2. CI. 3. *ibid.* 4. History of Chicago Board of Trade Battery. 5. Stephen E. Ambrose, *Nothing Like it in the World: The Men Who Built the Transcontinental Railroad, 1863-1869* (New York: Simon & Schuster, 2000). 6. LZ. 7. IN. 8. LZ. 9. Charles O. Eames, Sr., Train Robberies on Missouri Pacific, internal report. 10. Henri Chomeau obituary, PD, 8/18/29. 11. CI. 12. LW, written in scrapbook. 13. CW. 14. LZ. 15. LZ. 16. CI. 17. Newspaper clipping, ca. 1910. 18. CI. 19. *ibid.* 20. *ibid.* 21. CW. 22. CI. 23. AO. 24. CI. 25. *ibid.* 26. *ibid.* 27. LZ. 28. NB. 29. IN. 30. CI. 31. NB. 32. CI. 33. CI. 34. "School Class Looks Back on 50 Years," PD, 6/16/75. 35. LW. 36. CI. 37. CI. 38. CI. 39. CI. 40. CI. 41. SL, 12/1925. 42. NB. 43. Izzy Millstone, conv., StL, ca. 1/00. 44. Adele Starbird, "Devonair Charlie," PD, ca. 1975. 45. CI. 46. *ibid.* 47. JK. 48. LZ. 49. Michalene Seiler, conv. with Washington Univ. administrative office 4/4/2001. 50. SL, ca. 1928. 51. ED. 52. CI. 53. NB. 54. NB. 55. Conv., StL, ca. 1992. 56. LX. 57. NB. 58. HJ. 59. CI. 60. CI.

CHAPTER 6: 1. LC 288:3. *ibid.* 3. *ibid.* 4. "May Go on the Road," *Stockton Independent,* 2/18/1895. 5. SD. 6. "The Boy Manager," *Stockton Evening Mail,* 12/22/06. 7. KE. 8. AO, cover of RE notebook, ca. 1935. 9. LC 288:11. 10. SD. 11. LC 288:11. 12. Midge Kaiser, phone conv., 12/16/00. 13. KP. 14. *ibid.* 15. ED: 18. 16. RX. 17. KP. 18. MM. 19. KE. 20. MM. 21. KP. 22. LC 288:8. 23. "Opening Bill for New Theater has been Announced," *Sacramento Bee,* 8/13/20, LC 288:3 "State Jammed for Opening". 24. RX. 25. Samuel Leask, to Alex Kaiser, 1/31/22. 26. BR. 27. *ibid.* 28. *ibid.* 29. *ibid.* 30. *ibid.* 31. *ibid.* 32. *ibid.* 33. RX. 34. *ibid.* 35. MM. 36. RM, 5/12/32. 37. RX. 38. *ibid.* 39. *ibid.* 40. BB. 41. RX. 42. BB. 43. *ibid.* 44. KE. 45. MM. 46. BR. 47. RM, 4/4/39. 48. RM, 4/11/36. 49. RM, 9/5/36. 50. RM, 1/2/39. 51. RM, 1/25/39. 52. RM, 2/2/39. 53. RM, 1/25/39. 54. RM, 3/7/39. 55. RM, 1/13/39. 56. RM, 8/20/37. 57. RX. 58. *ibid.* 59. LC 222:4. 60. Lee Krasner, to RE, 2/28/38. 61. RM, 1/10/39. 62. RM, 1/29/39. 63. RM, 1/25/39. 64. RM, 2/2/39. 65. RM, 5/20/39. 66. RM, 2/6/36. 67. RM, 3/7/39. 68. *ibid.* 69. CP: 7. 70. *ibid.*: 1.

CHAPTER 7: 1. JB. 2. CI. 3. LX. 4. BB. 5. LZ. 6. *ibid.* 7. PD. 8. NE. 9. PD. 10. LZ. 11. NA. 12. NE. 13. NE. 14. LZ. 15. IN. 16. *ibid.* 17. HJ. 18. *ibid.* 19. AG. 20. HJ. 21. LZ. 22. HJ. 23. LX. 24. *ibid.* 25. *ibid.* 26. *ibid.* 27. *ibid.* 28. "A French Town House," PD, 10/22/34. 29. PD. 30. RX. 31. AG. 32. *St. Mary's Church 1936–1998* (Helena, AR: St. Mary's Church, 1998). 33. *ibid.* 34. Mary Kesl Bussell, int., Helena, AR, 3/10/92. 35. AG. 36. *ibid.* 37. *ibid.* 38. CI. 39. AG. 40. *ibid.* 41. *ibid.* 42. *ibid.* 43. *ibid.* 44. Catherine Eames, to Adele Eames, 1938 (LW). 45. LX. 46. *ibid.* 47. CQ. 48. CI. 49. CE, application to Cranbrook, 1938. 50. *Interiors Magazine,* 4/58. 51. Gregory Wittkopp, *Saarinen House and Garden: A Total Work of Art* (New York: Harry N. Abrams, 1995). 52. *ibid.* 53. IN. 54. RP. 55. *ibid.* 56. *ibid.* 57. CR, 3/11/41. 58. TK. 59. *ibid.* 60. CI. 61. LW. 62. "Carl Milles, Cranbrook's Favorite Sculptor," *The Detroit News,* 5/01. 63. CI. 64. TK. 65. NE. 66. *ibid.* 67. *ibid.* 68. CQ. 69. LZ.

CHAPTER 8: 1. RM. 2. NB. 3. CR, 2/24/41. 4. LW. 5. RE, application to Cranbrook, 1940. 6. RX. 7. ED: 23. 8. CR, 3/11/41. 9. JM. 10. *ibid.* 11. CR, 1/2/41. 12. CR, postcard, 1/41. 13. CR, 2/18/01. 14. CR, 3/16/41. 15. LZ. 16. CR, 4/22/41. 17. CR, 2/5/41. 18. *ibid.* 19. *ibid.* 20. *ibid.* 21. CR, 2/24/41. 22. CR, 2/27/41. 23. CR, 2/22/41. 24. CR, 2/24/41. 25. *ibid.* 26. CR, 3/11/41. 27 . CR, 2/22/41. 28. CR, 4/9/41. 29. CR, 3/11/41. 30. CR, 3/14/41. 31. *ibid.* 32. Ryland Breen, conv., New Jersey, 3/13/92. 33. Celine Eames, to CE, 5/4/41. 34. LW. 35. *ibid.* 36. CR, 3/16/41. 37. Helen Donnelly, to RE, 4/8/41. 38. CR, 5/2/41. 39. CR, 3/25/41. 40. CR, 6/8/41. 41. CR, 5/10/41. 42. CR, 6/7/41. 43. CR, 4/29/41. 44. NE. 45. RP. 46. BR. 47. ED: 27. 48. *ibid.* 49. CN, 9/2/41. 50. FB. 51. *ibid.* 52. CE, to Richard Neutra, 5/18/49. 53. LB. 54. CL, ca. 10/43. 55. CL, ca. 11/41. 56. CE, to Richard Raseman, 6/42. 57. JB. 58. FB. 59. PH. 60. *ibid.* 61. FB. 62. Glodean Gates, on-line guest-book (www.eamesoffice.com, 1997). 63. LX. 64. CC. 65. *ECS,* film, CE & RE, 1961. 66. CC. 67. RZ. 68. AK. 69. *ibid.* 70. *ibid.* 71. *ibid.* 72. *ibid.*

CHAPTER 9: 1. RX. 2. FB. 3. LC 30:9. 4. PH. 5. ED. 6. PH. 7. DA. 8. Celine Eames, to Leonie Lawrence, 12/45. 9. LZ. 10. LC 221:2. 11. HM. 12. LZ. 13. Ralph Caplan, *The Design of Herman Miller* (New York: Whitney Library of Design, 1976). 14. *ibid.* 15. RX. 16. *ibid.* 17. RZ. 18. NE. 19. DA. 20. CI. 21. DA. 22. LG: 71. 23. PS. 24. ED: 97. 25. FU. 26. *ibid.* 27. DA. 28. *ibid.* 29. FU. 30. SG. 31. *ibid.* 32. *ibid.* 33. SG. 34. LB. 35. CH. 36. John Wills, phone conv., 2/7/01. 37. *ibid.* 38. SG. 39. IG. 40. *ibid.* 41. *ibid.* 42. SG. 43. IG. 44. SG. 45. *ibid.* 46. DH. 47. RX.

CHAPTER 10: 1. MM. 2. LZ. 3. *Think Magazine,* 4/61. 4. LC 222:4. 5. AN, Wellington, New Zealand, 4/01. 6. LC 222:7. 7. *ibid.* 8. QA. 9. PM. 10. JM. 11. JB. 12. BW. 13. DA. 14. *ibid.* 15. Mara Bailey, int., ca. 1997. 16. BD. 17. MS. 18. *ibid.* 19. MM. 20. MS. 21. *ibid.* 22. ND. 23. *ibid.* 24. *ibid.* 25. *ibid.* 26. DR. 27. LZ. 28. AF. 29. DR. 30. PM. 31. JB. 32. LZ. 33. SE.

CHAPTER 11: 1. Brief for Immaculate Heart (EO, 2/14/67). 2. "Sister Corita," www.immaculateheart.org,

5/1/2001. 3. Sister Magdalene Mary, int., 4/89. 4. Terence Conran, conv., London, 1998. 5. CN, 8/41. 6. EM: 9. 7. EM. 8. RX. 9. LX. 10. EM, p57. 11. Eames Demetrios, *Powers of Ten Interactive*, CD-ROM (Pyramid/EO, 1999). 12. FU. 13. CP. 14. ED: 109. 15. FU. 16. Ford Peatross, e-mail, 7/10/01. 17. EM: 54. 18. *ibid.* 19. JK.
CHAPTER 12: 1. Digby Diehl, Q&A with CE, *LA Times West Magazine* 10/7/72. 2. PS. 3. Michael Webb, conv., 1989. 4. RZ. 5. AF. 6. *The Films of Charles & Ray Eames* 2 (Pyramid, 1989). 7. RX. 8. CE, to Ian McCallum, 9/3/54. 9. EB. 10. *Toccata for Toy Trains*, film, CE & RE, 1957. 11. PM. 12. AF. 13. Vida T. Johnson, *Films of Andrei Tarkovsky: A Visual Fugue* (Indiana University Press, 1994). 14. PS. 15. JK. 16. EB. 17. *ibid.* 18. PM. 19. RS. 20. EB. 21. Hugh DePree, *Business as Unusual* (HR, 1986). 22. PM. 23. EB. 24. *ibid.*
CHAPTER 13: 1. *Image of the City*, film, CE & RE (1969). 2. DS. 3. JB. 4. BD. 5. AF. 6. JO. 7. *ibid.* 8. AF. 9. NA. 10. AF. 11. *ibid.* 12. AF. 13. PM. 14. LX. 15. BA. 16. Con Boevy, int., Holland, MI 5/12/97. 17. *ibid.* 18. AF. 19. JK.
CHAPTER 14: 1. ED. 2. QA. 3. *ibid.* 4. *ibid.* 5. *ibid.* 6. PM. 7. PM. 8. RZ. 9. DA. 10. ED: 207. 11. lecture 3/68, LC 218:10. 12. PM. 13. HM. 14. *ibid.* 15. PM. 16. DA. 17. Sam Passalacqua, letter, 7/9/01. 18. DA. 19. JB. 20. DD. 21. PM. 22. *ECS*, film, CE & RE, 1961. 23. DD. 24. Ralph Caplan, *Making Connections: The Work of Charles and Ray Eames*, (UCLA Arts Council, 1976). 25. NE. 26. *ibid.* 27. CR, 2/27/01. 28. JO. 29. ED, 227. 30. RS.

CHAPTER 15: 1. LG: 39. 2. PS. 3. ED: 15. 4. ED. 5. LC 218: 10. 6. *ibid.* 7. LC 218: 10. 8. RX. 9. Ray Redheffer, int., 2/4/93. 10. *ibid.* 11. *ibid.* 12. NC. 13. PN. 14. JK. 15 OG. 16. NC. 17. PN. 18. NF.
CHAPTER 16: 1. ED. 2. PN. 3. *ibid.* 4. CE, int., National Public Radio, broadcast 8/78. 5. JK. 6. RZ. 7. CI. 8. LB. 9. LZ. 10. JO. 11. BD. 12. AF. 13. *ibid.* 14. JK. 15. MR. 16. EG. 17. DD. 18. PM. 19. DA. 20. Annette del Zoppo, seminar at LACMA 8/24/00. 21. JK. 22. HM. 23. RZ. 24. DD. 25. FU. 26. JO. 27. AF. 28. BC. 29. MR. 30. DR. 31. BC. 32. *ibid.* 33. JO. 34. AF. 35. FU. 36. JO. 37. PH. 38. JB. 39. RS. 40. Anne Enkoji, conv., 2/01. 41. BC. 42. Charlie Kratka, int., 2/2/93. 43. JO. 44. FU. 45. Deborah Sussman, "Credit Due in Eames World," *LA Times*, 6/21/99. 46. JO. 47. LG: 68. 48. LZ. 49. EJ. 50. JO. 51. JM. 52. DA. 53. *Arts & Architecture Magazine*, 4/44. 54. PH. 55. FB. 56. PM. 57. JO. 58. HM. 59. Amanda Dunne, int., ca. 1997. 60. LZ. 61. JB. 62. AK. 63. DS. 64. BC. 65. PM. 66. QA.
CHAPTER 17: 1. NE. 2. LC 221:2. 3. NC. 4. *Computer Day at Midvale*, film, CE & RE, 1965. 5. VU. 6. Paul Goldberger, "The Eames Team," *The New Yorker* 92 (5/24/1999). 7. VU. 8. JO. 9. IC. 10. ND. 11. AQ. 12. BC. 13. CR, 3/25/41. 14. AQ. 15. PM. 16. PS. 17. DA. 18. AF. 19. AQ. 20. NA. 21. EB.
CHAPTER 18: 1. AF. 2. *ibid.* 3. EJ. 4. LC 221:2. 5. RE, *Detroit Free Press*, 7/31/80. 6. LC 222-6. 7. DR. 8. *ibid.* 9. AF. 10. EJ. 11. BB. 12. PN. 13. NE. 14. LC 222:8. 15. LC 222:6. 16. LX. 17. FR. 18. Pat Kirkham, *Charles and Ray Eames, Designers of the Twentieth*

*Century* (Cambridge: MIT Press, 1995): 83. 19. Don Albinson, conv., ca. 1999. 20. LG: 47. 21. JK. 22. BC. 23. AF. 24. LC 222:5. 25. JK. 26. AF. 27. DD. 28. AF. 29. EB. 30. LG. 31. BW. 32. JK. 33. RX. 34. JO. 35. JB. 36. JO. 37. JK. 38. EB. 39. *ibid.* 40. BC. 41. SG. 42. JO. 43. EB. 44. BR. 45. JK. 46. *ibid.* 47. AF. 48. DS. 49. PM. 50. JO. 51. MS. 52. PN.
CHAPTER 19: 1. QA. 2. PS. 3. ND. 4. DD. 5. *ibid.* 6. Frank Newby, conv., London, 9/98. 7. EG. 8. House of Cards label, ca. 1990. 9. JK. 10. AF. 11. DS. 12. JK. 13. OG. 14. *ibid.* 15. *ibid.* 16. AF. 17. RX. 18. IG. 19. AF. 20. Gordon Ashby, int., Inverness, CA, ca. 1995. 21. JO. 22. *International Herald-Tribune*, 1/4/1975. 23. BA: 17. 24. *ibid.* 25. PM. 26. *Glimpses of the USA*, film, CE & RE, 1959. 27. OS. 28. LZ. 29. LC 221:2. 30. OS. 31. NC. 32. EB. 33. *ibid.* 34. NC.
CHAPTER 20: 1. EB. 2. LC 218. 3. AN, 1/92. 4. LC 218. 5. *ibid.* 6. JK. 7. LC 222:6. 8. Hilton Kramer, NT, 3/76. 9. LC 218:2. 10. Keith Yamashita, *15 Things Charles and Ray Teach Us* (EO, 1999). 11. *Eames at MOMA*, film by Perry Miller Adato (WNET, 1973). 12. PN. 13. PT. 14. NE. 15. Philip & Phylis Morrison, RE, *Powers of Ten* (New York: W. H. Freeman, 1982). 16. AF. 17. PT. 18. AF. 19. EG. 20. OG. 21. ND.
CHAPTER 21: 1. Dr. Stuart Bailey, conv., 7/17/97. 2. RX. 3. JK. 4. AF. 5. JK. 6. JB. 7. LZ. 8. EB. 9. AF. 10. EJ. 11. JK. 12. LX. 13. JO. 14. PM. 15. JK. 16. AF. 17. EG. 18. JK. 19. James Hoekema, int., Washington, DC, 3/92. 20. ND. 21. Steve Cabella, int., San Rafael, CA, 11/25/94. 22. ED. 23. RG.

# Index

Aalto, Alvar, 36, 90
Airport. See Tandem Sling.
Albinson, Don, 37, 38, 94, 108, 111, 112, 123, 145, 170, 171, 194, 199, 218
aluminum, chair, 176
American Abstract Artists (A.A.A.), 73, 74
*Aquarium*, 158, 208–12, 210–11, 222

Architectural Forum, 82
Art Students League, 69
Arts and Architecture, *100*, 101, 102, *103*, 133, 136–37, 140, 200
Aubuchon, Marie Adele, 50

Babbage, 95
Bachman, Larry, 102, 116, 193

Bailey (Neutra) House, 135, 138, 139, 145, 253
Baldwin, Ben, 73, 74, 75, 88, 93, 217
*Banana Leaf*, 78–79
Bauer, Dale, 202
Bernstein, Elmer, 146, 149–50, 151, 152, *152*, 175, 213, 219, 223, 235, 238, 239, 254

Bishop, Frances, 102, 103, 112, 200
*Blacktop*, 144–45, *144–45*, 152, 199
Blaustein, Julian, 102, 122, 156, 197, 254
Bloomingdale's, 37, 39
Boeke, Kees, 247
Borges, Jorge, 148
*Bread*, 165, 232

Bridge House. See Eames House.
Bronowski, Judith, 248
Bruhwiler, Paul, 249, *251*
Burns, Jehane, 165, 188, 192, 193, 201, 218, 229

*Cable: The Immediate Future*, 241, *242*
Cage, John, 129, 218
California Museum of Science and Industry, 179, 180
Cantata, Dolores, 202
Carles, Mercedes, 73, 74
Case Study Houses. See individual houses
*Cézanne*, 254
chair(s). See specific chairs
Charles, Barbara, 197, 198, 202, 210, 219, 222
Chomeau, Henry, 50
Civil War, 47, 48
*Clown Face*, 120, *122*
Cohen, I. Bernard, *200*, 209
Collette, Buddy, 193
*Comics of the Fifties*, 81, 239
*Communications Primer, A*, 8, 23, 146, *148–49*, 159, 230, 246
*Computer Perspective, A*, 57, 265
*Copernicus*, 126, 185, 188, 230, *230*
Cosmic View (Boeke), 247
Cranbrook Academy of Art, 36, 37, 74, 84, 85, 86, 87–89, 93–94, 95, 102, 144, 200, 247, 267

*Day of the Dead*, *78*, 199, 202
*Decorator Crab*, 211
Demetrios, Eames, *6*, 7
Demetrios, Xander, *259*
DePree, D.J., 12, 109, 110, 118, 169
DePree, Hugh, 109, 169
DePree, Max, 143, 169, 267
Depression, 59–60
Design diagram, *166*, 175–76, *177*
honest/unselfconscious use of material in, 42, 32, 228, 250
*Design Q&A*, 35, 122, 167–68, *168*, 173, 202,

227
Donges, Dick, *22*, 159, 193, 194, 195, 219, 256, 261
Donnelly, Helen, 69, 70, 99

Eames, Adele (Franks), *49*, 50, 54
Eames, Catherine Dewey (Woermann), 58–59, *59*, 60, 80–81, 83, 87, 89, 93–94, 96, 98, 99
Eames, Charles Ormond, Jr., *11*, *46*, *59*, *91*, *97*, *100*, *119*, *175*, *187*, *190*, *200*, *204*, *214*, *220*, *262*
at Cranbrook, 85, 87–89, 93, 97, 102
death of, 9, 159, 201, 255–57
death of father of, 53
in Mexico, 60, *76*, 77–79
Eames, Charles Ormond, Sr., 47–49, *48*, 51–53, *52*
Eames, Henry, 47–48
Eames, Lucia Dewey, 7, *59*, 60, 80, 81, 85, 87, 93, *94*, 98, 103, 104, 127, 134, *184*, 260, 267
Eames, Maria Adele Celine (Lambert), 49–51, *50*, 53, 98
Eames, Ray (Kaiser), *11*, *22*, *62*, *70*, *97*, *100*, *175*, *190*, *204*, *214*, *221*, *259*, *262*
at Cranbrook, 94–95
death of, 9, 28, 228, 260
death of parents of, 63, 68, 74, 93, 100
letters to mother by, 70–71
*Eames Design*, 191, 200, 258–60, 265
Eames House, 8, 12, *13*, 84, *130*, 132–33, *135*, 135–37, *138–39*, 140, 141, *141*, 144–45, 149, *150–51*, 152–53, *153*, 229, 253, *261*, 266
Eames Lounge Chair, 11, 35, 39, 170–73, *172*, *173*, 263
*Eames Lounge Chair*, 173
Eames Office, 42, 102–03, 108, 117, 162–63, 196, 266. See also 901 Washington Blvd
Enkoji, Ann, 198
Entenza, John, *100*, 101, 102, 108, 112, 199

Entenza House, *130*, 135–36, 139, 199, 266
Evans Products Molded Plywood Division, 43, *103*, 107, 108–09, 111, 112, 159
*Expanding Airport*, 170

*Fabulous Fifties, The*, 237–39
Fehlbaum, Rolf, 12
Fehlbaum, Willi, 173
fiberglass chair, 115–19, *117*, 119, 180
*Fiberglass Chairs*, 151
*Fifteen Things Charles and Ray Teach us*, 244, 265
*Fifties Dead Sequences*, 237, 238
film(s). See individual titles.
Fingerhut, Sol, 115–16, 117, *203*, 245
Fleck, Glen, 202
*Franklin and Jefferson*, 122, 128, 144, 158, 196, 202, 219, 241–45, *242*, *243*, 253
Franks, Adele, 50, 55p
Frei, Emil, 83, 85
Fuller, Buckminster, *154*, 236, 244
Fung, Ming, 11, 12
Funke, Alex, 12, 23, 158, 161, 192, 193, 196, 219, 248, 253
furniture. See individual titles

Garfias, Etsu, 194, 256
*G.E.M.*, *232–33*
Gingerich, Owen, 188, 230, 235, 250
Girard, Alexander, 176, 232, 244, 263
*Glimpses of the USA*, 11, 158, 202, 205, 230, 233–37, *234–35*
*Good Design*, 205
*Goods*, 156
Gorky, Arshile, 73, 74
Gray, Charles, 59–60
Green, Irv, 115–16, 117, 118–19, 232
Grotell, Maija, 95

Hellmuth, Charles, 56
Henry Ford Museum, 241–42

Herman Miller, Inc., 12, 21, 44, 109–12, 117, 119, 127, 143, 155, 159, 161, 162–63, 169, 171, 172, 176, 199, 217, 254, 266–67
Heywood-Wakefield Furniture, 23, 39
Hill, Lawrence, 57–58
Hodgetts, Craig, 12
Hofmann, Hans, 69–70, 73–74, *75*, 94
*House: after five years of living*, 149–51, *150–51*
House of Cards, 11, *13*, *15*, *17*, *19*, *127*, 133, 223, 228–29, 265
*House of Science*, 177, 185, 230
Hughes, Howard, 104

IBM, 21, 25, 124, 127, 128, 146, 161, *161*, 179, 206, 253, 257
*India* slide show, *26*, *28*
India Report, 27, 28, 29, *30*, 32, *33*

Jackson, Huson, 12, 79–80
Jayakar, Pupul, 29

Kaiser, Alexander, 63–68, *65*
Kaiser, Edna May (Burr), 64–65, *64*, 67, 73, 74, 75, 93
Kaiser, Elizabeth, 65–66
Kaiser, George, 63, 65
Kaiser, Maurice, 65, *66*, 68, 70, 93, 98–99, 100, 121
Kaiser, Maurice and Henrietta, 63, 64
Kaiser, Midge, 121, 125
*Kaleidoscope Jazz Chair*, *153*, *168–69*
*Kaleidoscope Shop*, 167
Kazam! machine, 41–42, *45*, 189
Kent, Sister Mary Corita, 132
*Kepler's Laws*, 188
Kesi, Vaslau and Oldrich, 83
Kleinhans Chair (Eames-Saarinen), 35, 36, *38*, 89–90, 107
Knoll, 109–10
Knox, Alexander, 103–05
Krasner, Lee, 70, 73, 74

Kuhn, Jehane Burns. *See* Burns, Jehane
Kuhn, Thomas, 185
Kwikset House, 143

La Chaise chair, 119, *119*, 159, 218, *262*
Lambert, Pierre, 50
Lecture 1, 104, 231
Leger, Fernand, 73–74
Library of Congress, 227, 241–42, 267
*Look of America*, 162
Los Angeles, 31, 41, *43*, 99
Lota, 32, *33*
Lounge Chair Wood (LCW), 11, *15*, *17*, *39*, *40*, 44, 107, 171, *228*
Low Cost Furniture Competition (MoMA), 112–13, *113*, 115, 119

*Mathematica*, 12, *17*, 126, *128*, 156, 158, *178*, *181*, *182*, 182–85, *187*, *204*, 205, 267
Matter, Herbert, 200
May Friend Bennett School, 68–69
Meek, Parke, 148, *150–51*, 152, 162, 167, 194, 200, 202, 223, 238, 261
*Meeting of Waters, The* (Milles), 84, 89
metal chair, 113–15, *115*
*Metropolitan Overview*, 212, *242*, 254
Meyer, Alice, 80, 83, 84
Meyer House, 80, 82, 83, 84, *84*, 85, *85*, 86, 255
MGM, 101–02
Milles, Carl, 84, 89
Millstone, Izzy, 57
Mitchell, Jill, 39, 94, 95, 122
Moore, Harlan, 171–72, 195, 201
Morrison, Philip, 186, 188–89, 192, 217, 224–25, 244, 247, 258
Morrison, Phylis, *22*, 186, 191–92, 224–25, 244, 258
motion-controlled movie camera, 255
*Movable Feasts*, *157*, *203*
multimedia, 160–61, 163, 174, 206–08, 230–39, 257–58, 265–66. See also individual titles

Museum of Modern Art, 23, 35, 36, 38, 39, 107, 108, *108*, 109, 111, 112, 115, 119, 170, 171, 220
*Music of the Fifties*, *237*

National Institute of Design (NID), 12, 29, 31, 267
Nehru, Jawahral, 27, 29, 31
*Nehru: The Man and His India*, 31
Nelson, George, 109, 110, 244, 263
Neuhart, John, 202, 238, 259
Neutra, Richard, 101, 133, 135
Neutra Apartments, 101–02, *101*, 123, 200
New Covetables, 124–25, 179
New Furniture by Charles Eames (MoMA), 220
Newton, Isaac, 21, 23
Newton Cards, *20*, 21–25, *22*, *23*
Newton's Method, *188*
901: after 45 years of working, 9
901 Washington Boulevard, 5, 25, 115, 145, 266
Norton Lectures, 163, *164*, 165, 174, 189, 206
Noyes, Eliot, 23, 36, 38, 41, 101, 107, *191*

opera, municipal, 60, *61*
Oppewall, Jeannine, 160, 195, 198, 200, *201*, 209, 232–33
Organic Chair, 36–41, *38*, 44, 98, 99, 100–01, 107
Organic Furniture competition (MoMA), 23, 35, 36–40, *38*, 95, 96

*Parade: Or Here They Come Down the Street*, 145, 205
Passalacqua, Sam, *201*
Pauley, Walter, 59–60
Pearce, Peter, 202
*Photography and the City*, 156
Picasso, death of, 229
Pilgrim Congregational Church, 60, *61*
pilot seat, *39*, *42*
plywood, *34*, *38*, 41–42, *42*,

106, 107, 108, *108*, *252*
Polaroid, 253
*Polyorchis Haplus*, *13*, *15*, *17*, *19*, 95, 211
*Powers of Ten: Rough Sketch*, 155, 202, *240*, 244–50, *246*, 248, 249, 250
*Powers of Ten*, 8, 11, *13*, *15*, *17*, *19*, 159, 202, 244–50, 248, 249, 251, 253
*Push Again*, 209

Quest, Charles, 83

Rapson, Ralph, 88, 100, 134
Raseman, Richard, 97
Red Lion Furniture, 38
Redheffer, Ray, 185–86, 188, 206, 247
Reese, Barney, 66, 67, 100, 223
*Revell Toy House*, *213*
Rich, Irene, 99, 100
Ripps, Michael, *22*, 196, 202
Rosenthal, Tony, 94
*Rough Sketch*. See *Powers of Ten: Rough Sketch*

Saarinen, Eero, 23, 35, 36, 37, 38, 40, 41, 50, 88–90, *91*, 96, 99–100, *131*, 133, 176, 186, 200, 205, 206, 244, 246, 247, 263
Saarinen, Eliel, 36, 82, 84, 85–90, *88*, 205
Saarinen, Loja, 84, *88*
*Sample Lesson for a Hypothetical Course*, 165, 205, 232
Schrader, Paul, 148, 149, 212
Shah, Haku, 28
shockmount, 117, 118, *118*
Sisters of Immaculate Heart College, 131–32, *133*
Smithsonian Gallery of Art, 90–91
*Sofa Compact*, 128
*Soft Pad*, 129
*Something About Photography*, 9, 174–75, *174*, 253
Spiller, Jane, 255
splints, 43–44
*St. Louis Post-Dispatch* model house, 82
St. Mary's Church, 82–83,

82, 84, 267
stadium seating chair, 119, *119*
stamping machine, 114
Staples, Bob, 176
Sullivan, Mike, 124
Sussman, Deborah, 12, 148, 155–56, *191*, 196, 199, 202, 205, 216, 223, 229
*SX-70*, 156, *157*, 159, 174–75, *174*

Tandem Sling Seating, *19*, 169–70, 176–77, *226*
*The Spirit of St. Louis*, 151
*Think*, *152*, 206–07, *207*, 209, 212
*Three Clients*, 174
*Toccata for Toy Trains*, 11, *13*, *15*, *17*, *19*, 132, *142*, 146–47, 147–48, 151–52, 180, 205, *215*, 246
Tondreau, Bill, 158, 255
*Tops*, *233*
*Two Baroque Churches in Germany*, 172
Two Piece plastic chair, 35

Usher, Fred, 199

Vitra Design Museum, 266

Walsh, Robert, 79–80, 82, 83
Washington University, 56–58, 81
Watson, Thomas, Jr., 21, 23, 25, 179, 253
Weese, Harry, 88
West House, 135
*What Is Design?*, 95, 174, 175
Wilder, Audrey, 207, *209*
Wilder, Billy, 151, 152, *152*, 173, 220
Wills, John, 116–17, *117*
Woermann, Frederick, 58–59, 81
Woermann Construction Company, 81, 84
World War II, 23, 43, 133–34, 136
World's Fair, New York, 11, *161*, 202, 206–07
Wright, Frank Lloyd, 57–58

Zenith Plastics, 115, 117, 232
Zogbaum, Wilfred, 70, 74